American Buddhism

Charles S. Prebish
Pennsylvania State University

Duxbury Press **North Scituate, Massachusetts**

Interior design was provided by Amato Prudente. The cover was designed by Oliver Kline.

Duxbury Press
A Division of Wadsworth, Inc.

Library of Congress Cataloging in Publication Data

Prebish, Charles S
  American Buddhism.

  Bibliography: p.
  Includes index.
  1. Buddhism—United States. I. Title.
BQ732.P73   294.3'0973   79-10858

ISBN 0-87872-225-4

Printed in the United States of America
1   2   3   4   5   7   8   9 — 83   82   81   80   79

Contents

Preface

For years I have thought that any responsible introductory study of Buddhism ought to consider the changing face of this diverse and fascinating tradition. To be sure, the scholarly and/or journalistic treatment of Buddhism in the modern world has created an ever increasing corpus of literature, about evenly divided between general studies and investigations of individual traditions. Even the most recent and notable of these volumes, *Buddhism in the Modern World* (edited by Heinrich Dumoulin and his assistant, John Maraldo), however, fails to give serious attention to Buddhism in the West. Of course Western Buddhism is mentioned, but only quite superficially. And in a world of ever decreasing size and increasing accessibility, this is both surprising and disappointing.

American scholars have been interested in modern religious movements for some time. Curiously though, very little of the recent literature has taken notice of the growing number of Buddhist groups on the American scene. Beginning with Hal Bridges's *American Mysticism: From William James to Zen* (which is still cited appreciatively by scholars although it gives little attention to Buddhism), Peter Rowly's *New Gods in America*, and Glock and Bellah's *The New Religious Consciousness*, scholarly studies of the new American religious sectarianism have almost exclusively ignored Buddhism. In addition, although Irving Zaretsky and Mark Leone published over 800 pages on marginal religious groups in America (*Religious Movements in Contemporary America*) and gained much critical acclaim for their admittedly useful volume, they hardly mentioned Buddhism at all. The notable exceptions to the volumes cited above are Jacob Needleman's *The New Religions* and Robert S. Ellwood's *Religious and Spiritual Groups in Modern America*, each of which has major sections on Buddhist groups, and Ellwood's *The Eagle and the Rising*

Sun, an interesting and important work that offers an excellent chapter on the Nichiren Shōshū movement in America. Nevertheless, the few books that do address the question of Buddhism in an American setting directly are either too restrictive (such as Louise Hunter's *Buddhism in Hawaii*), too outdated (such as Van Meter Ames's *Zen and American Thought*), or both. The crux of the problem, then, can be stated as follows: Can we expect specialists in modern American religions to set aside, or at least suspend, their avowedly Western (and valuable) pursuits in order to garner the training necessary to be able to meaningfully incorporate Oriental religions in America into their work? Can we expect specialists in Oriental religions to gain equal sophistication in working with the Western tradition (a sophistication far too often presumed but not possessed) so as to pursue studies of Oriental religions in America when there are so many questions in their own area as yet unanswered, and in the process, become mediocre generalists instead of good specialists? Of course the answer to each of these questions must invariably be the proverbial "Yes and No!" Yes, it would be valuable to have *good* research studies which *effectively* bridge the cultural gap, but no, it is not likely to happen. Consequently, we rely on pooled interests and methodological dialogue to inform our individual pursuits. The recent working Conference on the Study of New American Religious Movements, held at the Graduate Theological Union, Berkeley, California, in June 1977 was an important step in this direction. By bringing together those scholars who are aware of the above problem, this conference enhanced infracultural understanding. Without doubt, the Program for the Study of New American Religious Movements (located at the Graduate Theological Union) will continue to enhance this understanding.

It is impossible to properly thank all those who contributed to this study. Nevertheless, a few specific cases must be singled out. First, I offer my gratitude to the hundreds of Buddhist groups who cheerfully responded to my persistent and nagging inquiries. Since I could not visit all the groups personally, a steady flow of correspondence was necessary, and quite effective. I also offer my sincere praise to my students for serving as a somewhat captive audience for preliminary speculations in my experimental courses on American Buddhism. To the Department of Religion at Syracuse University (and particularly Joanna Rogers Macy), I offer my appreciation for the opportunity to participate in a workshop on "The Flowering of Buddhism in America" (from which I have taken the title for the second section of this book). To Claude Welch and the Graduate Theological Union, I express thanks for allowing me to share ideas and perspectives with the many great scholars who attended their aforementioned conference. To the Institute for the Arts and Humanistic Studies of The Pennsylvania State University, I am grateful for providing a grant which enabled me to complete my task earlier than I had anticipated.

Finally, I dedicate this work to my wife, Susan, and in so doing, offer her my professional affection for convincing me (on numerous occasions) not to abandon the project, as well as my personal affection for reminding me that Buddhologists do not live by Vinaya and Indian Buddhism alone.

Acknowledgments

The author gratefully acknowledges permission to reprint copy-righted material:

From Bob Dylan, *Ballad of a Thin Man.* © 1965 Warner Bros. Inc. All rights reserved. Used by permission.

From Michael Novak, *The Experience of Nothingness* (New York: Harper & Row, 1971). Reprinted by permission of the publisher.

From Agehananda Bharati, *The Light at the Center* (Santa Barbara, Calif.: Ross-Erikson, 1976). Reprinted by permission of the publisher.

From Martin Marty, *A Nation of Behavers.* © 1976 by The University of Chicago Press. Reprinted by permission of the publisher.

From *Namu Dai Bosa: A Transmission of Zen Buddhism to America* by Nyogen Senzaki, Soen Nakagawa, and Eido Shimano. Edited by Louis Nordstrom. © 1976 The Zen Studies Society, Inc. Published in the Bhaisajaguru Series by Theatre Arts Books, New York, and used here with the permission of the publisher.

From *Wind Bell*, vols. VIII (1969), IX (1970–71), and XI (1972), and "Zen in America" published by Zen Center, San Francisco. Reprinted by permission of the publisher.

From Harvey Cox, *The Seduction of the Spirit*, Simon & Schuster, 1973. © 1973 by Harvey Cox. Reprinted by permission of Simon & Schuster, Inc., and Wildwood House Ltd. (London).

From Robert Michaelson, *The American Search for Soul* (Baton Rouge: Louisiana State University Press, 1975). Reprinted by permission of the publisher.

From Frederick Streng, *Understanding Religious Life*, 2nd ed., rev. (Encino, Calif.: Dickenson Publishing Co., 1976). Reprinted by permission of the publisher.

Introduction

The idea for this book was born in the spring of 1972 when one of my students asked me what I thought of Philip Kapleau. Prior to that time, I had simply known Kapleau as the author of *The Three Pillars of Zen*, a fine book usually required of all serious students of Buddhism—nothing more, nothing less. When I proceeded to begin an exegesis of the book, in my usual fashion, the student soon interrupted me by saying, "That's not what I meant! I've read the book and can make up my own mind about its merits and shortcomings. I want to know what you think of Kapleau——rōshi." After recovering from the shock of a rather pretentious intrusion on my scholarly discourse, I realized that for me, prior to that moment, there was no Philip Kapleau—only a faceless force that had authored a reasonable book. The student had just returned from a short visit to the Zen Center of Rochester, established by Kapleau, and wanted his professor's personal appraisal of this captivating figure. Of course I had formed no personal appraisal of Kapleau or of any other Buddhist practicing in America. I do not mean to say that I was unaware of the Buddhist movement in America. To be sure, I knew that there was a Zen Center in San Francisco founded by an individual named Suzuki, a Buddhist vihāra in Washington, D.C., with Theravāda affiliation, and some lama (and ex-monk) up in Vermont who talked a great deal about gurus and openness. And of course there was Buddhist Churches of America, based in San Francisco. I knew about this latter group only because they sent an emissary to the memorial service of Professor Richard H. Robinson, who had died in 1970 while I was still at the University of Wisconsin. I did not, however, know they were a Jōdo Shinshū group until I met their representative in Madison. When I realized how little I knew about Buddhist groups in America I asked myself what I was going to do about my ignorance.

Was it, in fact, even worth bothering with at all? Would I simply brush it off as so many of my colleagues in Buddhist Studies and Religious Studies had, by noting the faddish nature of the entire enterprise? Besides, I was hard at work on the completion of two other, proper books. Consequently, I thought if I could secure a few appropriate statistics, it would be easy to set the matter to rest once and for all and return to "real" Buddhology. I consulted one of my colleagues at Penn State, a well-respected sociologist of religion, and with his help discovered that the usual sources revealed membership statistics for only one group, Buddhist Churches of America, but that they claimed 100,000 members. From here the problem got worse, not better! Were these 100,000 members all merely first or second generation Japanese immigrants who brought their religion to America with them? Were they all on the West Coast (as I suspected)? Were their practices conducted in English or Japanese? And on and on, to say nothing about the various Zen groups that proliferated after Jack Kerouac and Gary Snyder emerged from the beat movement with Zen in hand. Rather than making a quick and expected exit, I was being pulled more deeply into a quasi-investigation of American Buddhist groups. Eventually, I learned that Colgate University had sponsored a research project by an American Pure Land priest, Boris Erwitt, and that the fruits of his labors were now in the possession of Professor Kenneth Morgan of Colgate University. Helpful as always, Professor Morgan sent me the research from this now abandoned project (Reverend Erwitt later confessed to me that he once had intended to write a book on Buddhism in America, but was now too old to carry the task out). Much to my surprise (and dismay), I found that there were over 200 Buddhist groups listed in Erwitt's findings, as well as numerous photographs (in accord with Erwitt's background as a professional photographer). All of this newly discovered material was becoming much too inviting to pass up. To pursue my inquiry properly, though, would require both time and money. No matter how I tried, I could procure neither. Consequently, I utilized whatever "free" time I could glean to write what seemed to be an endless flow of letters and to gather information (for what reasons I could not discern, for I had absolutely no idea what to do with all this material). Within a year, I discovered that I had filled an entire five-drawer cabinet with information on Buddhist activities in America.

In the ensuing years, projects came and went, but this ominous file cabinet remained and grew. Finally, after being invited in the summer of 1974 to be a visiting professor of Sanskrit at the newly formed Naropa Institute (founded by the previously mentioned lama in Vermont, whose name I discovered was Chögyam Trungpa), I began to sort out some of the materials that I had gathered. A somewhat presumptuous master plan then developed to write the first book on Buddhism in America (as I then intended to call it). This grand plan has fallen by the wayside, not by design, but rather because Emma McCloy Layman's *Buddhism in America* was published in September 1976. What was at first a disappointment (at being up-staged, so to speak) has turned into a blessing in disguise. Ms. Layman has gathered a voluminous amount of data, certainly as much as (or more than) my own efforts yielded. Thus, this allows me to narrow my task, lest I duplicate her efforts. Further, I can concentrate on those aspects of Buddhism in America that I find most intriguing and that she, obligingly, omits or overlooks.

Professor Layman asks in her Introduction (p. xiii) what, for me, is the fundamental question in this area—one that has plagued me since my own research began in 1972: Is there a characteristically Ameri-can style of Buddhism? What she is questioning here is whether we have Asian Buddhism transplanted onto (but not necessarily into) American soil, or whether we have a new cultural amalgam that we should properly identify as "American Buddhism." Ultimately she is correct when she remarks that what is emerging is not "American," not "Western," and not even altogether "Eastern." At best, we have what Donald Swearer has called (in another cultural context) "Bud-dhism in transition." This book is intended to document the nature of this transition in America.

At the outset, I should state that this book assumes a basic familiar-ity on the part of the reader with Asian Buddhism. Rather than try-ing to condense a working knowledge of Asian Buddhism into one inevitably inadequate chapter, I refer the reader to *The Buddhist Religion* by Richard H. Robinson and Willard Johnson or my own *Buddhism: A Modern Perspective.* For a series of fine essays on modern Buddhism, refer to Dumoulin's *Buddhism in the Modern World.*

The following pages are organized into three major parts: (1) American Buddhism: The Iron Bird Flies, (2) The Flowering of Bud-dhism in America: Horses Run on Wheels, and (3) New Heaven and Earth: Dharma Comes to the Land of the Red Man. The first part of the book documents the important historical data concerning Bud-dhism's entry into America, both formally and informally. Further, it follows the development of the various Buddhist traditions from the late 1890s to the present day. At best then, we get a complex picture of an obviously bifurcated tradition. After these initial necessities, the first part attempts to confront the manner and degree to which Buddhism has been successful in adjusting itself to its new and rather foreign environment in the United States. What problems of cultural translocation have inhibited meaningful progress for Bud-dhism? What alliances have been pursued or disavowed? One cannot understand the actual reality of Buddhism in America without in-vestigating the cultural and sectarian traditions that are represented among American Buddhists and the varied membership of the dif-ferent groups. We must further explore the stated goals and ambitions of the Buddhist groups with an eye toward the degree to which ecumenism is considered valuable and/or a simple necessity for survival. The particular concerns of the various groups must also be considered, such as the purposeful (or otherwise) lack of an active monastic tradition. Finally, we must explore the different images that Americans have had of Buddhism, which is done in the section called "A Tradition of Misunderstanding: Two Buddhisms in America."

The second section of the book attempts to demonstrate, through application, some of the ways in which the issues cited in the first section are concretely manifested in the various Buddhist groups. Obviously, one could choose samples for study from hundreds of Buddhist groups that exist in America. On the other hand, one might adopt Ms. Layman's technique of offering a chapter on each tradition with special emphasis given to major groups. In seeking to avoid a mere hodge-podge of data, I have somewhat restricted my choice of groups for study, hoping to reveal more, by extended treatment, than a cursory examination might. Of the eight groups I have chosen to present, four are Japanese in origin, two Tibetan, one Chinese, and one Sinhalese. This selection of groups is roughly proportional to the numbers of practitioners in each tradition. Further, within each tradition there is diversity. For that reason, I have included discussions of differing sectarian groups: Jōdo Shinshū, Nichiren Shōshū and Zen for the Japanese tradition, as well as the rNying-ma-pa and bKa-rgyud-pa lineages for the Tibetan tradition. These and the other groups I examine have been selected because they are representative, growing, popular, and relatively stable. There is not as much geographic diversity as I would like (since six of the eight are located in or have headquarters in California). Nevertheless, while this may confirm for some their suspicion that Buddhist groups only serve Oriental communities, the bulk of which are in California, or communities of "freaks," the bulk of which also seem to be in California, this would prove to be a hasty judgment. Serving Oriental communities may have been the initial intention for at least one group (Buddhist Churches of America), but it is not the predominant factor. Even the one group cited now has 60 temples and 40 branches throughout North America. Other groups settled in California solely because the founder chose that state, rather than because of native communities.

The third section of the book concerns the future of Buddhism in America; of course, this section can only proceed from an evaluation of the current state of affairs. Unlike Ms. Layman's examination, which I feel overestimates Buddhism's impact on America, my treatment starts from the position that, to date, it has made almost no impact at all. I would argue that, taken collectively (a position about which I have some reservations), Oriental religion has influenced American culture, but that Buddhism is only one component of that larger cultural complex. The more appropriate question seems to be: Can it or will it significantly influence American culture? I will try to outline in the third section some of the directions Buddhism must

take if it is to become part of the fiber of American religious life.
Whether there are *distinctly Buddhist* answers to American problems
remains to be seen. Religious freedom accords a place in America for
Buddhism, but only if Buddhism becomes fully American and responsive to American religious needs and inquiries can it ever hope to add
something difinitive and integral to American religious life.

When the iron bird flies, and horses run on wheels,
The Tibetan people will be scattered like ants across the World,
And the Dharma will come to the land of the Red Man.

Attributed to Padmasambhava
(Quoted from the first volume of
Annals of the Nyingma Lineage in
America, p. 4)

PART ONE

American Buddhism: The Iron Bird Flies

And something is happening here,
But you don't know what it is,
Do you, Mr. Jones?

— Bob Dylan[1]

Boredom is the first taste of nothingness.
Today, boredom is the chief starting place of metaphysics.

— Michael Novak[2]

The scene is a bright apartment in the "hill" section of Boulder, Colorado, near the University of Colorado campus. It is the occasion of a weekly "party" held by students who are enrolled in the first half of an intensive ten-week "module" in which they will study Indian Buddhism, live and meditate together, and otherwise partake of the activities that Naropa Institute has provided for its Summer Program of 1975. Only in its second summer of operation, this not yet accredited university has offered perhaps the most diversified curriculum of any alternative form of education since Esalen Institute first appeared on the American scene. The main focus of the university is Buddhist studies, advertised in nonsectarian fashion in keeping with the wishes of the institute's founder, and that is what the party-goers are here to discuss: Buddhism. Seated on a sofa along one wall, two members of the experimental course are engaged in heated conversation. One is an instructor in the module, and the other is one of the students. Each of the two discussants normally teaches in a "regular" university during the academic year. With Coors in hand, the two figures debate the (Mahāyāna) doctrine of emptiness. After much talk, and little consensus, the module instructor asks the student to define emptiness. The student replies quickly and with confidence: "Emptiness means that we don't exist. That's what Nāgārjuna said, and that's what I believe." Quick to respond, the instructor asks, "But does that mean that we are not sitting here having this discussion right now?" "Yep," notes the student, "No you, no me, no apartment, no Naropa Institute. That's what it means." "Then what's going on here? What about Nāgārjuna's two levels of truth?" asks the instructor. The student, sensing imminent victory, goes on. "Nirvāṇa and Saṃsāra are precisely the same thing, so nothing's going on here." "But isn't that a statement made from the standpoint of ultimate truth, and doesn't Nāgārjuna also say, in the 18th verse of the 24th chapter of the Mādhyamika-kārikās, 'It is dependent origination that we call emptiness,' thus stressing the *relational* quality of things rather than their nonexistence?" the instructor answers. The student, now somewhat flustered and becoming uneasy due to the little grin readily apparent on his interlocutor's face, says, "Look, you're just testing my faith." "No," says the instructor, "I'm just demonstrating how right Nāgārjuna is— especially when he says, in the 8th verse of the 13th chapter of the kārikās, that those who treat emptiness as a viewpoint are 'incurable.'" "Now wait just a minute," the student says, getting quite angry. "You're just twisting my words." "Fair enough," quips the instructor. "How about if I demonstrate by pushing with no push the table which is no table into your nonexistent knee and laughing no laugh while you cry no tears?" "Look, we're not getting anywhere," says the student. "Why do you suppose my teacher told me all this if it wasn't true?" The instructor, eager for an opportunity to change subjects, asks, "Who is your teacher?" "Why Rinpoche, of course," the student responds. "Have you ever *met him personally? By that I mean have you ever had a *private interview* with him?" the instructor asks. "Yes, once," the student retorts. "Not too long ago, when Rinpoche visited Chicago." Sensing a chance for some firsthand information, the instructor continues this line of questioning: "What was it like? How long did it last? How did you feel? What teaching did you get?" The student, now smiling, says, "Well, I was given five minutes with him, but actually our interview only lasted about three minutes. He was so compassionate that when he recognized my nervousness, he stared out the window the whole time." "You're kidding," says the instructor. "What did you learn from that?" The student: "I learned how terribly messed up I am, and how important his teaching was for me." At this point the instructor moved on to another conversation.

The foregoing is a mildly fictionalized account of a real conversation I witnessed in which the student was (by his own definition) a serious American Buddhist who devoted a considerable part of every day to Buddhist practice. Why do I start what I hope will be a reasonably sympathetic book on Buddhism in America with such a profoundly disappointing demonstration? I do it because it must be clear from the outset that Buddhism in this country is a veritable "mixed-bag" of serious, mature, understanding students and practitioners, and a group of no less serious, but limited students who understand little, perceive less, and are wildly vocal. I do not mean to imply by my example that all students of the teacher in question are like the one referred to above. Quite the contrary is true. Nevertheless, some Buddhist groups in America are growing so fast, with so little concern for the meaning of this rapid growth, that it is possible to follow a teacher that one has met only briefly, if at all, and to shape one's entire life around the *supposed* meaning of this teacher's pronouncements.

How did Buddhism in America grow from a simple beginning in the latter half of the nineteenth century to the mass movement that it has become less than one hundred years later? How did it evolve to its present state, a state which prompted Agehananda Bharati to remark:

> Alan Watts once suggested that in another fifty years or so, people in India will drive around in cars, live in suburbia, and play baseball, whereas people in America will sit in caves in Oregon and in the Rockies and meditate on their navel and on ātman and nirvāṇa. This was meant to be a facctious, but forensically useful exaggeration. Still, the trend is certainly there.[3]

CHAPTER 1

The Historical Scene

A map is needed in order for people to find their way, to avoid being lost; even a map of familiar territory is necessary if one is looking for something in particular. Maps are also used to encourage further exploration.

—Martin Marty[1]

There is good reason to believe that as early as 1839, Japanese Buddhism of the Jōdo Shinshū variety was beginning to find its way to Hawaii, predominantly through the Japanese vessels that shipwrecked in or near Hawaiian waters.[2] Buddhism's official entry to Hawaii, however, is marked by the arrival of Sōryū Kagahi, a Jōdo Shinshū priest who sailed into Honolulu harbor in the spring of 1889.[3] It should be remembered that Hawaii did not become an American possession until 1898. Consequently, Buddhism in nineteenth-century Hawaii cannot technically be considered American. On the mainland, matters are not so easy to delineate. Chinese immigrants began to appear on the West Coast in the late 1840s. By the early 1850s, as news of the new gold discoveries began to spread, thousands of Chinese were in residence. Several Chinese temples were erected, most notably Kong Chow Temple and T'ien-hou Temple (both in San Francisco), but these were rather eclectic in nature and only mildly influenced by Buddhist teachings. In spite of the fact that these temples seem to have been prototypic for the modern day "Chinatown" temples, the real beginnings of Buddhism in America did not occur until considerably later.

Perhaps the critical event foreshadowing the entry of Buddhism was the World Parliament of Religions, held at the Chicago World's Fair in 1893. Several important proponents of Oriental religions were in attendance, among them two Buddhists: Sōyen Shaku (the disciple of Imakita Kōsen of Engaku Temple, a Rinzai master) and Anagarika Dharmapala (who was later to become the driving force behind the Mahbodhi Society in America). They aroused a great deal of interest, and Sōyen Shaku was to return to America slightly more than a decade later to promote the Rinzai school of Zen.

Other schools of Buddhism, however, were also interested in America. In July 1898, two Pure Land priests from Hompa Hongwanji in Kyoto arrived in San Francisco, founding the Buddhist Mission of North America the following year. Incorporated in 1942 as Buddhist Churches of America, this group now claims in excess of 100,000 members, and is the largest Jōdo Shinshū organization in America.

THE RINZAI SCHOOL OF ZEN

Sōyen Shaku returned to the United States in 1905 as a guest of Mr. and Mrs. Alexander Russell of San Francisco. Mrs. Russell particularly was a great friend to Zen Buddhism and was referred to by Nyōgen Senzaki as "the gate-opener of Zen in America,"[4] and she arranged for Sōyen Shaku to visit many American cities during his stay. When he returned to Japan in March 1906, Sōyen Shaku selected three of his closest disciples to promote the Rinzai lineage in America: Sōkatsu Shaku, D.T. Suzuki, and Nyōgen Senzaki. Each of these remarkable disciples has left a lasting imprint on the development of Zen in America.

Nyōgen Senzaki

Nyōgen Senzaki arrived in California in 1905, but did not begin to teach Zen until seventeen years later[5] and did not establish any permanent facility until the late 1920s. In the interim period he held many jobs ranging from waiter to hotel manager.[6] Louis Nordstrom has said of Nyōgen Senzaki:

> Nyōgen Senzaki had come to this country partly because he felt that Zen in Japan had begun to drift in the direction of decadence, and like Soyen Shaku before him, he hoped America would indeed prove to be the "happy field" of his teacher's dreams. He encouraged his students to be critical of all things Eastern and Oriental, thereby discouraging an unreflecting assimilation of dogma and mindless guru worship. What he hoped to bring about was a thoroughly international Buddhism, with an American base; a Buddhism that would transcend not only church and sect affiliation, but language affiliation as well. To achieve this transcendence of language affiliation, he went so far as to sponsor Esperanto, which he hoped would one day become the official language of Buddhism.[7]

Centers were eventually established in San Francisco (1928) and Los Angeles (1929), the latter of which he personally attended until his death in 1958. In an undated manuscript, Senzaki makes his abundantly optimistic hopes for America quite clear:

> When I first came to this country I was told that America had no phil-
> osophy of its own; that its thought was merely a derivative reflection of
> the thought of other countries and cultures. But I have found out that this
> is not wholly true. America has had philosophers as well as original
> thinkers who were true makers of history, even though their influence may
> not have extended abroad. In particular, I have in mind the American
> freethinkers, from Thomas Paine to Robert Ingersoll, whose books I enjoy
> reading very much. I also admire a great deal the American Transcen-
> dentalism of Ralph Waldo Emerson. It was after having read these writers
> and philosophers that I at last came upon William James's Pragmatism—
> the philosophy of practicality, the gospel of energy, whose chief criterion
> is success. Zen and American Pragmatism have much in common. Just as
> Pragmatism, according to James, was a new name for an old thought, so
> I say Zen is an old name for a new thought!
>   Americans in general are lovers of freedom and equality; for this reason,
> they make natural Zen students. There are eight aspects of American life
> and character that make America fertile ground for Zen:
>
> 1. American philosophy is practical.
> 2. American life does not cling to formality.
> 3. The majority of Americans are optimists.
> 4. Americans love nature.
> 5. They are capable of simple living, being both practical and efficient.
> 6. Americans consider true happiness to lie in universal brotherhood.
> 7. The American conception of ethics is rooted in individual morality.
> 8. Americans are rational thinkers.
>
> Pragmatism is truly an indigenous American philosophy. At the same time,
> however, it is but another name for one manifestation of the sparkling
> rays of Zen in the actual, practical world.[8]

This sort of approach gained Senzaki many disciples. His most immediate disciple, Robert Aitken, established the Diamond Sangha community group in Honolulu (which now has a branch in Haiku, Maui). Although the Diamond Sangha was not founded until 1959, one year after Senzaki's death, it did help to sponsor some of the early visits of Nakagawa Sōen Rōshi to America. Although he had visited America as early as 1949, at Nyōgen Senzaki's request Nakagawa Sōen returned to America after Senzaki's death to found the Los Angeles Bosatsukai (later called the California Bosatsukai). Both the Diamond Sangha and California Bosatsukai are under the leadership of Soen Rōshi. Nakagawa Sōen was also responsible for bringing Eido Tai Shimano to America. Settling first in Hawaii in 1960, where he assisted the Diamond Sangha, Eido Tai Shimano moved to New York in 1965 and soon became president of the Zen Studies Society. He eventually opened (in 1968) the New York Zendo Shoboji and in 1973 (less than a year after he received Dharma Transmission from Sōen Rōshi) opened the International Dai Bosatsu Zendo, named after a mountain in Japan. From the above progression of teachers and disciples, it is clear that Sōyen Shaku's student, Nyōgen Senzaki, left a firm imprint on the Rinzai Zen movement that was to follow him in America.

Sokei-an

Sōyen Shaku's second student, Sōkatsu Shaku, spent two years in America from 1906 to 1908 and later came back (1909, 1910) to continue his work. When he finally returned to Japan, he left behind his own disciple, Shigetsu Sasaki, to continue the teaching. Unlike his predecessors, Sasaki immediately cultivated the East Coast. Since he had been only a lay disciple, he felt it necessary to return to Japan to complete his training and in October 1919 left New York. He became an ordained Zen master in 1928 (at age forty-eight) and returned to America at the urging of his teacher. Having taken the name Sokei-an, he founded the Buddhist Society of America in 1930. (The group was incorporated the next year.) Five years before his death in 1945, Sokei-an married Ruth Fuller Everett, and in the year of his death, the organization was renamed the First Zen Institute of America. Always possessed of a quick wit, Sokei-an speaks of his early experiences teaching meditation in America:

> When I came to this country last time, I was teaching American young ladies to meditate—half an hour—and in three days no one came to my place. So five minutes! And that was very long, and I reduced it to one minute, and one young lady fainted![9]

In 1935, Sokei-an remarked, "It is an unhappy death for a Zen master when he does not leave an heir."[10] Nevertheless, this was precisely the case for the Dharma heir of Sōyen Shaku's second disciple in America.

Dr. D.T. Suzuki

When Sōyen Shaku lectured at the World Parliament of Religions, one of the members of the audience was Paul Carus, the owner of Open Court Publishing Company. Favorably impressed with what he heard, he asked Sōyen Shaku to stay on in America as an editor in his publishing firm. The venerable rōshi declined, but suggested in his stead Dr. D.T. Suzuki, the third of his students in America. Despite the pioneering achievements of Sōyen Shaku's other disciples, neither was as instrumental as D.T. Suzuki in bringing Zen to public awareness in America. D.T. Suzuki worked for Open Court in LaSalle, Illinois, from 1897 to 1909, at which point he returned to Japan. Although he would not return to America until 1936, Suzuki's career continued in brilliant fashion. Along the way, he married Beatrice Lane in 1911 and pursued his scholarly endeavors.

No single writer on Zen has been so prolific as Suzuki. Of his works still in print, the ones most often referred to are: *Manual of Zen Buddhism, The Training of the Zen Buddhist Monk,* and *Essays in Zen Buddhism* (published in three series). In addition to his Zen publications, Suzuki was also fiercely interested in Indian Mahāyāna, an area in which he published extensively. Of primary interest are his translation and study of the Laṅkāvatāra-sūtra (published as two separate volumes), his many articles in *The Eastern Buddhist* (an English language journal that he edited and published in Japan), and his translation of substantial portions of the difficult Gaṇḍavyūha-sūtra. A partial, but useful, bibliography of Suzuki's writings appears in *On Indian Mahayana Buddhism.* The book also contains selections of Suzuki's writings on this topic.

Suzuki spent the war years in Japan, but returned to America for a long stay between 1950 and 1958. During this time, he gave frequent lectures in American universities (the most notable of which were a series of talks he gave at Columbia University in 1951). Further, he served as president of the Cambridge Buddhist Association (founded in 1957),[11] although his leadership was mostly from a distance. Suzuki received assistance with his work from the Zen Studies Society of New York, founded by Cornelius Crane in 1956. After Mr. Crane's death in 1962, this organization was, for the most part, inactive until Eido Rōshi assumed the presidency.

Although D.T. Suzuki's scholarly efforts have not always been praised, the overall estimate of his work and mission must be unequivocally favorable, especially because it offered Americans a "serious" Zen amidst the curious "Beat Zen" and "Square Zen" that developed in the 1950s. In 1969, Gary Snyder gave the following appraisal of Suzuki:

> The reason people criticize Suzuki is that there almost aren't enough words to say how big he was. What other Japanese person has had so much influence on the world at large? We don't think of it that way because we take him to be so much our own, but he is Japan's greatest cultural contribution to the world so far. In Europe and America he has influenced everything—psychology, music, aesthetics, architecture, landscape design—and through his "disciples" like Christmas Humphreys, Edward Conze, Hubert Benoit, Bernard Phillips, John Cage, and Alan Watts, he has permeated all levels of society. He has been the catalyst of some real social changes, in attitudes towards the self, towards effort, towards involvement, in attitudes on the nature of creativity, on the value of verbalization and articulation as against the intuitive approach. All these things which are not "pure Zen" or Zen practice are nonetheless very important humanly.[12]

Prior to the upsurge of interest in Zen from the late 1950s on, D.T. Suzuki remained the single most significant force in Zen's presence in America—a fitting tribute for this exemplary disciple of Sōyen Shaku.

OTHER EARLY TRADITIONS

To a large degree, the history of Buddhism in America up to 1960 is, with the exception of the Buddhist Churches of America, really a history of Zen in America. Two other exceptions, however, must be noted. In 1912, the Koyasan Buddhist Temple was founded in Los Angeles, representative of yet another Japanese form of Buddhism: Shingon. Shingon is the Japanese form of Vajrayāna or Tantric Buddhism. Although Shingon has persisted in America for a long time, it has never gained any large measure of support or popularity. Equally unnoticed is the Lamaist Buddhist Monastery in Washington, New Jersey, founded by dGe-lugs-pa Tibetans under the directorship of Geshe Wangyal. Geshe Wangyal, born in 1900 of Kalmuck heritage, studied at Drepung Monastery in Tibet. After coming to the United States, he founded the Lamaist Buddhist Monastery in 1958. Perhaps due to brilliant scholarship and lack of "flashiness," the group working with Geshe Wangyal has attracted little attention. It has, however, played an important role in the careers of several fine young American scholars of Buddhism. Further, it offers serious practitioners an opportunity to learn Buddhist meditational techniques from a group of eminently trained lamas.

THE ZEN EXPLOSION

It was not until a full decade after the conclusion of World War II that America witnessed the "Zen explosion." By Zen explosion I mean that groups other than Rinzai affiliates began to take root in America. In this regard, two other forms of Zen now abound in America, the first being a mixture of Rinzai and Sōtō and the second being Sōtō Zen itself. The former group owes its beginnings to Sogaku Harada, although this master from Hosshin Temple never set foot in the United States. Harada's impact is felt primarily through the teachings of three of his disciples: Taizan Maezumi, Hakuun Yasutani, and Philip Kapleau.

Taizan Maezumi Rōshi
The earliest of Harada's three disciples to teach in America was Taizan Maezumi Rōshi. Originally trained as a Sōtō priest at Eihei Temple, this young man (born 1930) now represents three major Zen lineages, those of Hakujun Kuroda Rōshi, Hakuun Yasutani Rōshi, and Kōryū Ōsaka Rōshi. He arrived in Los Angeles in 1956 and established the Zen Center of Los Angeles. Like Sogaku Harada, he emphasizes both kōan practice and shikantaza, adjusting the method selected to suit the needs and temperament of the individual student. The Zen Center of Los Angeles trains both priests and laymen, with Maezumi Rōshi emphasizing strict discipline for all. With the assistance of one of his senior training monks, Bernard Tetsugen Glassman, Maezumi Rōshi has edited two extremely useful volumes on Zen practice, emphasizing his multifaceted approach.

Hakuun Yasutani Rōshi

Hakuun Yasutani Rōshi visited the United States for the first time in 1962. During this trip he held sesshins in Los Angeles, Philadelphia, New York, Boston, and Washington, D.C. The following year he returned to America, but continued to give lectures in England, France, and Germany. These periodic visits continued until Yasutani's death in 1973 (at the advanced age of eighty-eight). Somewhat an "itinerant" in America, he served as Zen master for many groups (including the Diamond Sangha, California Bosatsukai, and Zen Studies Society of New York). A long-time schoolmaster, Yasutani had his head shaved at age five as a symbolic induction into the priesthood. He was sent to live in a Zen temple, where he remained until he became a novice at age thirteen. His schooling continued, and at age thirty he married, eventually raising five children. No temple was available for Yasutani, so he utilized his education and turned to teaching. It is said that he broke with the Sōtō sect because the great teachers in this lineage were vague about the nature of satori. At forty, he met Harada Rōshi, abandoned his work as an educator, and became a temple priest. While participating in his very first sesshin with his new master, he gained the kensho experience. Many years later (at age fifty-eight), he was named a Dharma heir by his teacher.

Philip Kapleau

The most influential of Harada's disciples in America is Philip Kapleau. Kapleau had some acquaintance with Zen prior to his decision to pursue its practice, as he was a court reporter for the War Crimes Trials in Tokyo in 1946. After returning to America, he began to attend D.T. Suzuki's lectures at Columbia University in 1951. Nagging discontent with "intellectual" Buddhism and recurring illness led to Kapleau's resolution to travel to Japan to seek enlightenment. He arrived in Japan in the fall of 1953, eventually living at Ryutakuji Temple and practicing under Nakagawa Sōen Rōshi. After a six-month stay, he traveled to Hosshinji Temple to practice under Harada Rōshi. For just under three years he stayed at Hosshinji as a lay monk. In 1956, Nakagawa Sōen took Kapleau to Yasutani Rōshi, and it was Yasutani Rōshi that urged Kapleau to bring Zen to America. Two years later, Kapleau had the kensho experience. Prior to his return to America in 1966, Yasutani Rōshi authorized Kapleau as a teacher. During the year of his return, *The Three Pillars of Zen* was published in America (it was published in Japan the previous year). In August of 1966, the Zen Meditation Center was founded in Rochester, New York. Perhaps more than any other practitioner of Zen in America, Philip Kapleau has attempted to promote Zen as an American religious practice. Such innovations as adopting Western clothing for zazen, adapting Zen rituals to an American audience, chanting in English, and the like, are all in evidence at Kapleau's center. To a large extent, it was these "deviations" from the traditional forms of Zen that led to Kapleau's break with Yasutani Rōshi in 1967. Nevertheless, Kapleau remains one of the most sincere, hard working, and *effective* teachers of Zen in America.

Sōtō Zen

The Sōtō Zen tradition did not really commence in America until the mid-1950s. At that time, Soyu Matsuoka Rōshi founded the Chicago Buddhist Temple. Matsuoka Rōshi too has served many Buddhist groups (particularly in California), leaving the Chicago group in the hands of his disciple, Richard Langlois Roshi (one of the few American rōshis). By far, the most influential proponent of Sōtō Zen has been Shunryu Suzuki Rōshi, who arrived in San Francisco from Eihei Temple in May of 1959. By 1961, he had a substantial following of Americans, and the San Francisco Zen Center was opened. His determination and rigorous practice resulted in the purchase of Tassajara Hot Springs, which was turned into a monastic training center in 1967. Before Suzuki's death in 1971, he had assistance from Daimin Katagiri Rōshi, who came to America in 1964. Shortly before he died, Suzuki Rōshi passed on the Dharma mantle to his disciple, Richard Baker Rōshi, who now heads the San Francisco Zen Center.

Also noteworthy in the Sōtō lineage is Jiyu Kennett Rōshi, an English woman (and almost lifelong Buddhist) who traveled to Japan in 1962 and studied as a priestess under the Chief Abbot of Sōjiji Temple: Chisan Kōhō Zenji. As the first woman admitted to either of the chief Sōtō training temples (Sōjiji and Eiheiji) since the fourteenth century, much was expected of this diligent practitioner. Not to disappoint her master, she received Dharma Transmission in 1963 and later that year was made abbess of her own temple. In 1969, she arrived in America, establishing Shasta Abbey the following year as a training center for Zen priests.

One should not infer from the above paragraphs that the Rinzai tradition has died out or abandoned its missionary pursuit in America. In 1962, still actively pursuing new disciples, Joshu Sasaki Rōshi arrived in California to found the Cimarron Zen Center in Los Angeles (in 1966) and the Mt. Baldy Zen Center (in 1971). Affiliates are now located in California, New York, and Canada. In addition, it should be noted that many other Zen teachers, too numerous to mention in these few pages, are in residence on the American scene.

NICHIREN SHŌSHŪ SŌKAGAKKAI

By 1960 in America, time was ripe for the influx of even more Buddhist groups. The first to appear on the scene was a small group

called Nichiren Shōshū Sōkagakkai. During 1960, the president of
the parent organization in Japan, Daisaku Ikeda, organized two chapters in the Western hemisphere: one in South America and one in California. During its initial phase in America, its appeal was primarily directed to Japanese Americans. Using the same ideology as the parent organization in Japan, it grew quickly, primarily through the promise of such items as better jobs, familial stability, increased personal wealth, better health, and the like. All the disciple had to do was chant the daimoku, a seemingly magical formula that meant "Homage to the Lotus Sūtra" (Nam Myōhō Renge Kyō). Fear of potentially declining membership, however, caused the leaders of Nichiren Shoshu of America (as the group was now called) to embark on conversion drives aimed at Americans. Immediately successful, this drive utilized the usual conversion tactics of the organization, although somewhat moderated on the American scene in keeping with Daisaku Ikeda's less fanatic approach than his predecessor's. From its few chapters in the early 1960s, the organization now has in excess of two hundred chapters and over 200,000 members.

THERAVĀDA BUDDHISM

The mid and late 1960s witnessed the entry and proliferation of two new kinds of Buddhism in America: Theravāda and the predominantly meditational (or practice oriented) traditions of Tibetan Buddhism. Theravāda made its entry on the East Coast, following the visit of an eminent Theravāda monk, Madihe Pannaseeha. One year after his visit, a permanent resident was sent expressly for the purpose of founding a Theravāda organization. Thus, in 1966, the Buddhist Vihara Society was born, under the presidency of the Venerable Bope Vinita. Located in Washington, D.C., it has since 1968 operated out of one building. Needless to say, its location is convenient for the international community present in the area. Other Theravāda groups in the United States are few and far between. On the West Coast, the Stillpoint Institutes is the new name of an enterprise under the direction of Anagarika Sujata, an American who, for some time, had been a Buddhist monk. Sujata originally set up a meditation center in Clearwater, Florida, but later moved to Denver, founding the Sasana Yeiktha Meditation Center (which included a monastery and nunnery). Finally, the entire operation was moved to San Jose, California, and renamed Stillpoint Institutes. The only other noteworthy and authentic Theravāda centers are Thai temples in New York and Chicago and a small Thai enclave (including monastery and temple) in North Hollywood, which has been serviced by a few Thai monks since the early 1970s. Also popular since the early 1970s is the Vipassanā technique of Theravāda meditation. The most popular group promoting this technique is the Insight Meditation Center in Barre, Massachusetts, run by Joseph Goldstein and Jack Kornfield.

TIBETAN BUDDHISM

The late 1960s marked the beginning of a significant Western interest in Tibetan Buddhism. Since the Tibetan Holocaust, Tibetan Buddhism had largely been relegated to exile in India, Bhutan, Sikkim, and Nepal, many of its leaders having fled over the mountain from Tibet in the late 1950s to escape the pursuit of the Communist Chinese. Eventually, some of the more distinguished scholars and incarnate lamas began appearing in America. The two best known of these are Tarthang Tulku and Chögyam Trungpa. Tarthang Tulku arrived in Berkeley, California, in 1969, having come to America the previous year. He then founded the Tibetan Nyingma Meditation Center, which has grown by leaps and bounds. Chögyam Trungpa came to America in 1970 to reside in Barnet, Vermont, at Tail of the Tiger Meditation Center (since renamed Karmê-Chöling), a facility organized by several of his students. Prior to that time he had studied in India and at Oxford and also had founded Samyê-Ling Meditation Center in Scotland. The fascinating details of his life are recounted in *Born in Tibet.* Trungpa too has a rapidly expanding following. He has adopted a more unorthodox style of teaching than Tarthang Tulku, but with no less success. While Tarthang Tulku's center is explicitly rNying-ma in affiliation, Trungpa's organization is predominantly bKa-rgyud-pa, although Trungpa has some link with the rNying-ma lineage as well. There is also a Sa-skya-pa group currently active in the United States, located in Kensington, California, under the direction of Lama Kunga Thartse Tulku.

CHINESE BUDDHIST GROUPS

In addition to the Japanese, Tibetan, and South Asian traditions of Buddhism in America, there is also a modicum of support for Chinese groups. Several, such as Buddha's Universal Church in San Francisco, Temple Mahayana in the Catskill Mountains, and the Temple of Enlightenment (Buddhist Association of the United States) in the Bronx, New York, have reasonable followings. The most significant and aggressive of the Chinese Buddhist groups, however, are the Sino-American Buddhist Association and one of its divisions, Gold Mountain Monastery. Located in San Francisco, the organization is led by the learned Hsüan Hua, a Ch'an and Tripiṭaka master. This group is pursuing an active monastic life, ordaining

American men and women as monks and nuns, as well as launching a vigorous translation project.

As is obvious, the preceding pages are not intended to provide a comprehensive history of the Buddhist movement in America. Rather, these pages are intended to provide some clear landmarks from which we can enlarge our study, both in scope and perspective. Obviously, many groups have been omitted, but since it is not my intention to provide a "directory" of Buddhist groups, such procedure is required. I have tried in these pages to document some major trends of development in Buddhism in America, most specifically the development of Zen (Rinzai, Sōtō, and their combination), Jōdo Shinshū, and Nichiren in the Japanese tradition, Vajrayāna (dGe-lugs-pa, rNying-ma-pa, and bKa-rgyud-pa) in the Tibetan tradition, Theravāda in the South Asian tradition, and Ch'an in the Chinese tradition. Now it is necessary to assess some of the problems of cultural translocation encountered by these groups as well as the way in which these traditions in general have developed and then to correlate this information with the parallel progress of some key issues in American religious life.

CHAPTER 2

Buddhist Beginnings in America: 1893-1960

Few faiths ever escape modification when they collide or interact with others. Most profit from such encounters.

—Harvey Cox[1]

With few exceptions, during its initial activity, Buddhism in America was represented by two sects of Japanese Buddhism: the Jōdo Shinshū tradition from Hompa Hongwanji in Kyoto and the Zen tradition, for the most part dominated by the Rinzai lineage of Imakita Kōsen of Engaku Temple. Apart from the almost exclusively Japanese communities that these traditions served, Buddhism was simply a curiosity for Americans. Needless to say, this led to some rather incongruous circumstances:

> The majority of Sokatsu's students in San Francisco, aside from the few Japanese in San Francisco who studied with him, were all missionary ladies who were going over to Japan to do mission work. There is somewhere a picture of Sokatsu—who was one of the handsomest men you ever laid eyes on—sitting in his clerical costume, which was a long coat buttoned up to the top something like the Indian swamis wear, with all the big busty missionary ladies in their white blouses with high lace collars and their pompadours and so forth, and a few Japanese sitting on the floor.[2]

Other Americans turned to Buddhism to quench an intellectual thirst, an inquisitiveness fueled by this seemingly exotic religion. In this regard, there is a striking parallel to the entry of Buddhism to China, probably in the first century A.D. With their Confucian and Taoist cultural patterns, the Chinese saw Buddhism as an overwhelmingly foreign and peculiar endeavor. Not only were Buddhism's rituals and modes of religious practice strange, buts its world view and philosophical basis taxed the Chinese mind and temperament. To complicate the matter further, the language differences between the Indic and Chinese traditions were considerable. Consequently, during its first several hundred years in China, Buddhism made little meaningful headway. Its inertia was compounded by the fall of the Han Dynasty around 220 A.D. and the political confusion and instability that ensued. To be sure, the political dysfunction in China gave rise to substantial doses of social instability and the resultant anomie.

Initially, Buddhism was forced to find similar doctrines in Taoism by which the new religion could be explained to the Chinese, and often relied on merely approximate vocabulary renderings for its technical terminology. Thus it was not until the coming of Kumāra-jīva, around 400 A.D., that China witnessed the influx of Buddhists who were credibly bilingual and sufficiently grounded in basic Buddhist ideals so that accurate inroads could be made for Buddhist notions. Gradually, Buddhism underwent a Sinicization process in which its precepts, doctrines, and practices lost their distinctively Indian flavor. In addition, Buddhist texts were being composed by Chinese adepts, culminating in the clearly Chinese schools of Buddhism such as T'ien-t'ai and Hua-yen. Only by the time of the Sui Dynasty (589–617) had the political situation stabilized and Buddhism in China matured sufficiently that we can speak of a "Chinese" Buddhism.

For Americans, Buddhism was no less foreign and curious than it was for the Chinese. America had its own variety of a double helix basis for religious and cultural patterns in the Judaeo-Christian tradition, and this is as anomalous with regard to Buddhism as Confucianism and Taoism were for the Chinese. Equally taxing for the American mind and temperament, as it was for the Chinese, was its attempt to understand a religious tradition that is essentially non-theistic, individualistic, and apparently esoteric, mystical, and antithetical to social ethics. Not only is time construed in nonlinear fashion, but we read of an endless chain of rebirths, suffering as the basic tenet of Buddha's preaching, and a meditational practice that many see initially as leading more to catatonia than to "enlightenment." Of course we should also not forget Robert Michaelson's gloss on Henri Bergson:

> Mystical ecstasy may seem to be repose, but it is a repose like that of a locomotive standing in a station under a head of steam. Such a person has the capacity to help effect a change in humanity.[3]

Occasionally, too, we would hear of the ubiquitous doctrine of "emptiness," which seems to have been interpreted by many Americans to mean that nothing exists, not even America. All of the above was complicated by the fact that long before Buddhism's introduction, America had already built a powerful mythic history that was profoundly religious.

Although it is likely that Americans during this period were attracted to Buddhism primarily out of curiosity or intellectual concerns (or perhaps even as a form of escapism), the American soil was fertile for further Buddhist development. The doctrinal basis for Buddhism has always been embodied in the teachings of Buddha's first sermon, a text which clearly espouses the Four Noble Truths of (1) suffering, (2) craving as the cause of suffering, (3) the possibility for the cessation of suffering, and (4) the path to that cessation. America during the 1920s and 1930s was virtually the embodiment of, initially, the second noble truth, and then of the first noble truth run wild. In the affluence following World War I, craving for material wealth in a rapidly changing world and society was rampant. We all know only too well that the unrestricted fiscal policies quickly gave way to the deep Depression of the 1930s that scarred more than just America's economic foundations. And it was then that America, no less than India in the time of the Buddha, began to realize the truth of suffering. Out of the political, social, and economic instability, it might well have been possible for the American Buddhists to identify the rise of the Roosevelt administration with the third noble truth, and the New Deal policies of recovery with the fourth noble truth. In so doing, Buddhists in America would have been able to discern that life in America was not as incompatible with Buddhist teaching as it might at first appear. Since virtually all the Buddhists in America were of Japanese ancestry, instead of remaining simply Japanese Buddhists in America, they might have approached the possibility of identifying themselves as Japanese Americans (long before this term was fashionable) who also happened to embrace Buddhism as a religious ideal. Nevertheless, these proto-American Buddhists either chose not to make this association or it simply did not occur to them. Buddhists in this period, despite the then current racial prejudice in America (which has militated against Asian American Buddhists throughout their history in this country), passed up a marvelous opportunity to begin building their own mythic history in America—a problem which continues to haunt them today.

PROBLEMS IN ACCULTURATION

The Sacred Centers

To this point in American Buddhist history, American Buddhism's ritual life focused on the reenactment of an exclusively Japanese mythic structure. Harvey Cox has noted that "rather than 'moving' people, a myth 'places' them in a history and in a universe of value and meaning."[4] For early American Buddhists, the sacred center was Japan and not America. This "placed" them more fully in that culture than in the one of their residence. Regarding the critical meeting point between the sacred and profane, Frederick Streng has aptly remarked:

> A temple, especially, is a specific place where divine power reveals itself. Since the temple is the point of contact between earth and heaven, it is only natural that the temple reveal symbolically the character of the divine realm.[5]

The temple was *in* America; but the temple, the sacred power in the ritual life enacted there, and the religious efficacy engendered by the powerful sounds of the ritual (especially if we remember the importance of the repetition of the Nembutsu in the Jōdo Shinshū tradition), were all *of* Japan. Further, when Streng rightly notes that "in all major religious traditions there is a concern to make spiritual life effective in everyday social existence,"[6] we must realize that social existence in America was a problematic area for the Japanese Buddhist. It was probably much more problematic for them than for non-Asian American Buddhists, since India has always been the axis mundi for Buddhists (as Jerusalem has been for Christians and Jews). Consequently, the lack of social identity confounded the problem of religious identity through this early period of Buddhist development in America.

Parallels Between the Two Traditions

The identity problem just discussed might have been overcome had the Japanese Buddhists in America noticed some of the obvious parallels between avowedly American values and the enigmatic Buddhist practices noted above. On the one hand, the Zen tradition, like all of the meditative threads of Buddhist practice, emphasizes complete self-reliance in the attainment of religious salvation. No outside agency could produce the appropriate answer to the Zen practitioner's kōan; no outside agent could perform his zazen for him. This intense self-reliance was not unlike the so-called rugged individualism that Americans are so fond of citing as demonstration of their resilient nature and ability to overcome personal obstacles in the path to success. Yet only a few of the Zen teachers, and virtually none of the American Zen practitioners, ever seemed to have noticed the parallel. On the other hand, in more explicitly "religious" endeavors, the many practitioners of Jōdo Shinshū rarely (if ever) saw the parallel between the saving grace of Amida Buddha and the notion of grace in the Judaeo-Christian tradition. (We should remember that it is not *identity* that is claimed, but only similarity, albeit in rather unsophisticated fashion.) The usual reaction to social change on the part of the early American Buddhists was one of simple retrenchment. In other words, they seemed to opt for something less than the middle path.

The Mystical East

A final handicap to Buddhist infancy in America was the lack of the Orient as a substantial "sphere of influence" in American political life. Unlike the post-1945 period, with Korea and Vietnam successively dominating the consciousness of many Americans, before Pearl Harbor the Orient was still regarded as the "mystical East" or the "inscrutable East," offering little for the mind's eye of the public. To be sure, the war with Japan was a potential death blow to American Buddhism, this period being particularly difficult for those in internment camps. Like the Buddhist persecution in China in 845, in which all the scholastic traditions faded to the background and only the predominantly practice-oriented sects survived, World War II demonstrated the resilience of these same "vest pocket" traditions on the American scene. Instead of snuffing out American Buddhism before it had taken hold, the Pure Land and Zen traditions survived. At a time when Buddhism in America was so limited in scope, with little diversity of traditions and sects, this survival was the foreshadowing of the great diversity and growth that was to follow.

POSTWAR GROWTH

After the Second World War, not only was the bitter taste of collective inhumanity (symbolized by both Pearl Harbor and the atomic devastation of Hiroshima and Nagasaki) still souring our mouths, but also a profound awareness of the Orient in general and Japan in particular remained in our minds. Shintō in Japan had been disestablished. Buddhism, on the other hand, in spite of its support for the war effort, fared considerably better, in both Japan and America. American veterans, having returned to colleges and universities, were more aware of things Oriental. Also at this time, American universities began to expand their offerings on Asia, with courses on Asian history, politics, sociology, and religion. Just as today it is not unusual to find Vietnam veterans in courses on Buddhism, after World War II it was also not unusual to find veterans studying Buddhism.

The postwar interest was enhanced by the reappearance of D.T. Suzuki and others who pursued university lecturing with vigor and integrity. The study of Asian religions was finally emerging as an academic discipline in America, one that required serious and painstaking language training if the task was to be meaningfully accomplished. Just as in the time of Kumārajīva's arrival in China, it was not long before scholars with more than appropriate credentials indirectly aided in the task of establishing Buddhism's first significant entry to America by providing excellent translations of Buddhist texts from virtually all the Buddhist traditions and languages.

It was to the good fortune of Buddhism that, with few exceptions, Buddhism in America still meant Jōdo Shinshū or Rinzai Zen, for because of this, no sectarian squabbles or discussions of whose rōshi was better appeared to impede the progress of Buddhism's growth. Continued focus on Asia, particularly due to the Korean War, enabled Buddhism to remain indirectly in the public's eye.

At this point, it is necessary to ask just *who* these Buddhists in America were. For the first time in Buddhism's short history on the American scene, it was beginning to make real inroads with the non-Asian populace. Even conservative Buddhist groups, like Buddhist Churches of America, were beginning to develop more multifaceted communities, fulfilling one of the prime requisites for Buddhist religious life: a substantial and active lay saṃgha. It is often forgotten that the Buddhist saṃgha has always included an active laity as well as a monastic constituency. And in some respects, the saṃgha has been the driving and *unifying* force throughout Buddhism's long history in Asia. Just as an increasingly important role has been cited for the laity in modern Theravāda in Asia, such was the case for Buddhism as it pursued growth on the American scene.[7] With the saṃgha now composed of Americans and Asians alike (and the Americans were of all ages, both sexes, from various family and religious backgrounds, and pursuing various professional and nonprofessional careers), certain accommodations had to be made to meet the needs of the new clientele.

Buddhism's Attraction for Westerners

These accommodations turned out to be the beginning of Buddhism's acculturation within the American scene. It is certainly difficult to offer very specific information concerning this sudden upswing in the growth of Buddhism. Of course, some of the factors already mentioned must be considered, but we are sorely lacking in hard data (and have no apparent mode of procurement). We do, however, know that the political stability that accompanied the Eisenhower administration freed a tremendous amount of energy with which Americans could begin to pursue other societal concerns. Needless to say, after two wars in rapid succession, Buddhism's supposed doctrinal affirmation of pacifism may well have been a central issue in many Buddhist conversions. Others probably at least noticed Buddhism in their search for communists during the McCarthy deluge.

There were other nagging problems, however, that needed attention: racism, drug addiction, a rise in mental illness, and a burgeoning crime rate (to cite a few). For each in its place, Buddhism provided reasonable answers. Buddha has long been regarded as a social reformer who reacted against the caste system in promulgating his own religious path. He is reputed to have accepted into the fold members from all castes. This has been no small issue in the Buddhist resurgence in India, and it is no small issue for America. At least several Buddhist sects (among them Jōdo Shinshū and Nichiren Shōshū) have special appeal to the downtrodden, affording them a chance at renewed dignity. Regarding drug addiction, Buddhism's position has always been firm: no intoxicants or psychoactive substances whatsoever. It can be noted that many former "users" of all sorts reportedly abandon drugs following their initial involvement with Buddhist practice. Since Buddhism has always been concerned with mental health, its appeal here is obvious. Much of Buddhist practice is devoted to making the mind healthy and free. Developed to its peak in the scholastic period, Buddhist psychology (as embodied in the Abhidharma tradition) still affords at least as sophisticated an approach to the mind and its function as any Western psychological mode. It has been the sects of Buddhism that stress formal meditation (Zen, the Tibetan traditions, Ch'an, and Theravāda) that have had the greatest appeal for Americans. It is not by accident that the Dhammapada, one of the most well-known and beloved of all Buddhist texts, begins with the words: "Mind is the forerunner of all states; mind is chief." Crime too was castigated by Buddhists from their earliest beginnings in India. For a monk or nun, theft was punishable by nothing short of excommunication, while for the laity, nontheft was included as one of the five vows taken by all members of the Buddhist laity. This profound respect for the property of others offered a potentially healing alternative to the then current trends in American society, which were not unlike recent trends in Asia.[8] However, just as earlier American Buddhists had not pursued their opportunity to develop the beginnings of a mythic history and American identity during the Depression, more modern Buddhists passed up the opportunity to utilize the high standards of ethical life maintained by Buddhists as a means of actively pursuing an American constituency. Many American Buddhist groups were still too actively involved in their retrenchment.

Nor did Buddhists cultivate the appeal to reason that was becoming such a prominent factor in American life. The tradition of logic in Buddhism represents the epitome of Buddhist philosophy, yet this extension of reason into the philosophical domain was not (and is not now) stressed. Even as the pragmatism that Americans search for develops into technology run wild, Buddhists are slow to remind Americans that the founder of their tradition was regarded, perhaps above all else, as a pragmatist. Many claim that his pragmatism was the basis for his long, puzzling silence on metaphysical issues. As Michael Novak suggests that today boredom may well be the starting point for metaphysics, might we postulate that Buddha was just not bored enough?

Beat Zen

By the mid-1950s, Buddhism in America was on the brink of several new developments. First, new forms of Buddhism were appearing on the American scene, particularly Sōtō Zen, Zen that combined Rinzai and Sōtō techniques, and the beginnings of Tibetan Buddhism. Second, and by far the most important development in Buddhism since its entry to America, was the emergence of "Beat Zen." Although the Beat movement had its official beginning at the now famous reading at the Six Gallery in San Francisco in 1955, the movement had roots that went back considerably farther, farther even than the initial meeting between Allen Ginsberg and Jack Kerouac near Columbia University in 1945. The Beats owed much to Whitman, Thoreau, and Emerson, while Ginsberg was profoundly indebted to William Carlos Williams, and Kerouac to William Burroughs.

Bruce Cook highlights the essence of the Beat movement when he notes:

> . . . the Beats had perceived and managed to touch something essential that was only then beginning to take shape in America in the 1950s. It was a very important and widespread something, compounded of a deep hunger for individual recognition, a desire to speak frankly and honestly about things that mattered, and, finally, a need for passionate personal involvement in major undertakings.[9]

Cook believes that the appeal of the Beats was founded on the basis of their American heritage, a heritage which they also, in large part, rejected:

> And what they symbolized to a world grown dyspeptic from swallowing too much of the American myth was the relief of regurgitation. The Beats rejected. They vomited up the American dream and left the mess quivering on the floor for the world to walk around. They said they didn't want the sort of material success that everyone else in America was working so hard to achieve. And if a chance to hit the jackpot was all a culture could offer, then, they declared, that wasn't much, was it? The reputation they soon acquired as nay-sayers helped the Beats create a myth of their own. Theirs was a sort of antimyth; one that turned the idea of America inside out. Instead of American cleanliness, the Beats offered dirt; for industry, sloth; and in place of the official, fundamentally Protestant ethic, they presented their own, a morality with principles but no rules. This was how the Beats looked to the world at large. Accepting them, it was possible to reject some aspects of American culture, and still retain affection for those qualities of the national character that have always been most appealing—informality, enthusiasm, openness to adventure, and a kind of bold, plain-spoken honesty.[10]

In building a myth of their own, the Beats replaced what they rejected of American culture with Zen culture. As Theodore Roszak perceptively remarks:

> The way out of this corner was to arrive at a vision of sordidness and futility that made of *them* "spiritual facts" in their own right. The world might then be redeemed by the willingness to take it for what it is and to find its enchanting promise within the seemingly despiritualized waste.[11]

Further, Roszak goes on:

> It is indisputable, however, that the San Francisco beats, and much of our younger generation since their time, *thought* they had found something

in Zen they needed, and promptly proceeded to use what they understood of this exotic tradition as a justification for fulfilling the need.[12]

The parallels between Zen and what the Beats *thought* they (them-selves) represented are all too apparent. In the first place, the Beats identified with the spontaneity of the Zen tradition. Perhaps the most significant example of this, on the literary level, is Kerouac's "spontaneous prose," written on long rolls of paper, quickly and with no revisions. Just as Buddhists choose not to cling to a past that is already dead, Kerouac refused to polish his work. On the personal level, the Beats practiced a sort of perverted situation ethics. For them, the unifying character of this ethical system was (assumed) freedom, manifested in their blatant antinomianism. In addition, the Beats rather naively assumed that because some Zen monks wandered over the countryside as apparent "lunatics," in a style consistent with their satori experience, *all* Zen monks followed this practice. In so doing, the Beats not only ignored the very basis of Zen monastic life and its incumbent discipline, but they used this assumption to form the basis of a normative model (and justification) for their own itinerant lifestyle. The Beats also prostituted the supposed ecstasy of Zen experience. Consequently, the erotic quality of life was over-emphasized, as were their frequent excursions into the world of drugs and alcohol. Even in the musical styles favored by the Beats, they sought to convey the nonintellectual, intuitive style of Zen, exemplified by their fascination with jazz improvization. All of these themes are captured in the printed postcards sent out by Allen Gins-berg to advertise that momentous event in 1955:

> Six poets at 6 Gallery. Kenneth Rexroth, M.C., Remarkable collection of angels all gathered at once in the same spot. Wine, music, dancing girls, serious poetry, free satori. Small collection for wine and postcards. Charm-ing event.

And of course it was at this event that Ginsberg first read his much acclaimed poem "Howl," a proclamation for the need to experience life directly in all its fullness.

The Beats had come close, with their zany antics and the supposi-tions that they were founded on, to providing a real *American* begin-ning for Buddhism. Had they only understood more fully the Zen tradition they associated with, and incorporated an authentic Zen *lineage* into their tradition, genuine success might have been achieved. Of the lot, it was only Gary Snyder who had any acumen in properly understanding the meaning of Zen. Having studied Chinese and Japanese at Berkeley, he went to Japan (in 1956) to learn meditation from the great masters. As it turned out, Gary Snyder became the disciple of Seesō Oda Rōshi (who was a disciple of Sōkatsu Shaku's student, Zuigan Gōto), and he studied with Oda Rōshi until the master's death in 1966. Of his difficult path, Snyder has said:

> The first thing that always throws off the people that have come over from the mid-50's on is this language problem. They are just disappointed and

depressed by realizing how much work it would take before they could do any real Zen study with a teacher.

Then the second thing that has been a big obstacle has been the attitude of the Buddhist world, which is not very open, not very friendly. And there have never been more than two or three places where foreigners could go and sit or hope to be accepted as disciples if they did sit. So that the number of people who stayed and did anything with a Rinzai Roshi and have continued for any length of time is very, very small. It turns out to involve such a tremendous commitment of time. I was studying Japanese and Chinese at Berkeley before I ever went over there and I had kind of a feeling for sinology and for that kind of scholarship so I enjoyed doing it, but at the same time it always seemed a little bit paradoxical because one of the things that first attracted me to Zen in Suzuki's books was getting away from scholarship and learning and not relying on books, words and doctrines. But you get into that anyway and you have to see it from another standpoint and accept it.

And then the attitude of my Roshi and Walter Nowick's Roshi and all of the Roshis who take foreigners as students is that "We will make no adjustments for you as foreigners, we will teach you strictly the orthodox Zen way we teach everyone else. And if you wish to change it in any way for people in your own country, that's your business, but we will make no adjustments."[13]

It is curious and puzzling why the Beats did not adopt an approach more consonant with the one taken by Gary Snyder, apart from the fact that it may have required more responsibility than they seemed to possess. Whatever understanding Ginsberg may have attained seems to have come much later, and it is just not clear that Kerouac ever understood Buddhism very well, in spite of the fact that several of his novels (for example, *On the Road* or *The Dharma Bums*) were clearly Buddhist inspired.

Frank Reynolds and Joseph Kitagawa have noted that "throughout Southeast Asia modern reform Buddhism has been associated with the emerging urban elite. . . ."[14] It could also be argued that a similar claim might be made for "Beat Zen." How strange it is that none of the Beats ever sought to identify the city as the domain of the American Zennist's search for satori, as the wilderness in which religious wholeness might be found. Had such a notion been propounded and accepted, not only would the superficial layers of the forthcoming "back to nature" movement have been seriously undercut, but also the belief that the city is symbolic of inherent evil and darkness might have lost some of its apparent support, all with the result that Americans of the 1960s and 1970s would not incorrectly surmise that in order to practice Buddhism properly Americans must desert the city and run to the naked wilds, raping it in the process.

The "Square Zen" of Alan Watts

If the Beats are reputed to have publicized Zen while possibly damaging it in the process, the other side of the proverbial coin was represented by the "Square Zen" of Alan Watts. Theodore Roszak, in a very sympathetic treatment of Watts (only some of which seems

Alan Watts (Photo by Boris Erwitt.)

to be justified), notes that one academic referred to Watts as "the Norman Vincent Peale of Zen." Perhaps "the Werner Erhard of Zen" would be more appropriate. Watts's influence has been more significant than that of the Beats, primarily through his prolific production of popular books; but in his somewhat amateurish attempt to explain Zen in the context of modern science and psychology, he had neither the Buddhological sophistication of D.T. Suzuki nor the deep, personal experience of Philip Kapleau or others. What Watts did have was a unique flair for writing to the average American in a fashion that was both provocative and romantic. He made Zen appear to be possible; that is, its fruits could be tasted by anyone who had sufficient perseverance to sustain its formidable rigors. What Watts sacrificed in accuracy, he made up for in zeal and by directing people onto the path and into the counsel of Zen masters who were capable of correcting the misunderstandings fostered by Watts's books. Nevertheless, Watts, like the Beats, was sorely misunderstood and insufficiently appreciated.

My own suspicion is that it is movements like "Beat Zen" and "Square Zen," due to their ample visibility and flexible attitudes, that cause scholars to grossly underestimate the integrity of the Buddhist movement in America, leading to generalizations like the following:

> Wheresoever two or three yoga or Zen students gathered, conversation almost never had to do with intellectual constructs but with liberation

from them. These religions dealt not with institutions but with transcendence of them; with alternatives to, not expressions of, political and social concern.[15]

Thus by 1960, Buddhism in America was still groping for leadership, a Western identity, and a solid community of participants. Further, it was destined to be only a short wait until the Kennedy era was superimposed on the Beat movement, transmuting it into Hippiedom, and the "Death of God" theologians were to have their day.

CHAPTER 3

The Consciousness Explosion: 1961-1970

These days people begin their quest along many bizarre roads. They grope, they stumble often, they follow false lights, they too easily mistake the theater for the temple, the circus for the sanctuary.

—Theodore Roszak[1]

In the decade of the 1960s Buddhism was to experience the largest, fastest, and most dynamic growth spurt in its short history on the American scene. Its rapid rise presented Buddhism with as many potential liabilities as it did opportunities; liabilities which, without proper care and attention, could have fragmented Buddhism in America quite severely.

THE VIETNAM WAR AND AMERICAN BUDDHISM

In the first place, the undeclared war in Vietnam again focused continued awareness on the Orient. Like Japan and Korea, Vietnam was a predominantly Buddhist country and culture. The war was an unpopular involvement which, as was evidenced with Japan and Korea, left Americans with a strange "animosity-curiosity" complex, manifesting itself in a divisiveness that was to be felt throughout American culture. As reports of supposedly pacifist Buddhist monks engaging in acts of self-immolation began to filter back to America in the media, a proliferation of books appeared, prepared by journalists and scholars alike, with Jerrold Schecter's *The New Face of the Buddha* being a significant example of the former effort. Further, Vietnamese Buddhists, in seeking to explain the situation from their own perspective, began to write to an American audience, as witnessed by Thich Nhat Hanh's *Vietnam, Lotus in a Sea of Fire: The Buddhist Story.*

In academia, Buddhist Studies began to emerge as an independent discipline, usually embodied as an aspect of the many developing Area Studies Programs in American universities. The most notable of these was the Buddhist Studies Program at the University of Wisconsin, a program founded in 1961 under the able guidance of Richard Hugh Robinson. Although cloaked within the (then) Indian Studies Department of the university, the program focused on all aspects of Buddhist Studies in all areas and had an interdisciplinary flair as well. Shortly thereafter, Columbia University (under Alex Wayman) and the University of California at Berkeley (under Lewis Lancaster) were to offer balanced programs in the study of Buddhism.

Now I do not mean to imply that the Vietnam conflict was the cause of the programs just mentioned, and it may not have even been a significant factor in the appearance of the programs, but it was a contributing factor in attracting large numbers of undergraduate students and a devoted number of graduate students as well. It began a trend that, according to enrollment statistics, did not peak until 1971–72.

Balanced against the above responsible effort on the part of journalists, Buddhists, and scholars was the general media reporting of the events, often citing the gruesome spectaculars of the week-to-week or day-to-day happenings, blaring the sounds of war and the citations of the number of dead and wounded across millions of television screens nightly. All of this attention made Buddhism big news, but with a predominantly negative tinge. Thus it seems somewhat paradoxical that the 1960s should represent the decade of Buddhism's most dynamic growth in America.

The story of Buddhism's growth in the 1960s must be cast against the backdrop of two general, umbrellalike trends that were just beginning to come to full fruition: the rampant social and religious unrest. These two trends, in a country founded on social and religious freedom, were to interpenetrate in an exciting but disruptive fashion. The complexity of life in the 1960s must, however, be restricted somewhat so as to focus on those issues most relevant to the major concern of this study.

THE COUNTERCULTURE'S EFFECT ON BUDDHISM IN AMERICA

In the social domain, the most significant development for Buddhism in America was the emergence of a considerable counterculture, from which Buddhism was to recruit some of its most ardent supporters. Roszak, in his influential *The Making of a Counter Culture*, notes that "the counter culture is, essentially, an exploration of the politics of consciousness,"[2] and we must recognize at the outset that this "exploration of the politics of consciousness" had deep roots in both the burgeoning psychedelic pandemonium and the closely related hippie movement. Neither of these twin spires of the counterculture foundation was particularly new, however. One scholar has even argued that ". . . the American counterculture of the present is really as American as apple pie, motherhood, and the Fourth of July. It is one more manifestation of a long series of signs and symbols of American naiveté."[3]

Nevertheless, the most immediate predecessors of the hippies were the Beats of the 1950s. Kerouac himself, for example, conceded to Bruce Cook that the hippies were the descendants of the Beat Generation.[4] Further, just as the Beats sought temporary release from the agonies of existence through drugs, it was perhaps only logical that their descendants should follow suit. This theory was certainly borne out well in the character of Neal Cassady, one of the figures personified in Kerouac's *On the Road* (as Dean Moriarity) and a central figure in the rise of the hippie movement. When Ken Kesey's Merry Pranksters (the subject of Tom Wolfe's *The Electric Kool-Aid Acid Test*) drove their bus, painted with psychedelic colors, on a cross-country trip to New York in 1965, the driver was Neal Cassady.[5] Consequently, when Alan Harrington quipped that the hippies are "no more than Beats plus drugs,"[6] he seemed well supported in his contention. Just as Kerouac utilized the novel as a literary medium for espousing Beat notions, Kesey followed suit for the hippies, each man's perceptions being shaped by the times and conditions. It might also be suggested that the Beat poems of Allen Ginsberg and Gary Snyder were also mirrored, in transmuted form, in the poetic offerings of social protest, exemplified by the lyrics of Bob Dylan and Phil Ochs. Signs of the times were clear as jazz improvisation gave way to a mind-boggling acid rock.

The hippies, however, unlike the Beats, intended to gain more than just a mere reputation as critics of society. They responded to technology run wild, to what Alvin Toffler refers to as the superimposition of the future on the present, in a personal active fashion. Charles Glock has stated:

> The way of viewing the world I wish to assert was dominant in America's past, and which is perhaps, indeed probably, dominant today, is one that conceives of human beings as essentially in control of what happens to them in this world and, if they believe in it, the next. In its earliest formulation, this view included a conception of God as having granted mankind this control—"God created human beings in his own image but left them free to choose for or against him." As time went on, the idea that human beings were in control gained ascendency, so that it became the operating assumption, whether God was believed in or not.[7]

The notion Glock espouses is precisely what the hippies sought to exercise. Of course the hippies would have rejected Glock's positing of a second mode of consciousness coexisting with the first, which states that "the principal agent of control in this second view is not humankind but God,"[8] for they could not accept anything that questioned their ability to make a profound impact that would effect radical, sweeping social change. Here also one sees a clear affinity between the pure self-determinist notions of the hippie movement and the law of karma as stated in Buddhism. Despite a present shaped by past actions, freedom of action in each new moment persists, enabling the practitioner to claim complete responsibility for and control over the future, religiously and otherwise. Further, the practitioner is enjoined not to look outside of himself to any agency of control such as God.

The Death of God

Indeed, in the 1960s the entire religious situation in America was in turmoil. There was a continuous drop in church attendance, possibly indicative of a declining faith in the value of religion or its importance in a secular society. The "death of God" theologians such as Thomas Altizer, William Hamilton, and Richard Rubinstein were creating a fuss in both the public and private domain, and "the erosion of the legitimacy of the American way of life"[9] prompted Robert Bellah to conclude (regarding this loss of legitimacy in the old order):

> The deepest cause, no matter what particular factors contributed to the actual timing, was, in my opinion, the inability of utilitarian individualism to provide a meaningful pattern of personal and social existence, especially when its alliance with biblical religion began to sag because biblical religion itself had been gutted in the process. I would thus interpret the crisis of the sixties above all as a crisis of meaning, a religious crisis, with major political, social, and cultural consequences to be sure.[10]

Given the intensified secularization of the 1960s and its attendant pluralism, America was ripe for Buddhism to advance more fully than it had before. When Harvey Cox's *The Secular City* appeared in 1965, it made no less impact than John Robinson's *Honest to God* had two years earlier. When Peter Berger contends that secularization follows from modern industrialization, he also notes that "secularization brings about a demonopolization of religious traditions and thus, *ipso facto*, leads to a pluralistic situation."[11] He goes on to say:

> The key characteristic of all pluralistic situations, whatever the details of their historical background, is that the monopolies can no longer take for granted the allegiance of their client populations. . . . The pluralistic situation is, above all, a *market situation*.[12]

If we follow Berger's argument to its conclusion, we learn that some of the results of this secular, pluralistic situation are *ecumenicity*, in which religious collaboration results; perception of one's rivals as "fellows" rather than "enemies"; elimination of "supernatural" elements from the traditions (in extreme cases); and a new emphasis on the laity.[13] The demonopolization of predominantly Western religious traditions created an environment in which many persons saw Buddhism as a religious option that deserved exploration.

Buddhism took advantage of the mitigation of its somewhat alien appearance by the religious fellowship inherent in the ecumenical movement to gain new footholds in the American domain. Thus the 1960s witnessed more new Buddhist groups with a greater diversity of traditional and sectarian affiliations than ever existed before in America. Buddhism's lack of a God concept to express ultimate reality made it attractive to those persuaded by the "Death of God" argument and to those feeling the fallout of the declining super-natural thrust of traditional religion in America. Renewed interest in the laity on the part of Western religions only worked to Buddhism's advantage, because it had yet to establish a monastic community (or even a large community of religious officials) on American soil. A corollary of this last point is that unlike the Hare Krishna move-ment, conversion to Buddhism did not entail "an emphatic rejection of conventional affluent America."[14] Rather, Buddhist laymen searched for a Buddhist way to live within such a context, just as earlier laymen had done in their Asian homeland.

Discussing the atmosphere outlined above, Robert Bellah rather accurately summarizes the inroad for Asian religion in general:

> In many ways Asian spirituality provided a more thorough contrast to the rejected utilitarian individualism than did biblical religion. To external achievement it posed inner experience; to the exploitation of nature, harmony with nature; to impersonal organization, an intense relation to a guru. Mahayana Buddhism, particularly in the form of Zen, provided the most pervasive religious influence of the counterculture; but elements from Taoism, Hinduism, and Sufism were also influential. What drug experiences, interpreted in oriental religious terms, as Timothy Leary and Richard Alpert did quite early, and meditation experiences, often taken up when drug use was found to have too many negative consequences, showed was the illusoriness of world striving. Careerism and status seeking, the sacrifice of present fulfillment for some ever-receding future goal, no longer seemed worthwhile. There was a turn away not only from utili-tarian individualism but from the whole apparatus of industrial society. The new ethos preferred handicrafts and farming to business and indus-try, and small face-to-face communities to impersonal bureaucracy and the isolated nuclear family. Simplicity and naturalness in food and clothing were the ideal, even though conspicuous consumption and one-upmanship ("Oh, you don't use natural salt, I see") made their inevitable appearance.[15]

Three themes noted by Bellah need further consideration: the role of the "Drug Culture" in the Buddhist movement, the general revolu-tion in consciousness that in part resulted from it, and the appearance of alternative lifestyles consonant with the Buddhist world view.

The Drug Culture

A consideration of the Drug Culture brings the hippies, once again, into immediate view. Roszak sees what he calls the "psychedelic obsession" as a symptom of "cultural impoverishment."[16] Just as the hippies' concerns with social evils have their basis in a culture that has always considered civil disobedience as a valid form of dissent, the culture's concern with drugs goes back farther than just the Beats. The drug lineage in America traces its origins (omitting, in this context, Native American Religions) to William James, Havelock Ellis, and others. James's *The Varieties of Religious Experience,* Aldous Huxley's *The Doors of Perception,* and Alan Watts's *The Joyous Cosmology: Adventures in the Chemistry of Consciousness* all became counterculture bibles before Timothy Leary became "High Priest" and Richard Alpert was transformed into Baba Ram Dass. Leary, in fact, came somewhat late to drugs, having taken his first psychotropic mushrooms in Mexico in 1960, a mere three years before he was fired from Harvard. It was not until 1966 that he founded the League for Spiritual Discovery (which regarded LSD as a sacrament), and 1968 that *High Priest* was published. The "cosmic connection," however, antedates all of this. Even in the so-called historical religions, we find the Vedic references to the cult of soma, a powerful drug in the shaman's world, eventually resulting in the personification of the deity Soma. In the Vedic world, the gods attained their immortality by drinking soma. It might be possible to postulate that the psychedelic rituals of the 1960s were an inadvertent "myth of the eternal return," especially if one considers the role of soma in Huxley's *Brave New World* and the appearance of the Society of Mental Awareness (SOMA) in Great Britain.

In comparing the two giants of the psychedelic world of the 1960s, Roszak says:

> But Kesey's sessions were mainly fun and games: LSD served up in a heady brew of amplified rock bands, strobe lights, and free-form dance. The intention was, at best, aesthetic and entertaining. Leary, on the other hand, preferred to come on with all the solemnity of the risen Christ, replete with white cotton pajamas, incense, and the stigmata of his legal persecutions—though the light and sound effects were still part of the act.[17]

For Kesey, we might say:

> Marijuana and psychedelics, for example, offer a return to pure experience, to unencumbered sensation. People take them to encounter the world in terms of what it is rather than how it can be used. . . . They want to stop treating themselves as machines.[18]

The author of this statement, Philip Slater, goes on:

> People who take drugs regularly to alter their consciousness in some way are behaving like good American consumers. The mass media are always

telling us to satisfy our emotional needs with material products—particularly through oral consumption. . . . The drug world simply extends this process in its effort to reverse it. If the body can be used as a working machine, and a consuming machine, why not an experience machine? Drug consumers make the same assumption as all Americans—that the body is some sort of appliance. Hence they must turn on and tune in, in their unsuccessful effort to drop out. They may be enjoying the current more, but they are still plugged into the same machine that drives other Americans on their weary and joyless round.[19]

It was Leary, however, who returned to the themes of James and Huxley and promoted psychotropics as a religious endeavor. Since Leary and the other promoters of these substances were familiar with the rudimentary tenets of Oriental religions, they promoted it in these terms. Robert S. deRopp, author of *The Master Game*, rather sarcastically remarks:

. . . these explorers sing the praises of bottled *samadhis* or encapsulated *satoris* and eagerly spread the word that a short cut exists and that the efforts made by yogis, Sufis, mystics, and magi to break into the triple-locked fourth room were needless. All that these seekers had to do was introduce into their metabolism certain chemicals and all locked doors would open by themselves.[20]

While deRopp is disdainful of the role of LSD and other psychoactive substances in promoting genuine religious experience, Leary's theories do have support, occasionally from well-respected sources. Agehananda Bharati, Chairman of the Department of Anthropology at Syracuse University and, for many years prior to his chairmanship, a Hindu monastic, suggests in *The Light at the Center* (1976) that LSD may indeed serve as a trigger for what he calls "the zero experience." Regarding his own pursuit, he goes as far as to say:

Judging from my own childhood and adolescence, had there been LSD, willing maidens available for all experiments, plenty of Indian LP records, incense, etc., I might well have chosen those rather than seeking out, with Teutonic doggedness, the few sources that were obtainable in pre-War II Austria and Germany: university libraries, a few departments and seminars of Asian studies, and, of course, the Vivekananda-type pamphlet literature.[21]

The key here is that some Oriental religious groups utilized the obvious association made by Leary and others in order to promote their own purposes; for example, a large poster on the wall of a Hare Krishna temple in San Francisco began with the words "Stay High Forever."[22] Buddhism never promoted such claims and constantly sought to disavow any of its adherents' suspicions to the contrary. Nevertheless, not only had many 1960s Buddhists in America used drugs in the past, but they also seemed to hope for the "organic trip," which was more powerful than the drug experience but safer. The wisest of the Buddhist teachers in America did not stress the exotic experiences to be attained through Buddhist meditational systems, but constantly cited the "ordinariness" of Buddhist experience and the necessity of relating to the world "as it is" rather than as it can be adjusted.

The Human Potential Movement

It was in the language of the Human Potential Movement that Buddhism was to find an impressive and useful (as well as unknowing) ally. The landmark work of Abraham Maslow, Fritz Perls, and others was to coalesce in the 1960s under the rubric cited above. Donald Stone summarizes the thrust of the movement in the following way:

> Rather than taking direct action to change the political structures or setting up an exemplary countersociety, members of these groups seek to transcend the oppressiveness of culture by transforming themselves as individuals. They see that, if society is to realize its potential, they must first realize theirs.[23]

Encompassing a wide variety of techniques and therapies, the Human Potential Movement was symbolized by Esalen Institute, where many of the superstars of the movement came to offer seminars and programs. Of his involvement with Esalen Institute, Harvey Cox says:

> It's like an episodic love affair with a woman whose nutty ideas embarrass me but whose presence is warm and inviting, who knows I'm kidding a bit in the attention I pay her, but who doesn't really care because she has lots of other lovers, and for some reason she likes me too.[24]

The Human Potential Movement has often utilized techniques of Eastern spiritual disciplines, and because of this a growing number of Americans have become aware of Oriental religions. Buddhism in America in the 1960s (and 1970s) was also beginning to learn, however, that appropriation of the terminology (and to a lesser extent, the techniques) of the potential movement might enable Buddhism to attract some of the several million Americans who had (by the mid-1970s) associated with the movement. Consequently, it was not unusual to hear words like "growth," "openness," and the like in newly emergent Buddhist centers. "Peak experience" was a frequent synonym for nirvāṇa, and often one would hear a discussion of Charlotte Selver or "Rolfing" in place of the expected discussion of D.T. Suzuki or satipaṭṭhāna.

The 1960s again made people aware of suffering, a theme that seems to run throughout twentieth-century American history, and the Human Potential Movement gave Buddhists a new language for expressing human problems. The great suffering that was manifested in the Vietnam War and in social injustice was not unlike the overwhelming expressions of pain released through the various therapies (like Arthur Janov's "Primal Scream"). As Americans expressed their collective anguish, Buddhists could say, "Aha! That's just what we mean when we say that all life is suffering." Of course Buddhists did not say that and are just now beginning to realize that they could have. Nor did Buddhists say that the cause of suffering was "blocked growth" through living in a society that violated human dignity and freedom. They didn't even say, as quoted above, that they were "seeking to transcend the oppressiveness of culture by transforming themselves as individuals," and that this path was the pragmatic expression of the potential "peak experience" that existed for all of us. Some of these associations are just now finding their way into practice in Buddhist projects such as Chögyam Trungpa's *Maitri* program and Tarthang Tulku's *Human Development Training Program* (each of which will be discussed in Part II).

In the 1950s, Buddhists sought either to retrench and ignore their association with America altogether, to reject America and its culture and replace it with a perverted Zen culture (as the Beats did), or to popularize Zen in a less than effective or accurate fashion (as Alan Watts did). In the 1960s, however, Buddhists in America became much more aware of their potential American identity, and even took the first small steps towards achieving it. Of course this does not dismiss those who were attracted to Buddhism precisely because of its "otherness." For many, the newness, supposed rootlessness, and hoped-for ecstasy made Buddhism attractive in quite the same fashion as other counterculture expressions of antiformalism and pursuits of a seemingly elusive wholeness. Consequently, we find the somewhat paradoxical situation of Buddhism gaining adherents in some circles because of its sameness with American ideals and in other circles because of its separateness.

THE SEARCH FOR A LIFESTYLE

In spite of the above, Buddhism in the 1960s was still searching for a lifestyle consonant with its pursuits in America. In the first place there was virtually no monastic saṃgha present, and there were almost no Buddhist monks or nuns in residence. Thus Buddhist community meant *lay* community, and, to a large extent, *city* community. Regarding the critical question of commitment within the community, Rosabeth Kanter has stated (in her work on utopian communities):

> But for permanent commitments to result, persisting over long periods of time and independent of the presence or existence of any one person, charisma throughout the corporate group is required. Charisma in this form may be called "institutionalized awe." It is an extension of charisma from its original source into the organization of authority and the operations of the group, but not necessarily attached to a particular office (status) or hereditary line.[25]

Most Buddhist communities that were appearing and/or growing in the 1960s, whether they were church groups or meditational groups (centering around the figure of a guru or rōshi), managed to implement a hierarchy consonant with permanence and thus developed just the sort of "institutionalized awe" that Kanter identified as a requisite for permanent commitment. In fact, most Buddhist groups would score quite well in Kanter's six commitment mechanisms: sacrifice, investment, renunciation, communion, mortification, and surrender.

Buddhist communities, however, faced other problems that have proved more difficult. First, as Kanter suggests, "successful communities provided not only guide for work but also free time and recreation in line with the group's ideals."[26] Buddhist groups were notably remiss in providing such guidelines. Consequently, not only did a transcendence facilitating tradition not develop, but community members (many of whom were dropouts of some kind) found it too easy to fall back into their old patterns or to transfer their Sunday morning Protestantism into Sunday morning Buddhism. In many cases, Buddhist communities defined themselves in terms of what they rejected rather than what they affirmed, which allowed a severe sense of ambiguity to persist. In other words, Buddhist communities sought legitimation with no greater success than attained by their Western counterparts. And since the sectarian distinction among Buddhist groups in America was now becoming more apparent, American Buddhists were finding themselves in the midst of their own identity crisis, one not alleviated by their community life.

The Sacred Center

With an increasing emphasis on the laity as a result of secularization and pluralism, Buddhist lay communities needed, more profoundly than in previous decades, to find a means by which they might participate in the sanctity inherent in the sacred center of their religion. As is the rule in postprimitive religion, the *actual* center itself remains at a distance (in this case, in Asia), but it is *transposed* into an *American* sacred center through its embodiment in American Buddhist temples and the ritual life enacted there. And this is critical, since the sacred center is the place of creation and renewal, the realm of absolute reality, the place where chaos becomes cosmos. Unfortunately, in the 1960s the Buddhist temples in America were for the most part not only Asian in design (obviously manifest in their architecture), but also in *ritual function.* Thus, robbed of sacred American centers, American Buddhists—even the large number of non-Asians that had become part of the Buddhist movement— found themselves expressing a religious ideal and creativity more appropriate for Asia than for America. Buddhist community life in America was consequently handicapped by its lack of mythic meaning, relegating its activities almost exclusively to the profane rather than sacred realm.[27]

City Buddhism and Country Buddhism

As noted above, the Buddhist movement in America, and specifically Buddhist community life, has been a city movement. Nevertheless, in the 1960s a large number of Buddhists deserted the city and sought to practice their religion in a wilderness setting. Some of these practitioners simply rejected the evils of city life; others seemed to be motivated by a concern for the preservation of a sane ecological environment; and a goodly number were naïvely pursuing a "back-to-nature" style of life. Many American Buddhists had been blindly seduced by the rural settings of monastic institutions in Asia or the rustic settings of Japanese landscape painting and were convinced that Buddhism could *only* be practiced in the pristine wilds. In any case, these Buddhist practitioners searched for a peaceful spot in which, they were certain, it would be much easier to "actualize themselves." Most have returned to the city, but they do not seem to know why.

Now we all know the importance of the wilderness symbol in American religious history. Filled with trials and tribulations, it was a place for faith to be tested, with mastery; it was also a locus of creativity in which the recreation of the Garden motif was predominant. The key issue here is mastery, not a mastery that is dependent on the destruction of the environment, but one that depends on a consonance and resonance with the environment. And as the wilderness is mastered, so is the individual mastered and sacredness restored.

American Buddhists had no intention of mastering the wilds. It was simply a physical depository for their cumbersome bodies, enabling them to pursue their "spiritual" quest in an ideal environment, free from the responsibilities of city life. Apparently they did not realize that the wilderness imposed its own responsibilities, and it took little time to discover that they were no better prepared to master themselves isolated from the urbane life they had grown used to, than they were in the city.

Buddhism has always maintained that the best place to practice Buddhism is precisely *where you are,* and that the environment that needs tending is the *interior* environment. Of course this does not mean abandonment of concern for the ecological balance. It just means that one needs to be painfully honest about what one is pursuing in the first place. An old Buddhist saying remarks, "When the cart does not go, which do you whip, the cart or the horse?" As I have hinted at earlier, Buddhists would have been more consonant with the actual situation of their American quest if they had identified the city as the new American wilderness. Just as the biblical wilderness was inhabited by monsters, the city-wilderness has its own monsters in crime, racism, drug addiction, and other demons. Just as the biblical wilderness represented uncultivated lands, the city-wilderness has its own uncultivated lands in the inner city and ghetto. Thus the city symbolizes the pre-Creation chaos, which highlights the negative aspects of the wilderness; but it also symbolizes, in positive fashion, the potential for taming and creativity.[28] Consequently, settlement or establishment in the city is a mythic act of creation, and like all acts of beginning, it would have afforded Buddhism the truly American basis that it avowedly sought. Buddhism now finds itself, somewhat unawares, creating its first true acculturation in the wilderness of the American city. This acculturation in the city should not be surprising, for as Harvey Cox has observed:

> The religion of *homo urbanitas,* the dweller in the city, is a special kind of religion. Regardless of his or her religious past, once the city really makes its impact on the psyche, any city person's religion begins to have more in common with that of other city people than it does with the faith of people of his own tradition who still live, either physically or spiritually, in the countryside or small towns.[29]

The above has been only one aspect of Buddhism's search for identity and lifestyle in America. And it is a general one. Specific aspects of that lifestyle might also be considered, such as the mode of interpersonal or transpersonal relationships inherent in the Buddhist endeavor. Needless to say, the 1960s wreaked havoc on Buddhism as well as on other religious traditions present in America. In a permissive era, Buddhism, both in Asia and America, was struggling in the attempt to redefine its ethical patterns that had been fixed so long ago and reexamined only too infrequently. With the task of finding its American identity, the question of the specifics of lifestyle was to become the chief concern for American Buddhists in the 1970s.

By the close of the decade of the 1960s, America had virtually the full range of Buddhist traditions and sects active on its soil. Regarding the Buddhism of the counterculture, Catherine L. Albanese remarks:

> Hence, the eclectic Buddhism of the counter-culture represents one form of Buddhist acculturation in the United States. Buddhism has here been assimilated to a major component of the American myth and thus the American culture. The process has been an ordinary historical story of the appropriation of those nuances in one tradition which have supported the deep structures of consciousness in a second. Buddhism could provide a path for innocence and a means for direct experience in ecstasy. It could support an anti-intellectual individualism and appeal to an inherent pragmatism, both of which, so many scholars tell us, characterize American existence. Buddhism could speak to collective ideas which Americans do not merely hold or possess but which they most basically *are.*[30]

While it is clear that the Buddhist movement in America gained a broad-based support in the youth culture during this decade, it was not the youth culture alone that swelled its ranks. From 1960 on, Nichiren Shōshū appealed to all of America's downtrodden to recite the daimoku and reap its benefits. Jōdo Shinshū has never had much appeal to America's youth, but its membership grew as well. And Tibetan Buddhism was gaining a foothold that was soon to multiply rapidly, not altogether due to its erotic art forms and notorious (as well as misunderstood) sexual practices. To some degree, although it is difficult to estimate accurately, the problem of acculturation was exacerbated in the late 1960s by a kind of "Dharma hopping,"[31] or moving from one spiritual scene to another, inhibiting a sense of commitment to one specific group. Still, more than ever before, the American Buddhist is now American rather than Asian, of any age, of any career, of any degree of seriousness. The sexes are about evenly split, and the educational level of American Buddhists is higher than ever before. Perhaps the most telling comment on the 1960s (and its bizarre events) is Robert Bellah's quip that "neither the political movement nor the counterculture survived the decade."[32] Buddhism did, however, and it approached the 1970s having completed an incredible growth spurt in ten short years. Now it had to contend with problems that it had ignored during its growth spurt, and this would prove to be no small matter indeed.

CHAPTER 4

In the Aftermath of Chaos: 1971–

All systems determined by the law, whether religious or secular, are systems of compromise.

—Paul Tillich[1]

If the decade of the 1960s can be characterized as bizarre, the first half of the decade of the 1970s is no less unusual. Following our somewhat tardy withdrawal from Vietnam, and with the legacy of Watergate to haunt us continually, America finds itself with more than a fair share of political instability and social anomie. As inflation persists and values erode, many Americans are faced with a pervasive loss of wholeness. The average American is no longer the "rugged individualist" or "organization man," but rather the "bifurcated searcher," struggling against polarizing forces in virtually every aspect of his life. And of course the complicating variables appear to be unending. In an age of mass media, data input systems, and intensified social fluidity, America is flexing its collective muscles in the search for human completeness amid Theodore Roszak's projected "Wasteland," and an overwhelming (and perhaps alarming) variety of alternatives is appearing in the social, cultural, and religious spheres: alternative marriage styles to combat an alarming and constantly rising divorce rate, electronic music and computerized art forms to tantalize the avant-garde, and esoteric cults promoted by self-styled gurus of the "pop" scene. Even a new literature has emerged to delineate the problems and/or offer alternatives, such as Robert Pirsig's *Zen and the Art of Motorcycle Maintenance* and George and Neena O'Neill's *Shifting Gears*. Yet the problems persist, arousing the appearance of psychotherapies so exotic that the title "marginal" would be complimentary. It is no wonder that amid the fallout of America's orgasmic quest for wholeness, America is making itself more vulnerable than ever to the proliferation of techniques from outside its own boundaries. While Harvey Cox, in a 1975 lecture at Naropa Institute in Boulder, Colorado, warned against being fooled by the mystique of the East, noting that "the Western Soul looks somewhere else for what's right here,"[2] we are nevertheless faced with an incredible array of Buddhist teachers and practitioners in America.

Curiously though, as the 1970s proceed there is a distinct leveling off with regard to new Buddhist groups. Thus, by mid-decade, we have the following general schema for Buddhist traditions and groups:

Japanese Tradition
- Jōdo Shū (Pure Land)
- Jōdo Shinshū (True Pure Land)
- Rinzai Zen
- Sōtō Zen
- Syncretistic Zen[3]
- Nichiren Shōshū
- Shingon

Tibetan Tradition
- rNying-ma-pa
- bKa-rgyud-pa
- sa-skya-pa
- dGe-lugs-pa

Chinese Tradition
- Ch'an
- Ching-t'u (Pure Land)

Korean Tradition
- Chogye Chen (Zen)

Sinhalese and Burmese Traditions
- Theravāda

It is interesting to note that the Japanese tradition has the largest number of groups in America (and the largest number of members as well). I suspect that this is due not to the large number of Japanese Americans alone, but also to the fact that Japan's culture and technology most nearly resembles our own, making its Buddhism, at least theoretically, the easiest to "transplant" to American soil.

Despite the stabilizing of new "imports," the numerical expansion of Buddhist practitioners abounds, yielding a rather peculiar paradox: in the age of the supersonic transport, where boundaries between countries, continents, and cultures dissolve with no larger price to pay than "jet lag," the growth of Buddhism in America no longer is dependent on a continued focus on Asian developments. Indeed, with multinational corporations, SONY products, and advanced technology, even Japan hardly seems "Buddhist" to most Americans. As predominantly Buddhist cultures in Asia grudgingly modernize, they are rapidly learning that what Agehananda Bharati refers to as the "aloha-amigo" syndrome (which Bharati describes as "pathological eclecticism") may well be a product of the American mentality, but that it is highly contagious.

WHAT CONSTITUTES A BUDDHIST?

No one knows how far the numerical expansion of Buddhism in America has progressed to date, partly because it has become difficult to know what constitutes a Buddhist today. In his classic book *The Practice of Chinese Buddhism 1900-1950,* Holmes Welch makes it clear enough that it is insufficient to simply ask, "Are you a Buddhist?" An affirmative response does not rule out the possibility that a similar response might be evoked from the same person to the question, "Are you a Taoist?" A more appropriate question might be (as Professor Welch suggests): "Have you taken the Three Refuges?" Further, "Do you practice the five layman's vows?" If these questions were the standard for identifying Buddhists, we would be forced to estimate the number of Buddhists in America—and in Asia—considerably downward. The issue is further complicated by the fact that various groups determine "members" in diverse ways. For example, some groups designate financial contributors as members, and thereby as Buddhists. Others identify members as those who frequently attend services or meditation sessions. The methods for determining membership and Buddhist standing are too numerous to cite here. The result, however, is that membership rolls are inflated, at least with respect to the traditional criteria for determining Buddhist affiliation.

The above discussion of membership determination ignores a consideration of the *quality* of membership and *commitment* to the tradition. Consequently, we must consider whether new modes of standardization and new criteria are more appropriate today, and whether it is possible or valuable to maintain multivalent allegiances in such matters. When William Johnston, author of *The Still Point,* writes about the similarities and dialogue between Christianity and Zen, and Dom Aelred Graham writes on *Zen Catholicism,* may we postulate the Jewish Buddhist? Are such distinctions useful, meaningful, and fair? Martin Marty apparently thinks so, but only because the new religions exert influence on America as "suffusive forces." According to Marty, ". . . they offer some features that will suffuse, will cast a glow upon, will subtly soften or open or alter the Jewish and Christian faiths and the secular style."[4] In a somewhat more sympathetic treatment, Harvey Cox suggests that sovereign states and religious denominations are problematic because:

> First, they stress *exclusive* loyalties by teaching that you can't be an American *and* a Russian at the same time, or a Catholic *and* a Hindu. Second, they focus loyalty at the wrong *level.* What we need now are communi-

ties of shared symbol and decisional power that are *nonexclusive* in character and *global-local* in focus.[5]

In light of the above, it does seem clear that if Buddhism is to acculturate fully to its American setting, it must allow its adherents to incorporate their American cultural heritage into their religious life rather than requesting (or demanding) that they reject it summarily. And in so doing, not only are these questions valid, but they are imperative if Buddhists are to discover that tenuous brew of American culture and Buddhist ideal that will assure their success. Further, they will be repeating, in the process, the archetypal methodology by which Buddhism acculturated in each new country it entered on the Asian scene. Thus, in summary, we might conclude that while Buddhism grew in numbers by leaps and bounds in the 1960s, it was unable to consolidate these gains due to its somewhat untimely association with a counterculture that, in large part, rejected American culture and values and, as Robert Bellah pointed out, did not survive the decade. The American Buddhist of the 1970s, on the other hand, is beginning to express his identification more fully with American culture, and in the process, has been able to achieve a greater and more enduring growth.

It might be inferred that my sympathies rest with the older, traditional forms of Buddhism; that I assume the only valid form of a religious tradition is its pristine expression. Each claim, however, would simply be ungrounded. Rather, I would suggest that a study of Buddhism in Asia reveals that the more bizarre the various Buddhist manifestations in a given culture, the more ephemeral they were as well. Of course there is no *Ur*-Buddhism, but we must ask at what point the "aloha-amigo" amalgam becomes so strange and fantastic that it ceases to be *Buddhist, American,* or a *meaningful combination of the two.*

BUDDHISM'S RELUCTANCE TO CONFRONT MODERNITY

Throughout its early history in various Asian countries, one of Buddhism's strongest attractions has been its profoundly rigorous ethical dimension. On the monastic level, fully one-third of the Buddhist Tripiṭaka is devoted to the promotion and maintenance of a proper ethical framework in which the religious professional can integrate exemplary conduct into his general and overarching quest for salvation. Perhaps the highest expression of this concern is found in one of the introductory verses of the Mahāsāṃghika Prātimokṣa-sūtra:

The Śramaṇa who is intent upon śīla crosses over;
The Brāhmaṇa who is intent upon śīla crosses over.

One who is intent upon śīla is worthy of worship by men and gods;
There is Prātimokṣa for one intent upon śīla.[6]

Here it is not just Vinaya, or the disciplinary code for the monastic, that is being praised, but rather śīla, a difficult word to explicate, but which refers to the *internally* enforced ethical framework by which the monk or nun structures his or her life. Thus, Buddhist ethical life operates under the double balance of the *externally* enforced monastic code, exemplified by Prātimokṣa, and the *internally* enforced guideline of śīla.

The monastic codes, however, were canonized quite early in Buddhist history, leaving the commentarial tradition as the sole means for amending or altering the ethical dimension of Buddhist monastic life. For quite some time, Buddhism had an active, vibrant commentarial tradition, but in recent centuries this tradition had slackened, resulting in the fossilization of this aspect of the Buddhist tradition. On the lay level as well, ethical life is governed by the traditional five vows and their explication in a few key texts that are over two thousand years old.

Now this is not to say that the ethical tradition in Buddhism does not demand a high degree of moral behavior. Quite the contrary is true. Nevertheless, until quite recently, Buddhism's lack of willingness to confront modernity, its lack of willingness to redefine itself in the context of rapid social change, had led to serious problems in its Asian homeland. The situation is no less difficult for Buddhism in America. Faced with the task of applying a somewhat outdated and outmoded ethical tradition to modern circumstances or innovating a genuinely new framework which integrates appropriate aspects of its once rich tradition (as Asian Buddhists are now doing), American Buddhists have vacillated. While Christians have taken a long, hard look at the changing face of modern society and offered to confront the chief ethical issues directly and forthrightly, if not altogether effectively, Buddhists have done neither. Were American Buddhists to offer an innovation of the magnitude of Joseph Fletcher's situation ethics, it would be hailed as a monumental advancement.

In recent years, only two volumes have appeared that purport to deal with the question of Buddhist ethics: Tachibana's *The Ethics of Buddhism* and Saddhatissa's *Buddhist Ethics*. Unfortunately, neither truly confronts the question. Only Winston King's *In the Hope of Nibbana* provides a responsible, serious treatment of the topic. King's work, however, apart from being somewhat dated (1964), is really specific only for Burma. Admittedly, King's initial two chapters ("The Framework of Self-Perfection" and "The Self: Kamma and Rebirth") are brilliant in their attempt to find the contextual locus of the ethical tradition in Buddhism. As we progress through the volume, though, we discover that in King's application of rather rigid Western categories (at least as he utilizes them) to the Theravāda tradition in Burma, he does justice to neither the Theravāda nor the

Western situation. To grant the Buddhist parity with the Westerner in pursuing individual perfection, as King does, only tells a partial story, for it ignores the aspect of social ethics in Buddhism. Of course King will not admit that Buddhism has social ethics at all, and it is here that he misses the point altogether.

What I am suggesting as an antidote to King is that both the monastic and lay ethical dimensions of Buddhism need to be reconsidered, and this has special relevance for America. Buddhism in America appears to need, on the one hand, a revitalized ethical system, emphasizing the laity and informed by modern advances in the human and physical sciences. Further, it must more actively incorporate those formulations in the traditional doctrines that are still relevant— or might be made relevant—in the modern world. I have in mind here a return to the practices known as the Brahmavihāras or the "divine abodes." These four practices, usually identified as *love* (maitrī), *compassion* (karuṇā), *sympathetic joy* (muditā), and *equanimity* (upekṣā), when explicated in their totality, are the highest expression of the Buddhist ethical domain. And they have clear application to American religious experience. On the other hand, Buddhism in America might reawaken the long-silent commentarial tradition in order to address, from American perspective, the critical issues prevalent today. Only a few Buddhist groups have begun to reassess and reassert Buddhist ethics on the American scene, and their effort to date has been modest; but like all pioneering attempts, this will take time. In spite of its unobtrusive beginning, the new emphasis on Buddhist ethics is starting to make some impact on the various American Buddhist communities.

In the wildly chaotic decade of the 1960s, Buddhists, like other Americans, were caught in the midst of the Free Speech Movement, the Sexual Freedom Movement, the era of assassination, the terror of urban blight, the Peace Movement, the proliferation of psychoactive drugs, and a host of other polarizing forces. In many ways, Buddhists' infant community life in America was more seriously disrupted than were those of more established communities in the mainstream of American culture. Consequently, through its association with the counterculture, Buddhist community life was to some extent a hotbed of current or defunct radicals, practicing everything from do-it-yourself macrobiotics to various forms of multilateral marriage.

In reaction to these elements in Buddhism, some Buddhist teachers in the 1970s returned to the traditional mode of instruction for laymen, emphasizing nonharming and abstention from theft, false speech, intoxicants and drugs of any kind, and illicit sexual behavior. In so doing, these teachers began to realize that the traditional mode was generally outdated (and consequently rendered ineffective or unbelievable) or ill-suited to modern America. In their attempt to extemporize meaningfully and responsibly, Buddhists are learning

that, for example, some drugs, although psychoactive, are valuable
therapeutic tools when utilized by a trained and licensed professional. In addition, Buddhists are learning that some forms of premarital (and perhaps even extramarital) relationships that include sexuality may provide valuable personal growth rather than social and emotional harm. The whole dimension of nonharming is being rearranged for American Buddhists by the stirring developments in medical ethics.

These problems are certainly not unique to Buddhists. Nevertheless, in confronting them directly, Buddhists squarely face not only the immediate problems in the ethical domain, but also the greater problem of American identity. For by struggling as Americans with critical issues in American life, Buddhists in this country are able to emphasize their sameness rather than their separateness. Further, in beginning to alter the traditional patterns of Buddhist ethics, they are for the first time creatively dealing with their plight in the modern world.

Buddhism and Science

In the 1970s, the problems resulting from the monumental advances in all aspects of technology, have become strategic concerns for American Buddhists. Theoretically at least, "Future Shock" has never been a frightening issue for Buddhists in that it is the logical, modern application of the Buddhist theory of impermanence and its development into the doctrine of momentariness. Traditionally, each experiential reality is composed of four consecutive moments: origination, decay, duration, and destruction (or in some variant theories, origination, duration, and decay). In simple language, each presently existing moment manifests a latent (but now inexistent) past and a potential (but not yet existent) future. The most adept Buddhist scholastics, namely the Sarvāstivādin school, on the other hand propounded that the past, present, and future all exist simultaneously. Although this school eventually died out in India, it left its heritage by shaping much of the Buddhism that was to follow it. It also provided a tool which, when applied to the seemingly premature arrival of the future in the present, identifies this phenomenon as congruent with the "normal" state of affairs.

Just as the on-going explication, in the Abhidharma period, of the Sarvāstivādin theory of momentariness demonstrated Buddhists' willingness and capability in addressing scientific matters, so too would this attitude be helpful in the 1970s. Not only does the present lack of confrontation inhibit their acculturation, but it also cannot be expected that modern American Buddhists will accept overly simplistic or naïvely undemonstrable tenets for much longer. Harold K. Schilling's argument in defense of complexity in "In Celebration of Complexity"[7] is an indication that matters are significantly more complicated than American Buddhists have admitted. While American Buddhists vainly chase the simplicity that they *think* Buddhism represents, they fail to recognize that the *context* has changed. Thus, as Americans consider the potential abandonment of their dream of the "innocent Adam," American Buddhists might do well to abandon their dream of the "innocent Buddha." Although the innocent Buddha may be transmuted into a cybernetic version of the HAL computer in *Space Odyssey: 2001* or Michael Crichton's "terminal man," Buddhists in America would find it advantageous to end their silence on the relationship between Buddhism and science (or end their *simplistic* approach to the relationship), and in the process, assert their sameness with the American mission rather than their separateness.

THE NEED FOR ECUMENICITY

In our consideration of the decade of the 1960s, we referred to some of the problems then encountered by the Western religious traditions in America. One of the most profound was the pluralism resulting from secularization and the ecumenicity it engendered as a combative measure. In the 1970s, with the full array of Buddhist traditions and sects represented in America, the need for Buddhist ecumenicity is being keenly felt. Regarding the Buddhist ecumenical movement, Emma Layman notes:

> This is taking several forms: (1) establishment of nonsectarian or inter-sectarian churches and monasteries; (2) intersectarian sharing of resources, for example, Sunday School materials and visual aids; (3) exchange of priests or ministers on occasion; (4) integration of meditational-type approaches into ceremonial-type churches; and (5) joint services involving different sects and/or non-Buddhist groups. In each of these ways Buddhists of different sects do get together in comfortable interaction, coexistence, or union.[8]

There is no question that Professor Layman is correct in stressing the Buddhist concern for cooperation in America. Such cooperation serves to insulate against potential fragmentation. Her fifth point, regarding the interaction of Buddhist and non-Buddhist groups, however, develops into a potential problem area. Earlier we referred to the dialogue that has begun between Buddhism (particularly Zen and its meditative tradition) and Christianity. While on the surface this appears to be mutually beneficial, there are precedents for questioning the efficacy of such an endeavor. We all know that Buddhism arose in a predominantly Hindu culture in India. As Buddhism grew and matured, it gained an enormous following, enhanced by the patronage of several Indian rulers (most notably Aśoka and Kaniṣka). Nevertheless, in the first centuries of the Common Era, Hinduism began to fully reassert itself, with some significant measure of its success resulting from its amoebalike ability to absorb the finest essentials of Buddhism and Jainism. In fact, Buddha is even considered an incarnation (avatāra) of Viṣṇu. One might make a similar example of Neo-Taoism in China, and other examples could be cited as well. Might one anticipate that, as the Christian-Buddhist dialogue progresses and deepens, Christianity will simply assimilate Buddhist elements into its own tradition (in the same amoebalike fashion as Hinduism), and in so doing, undercut the potential growth of Buddhism in America? Buddha is reputed to have stated that Buddhism could not be defeated from without, that it could only be undermined from within its own boundaries. However, it was only a few short centuries after Hinduism's resurgence that Buddhism, weakened by the encounter, began to lose its vitality, creativity, and applicability, thus making it easy prey for the invading Muslims. Further, Buddhism's growth in America, like the advancement of any religious tradition, depends on a host of variables over which it has little or no control. In this regard, the development of the Western religious traditions, still so uncertain, will impart a profound impact on the future growth of Buddhism in this country.

THE NEW ROMANTICISM

The above remarks hint that much of the future of Buddhism in the 1970s, or for that matter, in longer term perspective, is dependent on the changing face of American religious life in general. Many scholars would argue that America has been witnessing in the 1960s and 1970s a new romanticism. Some writers would even extend the estimate back beyond the 1960s. Nevertheless, the implications of such a proposition are clear enough, particularly with regard to two issues. The first, and from my perspective the clearly less substantial item, concerns the fascination for things oriental in the rise of any romantic movement. The above is noteworthy insofar as it explains somewhat the recent interest in the Orient. The second item has more direct consequence for Buddhism in America. Bellah has argued,

> A central belief shared by the oriental religions and diffused widely outside them is important because of its sharp contrast with established American views. This is the belief in the unity of all being. Our separate selves, according to Buddhism, Hinduism, and their offshoots, are not ultimately real. Philosophical Hinduism and Mahayana Buddhism reject dualism.[9]

Belief in the organic unity of all beings represents one of the major thrusts of the new romanticism. Consequently, if we are witnessing such a revival, and I suspect that we are, Bellah stands contradicted,

and his identification of Buddhism's nondualism as a chief (and critical) liability of the movement in America turns into an asset. If, on
the other hand, it turns out that the new romanticism is a fanciful
fiction or an ephemeral movement, I would still argue that Bellah is
wrong, for he ignores Buddhism's doctrine of the "two levels of
truth," particularly as espoused in Nāgārjuna's Mādhyamika-kārikās,
which does identify the appropriateness of mundane activity and
relative reality.

"WHY?" AND "WHO?"

As we conclude our consideration of the 1970s, two final questions
remain concerning Buddhism in America. These two questions can be
stated as "Why?" and "Who?" Emma Layman suggests in her chapter
on "Why Buddhism?" eleven basic motivational factors which she
feels are useful in determining why Americans choose Buddhism in
the midst of other (and perhaps more logical) alternatives. These factors include (1) familial-cultural affinity, (2) intellectual, scientific
appeal, (3) appeal of a rational cure for a sick society, (4) appeal of
pageantry, symbolism, and the esoteric, (5) do-it-yourself appeal,
(6) a wish to transcend the ordinary, (7) need for a wise and benevo-
lent authority figure, (8) need to rebel against the establishment, (9)
need for a relief for suffering, (10) need for a fuller, richer, and more
effective life, and (11) need to seek the truth.[10] While all of these factors may indeed be applicable to the question, it must also be argued
that each of the eleven factors might well be met by the more traditional religions in America. If we are willing to admit, and I am, that
they *are* being met by the more traditional religions in America, then
the question "Why Buddhism?" remains unanswered. Ms. Layman's
factors seem more reminiscent of man's general quest for ultimacy
and meaning and of man's attempt to confront the ultimate conditions of his existence (to use Bellah's approach). To date, Buddhism
is no better a mode of ultimate transformation (to use Streng's term)
than the traditional models of religion in America. Perhaps the most
unique quality of Buddhism that makes its choice so appetizing is its
primary focus on the individual as the *sole* instrument of salvation
and its emphasis on the potential for wholeness *in this life.*
With regard to the question of "Who?" Ms. Layman notes several
points that are worthy of mention. Apart from our earlier estimates
of the composition of the Buddhist movement in America, she finds
the largest concentration of Buddhists on both coastal areas and in
the large urban centers of mid-America. As for other areas, the task
of Buddhism in the 1970s will be to cultivate these potential arenas
of interest. Within the meditational Buddhist groups, most members
are reported to be under thirty-five, and there are more male than fe-

male members. These disproportions will have to be corrected if meditational Buddhism is to become more pervasive.

A TRADITION OF MISUNDERSTANDING: TWO BUDDHISMS IN AMERICA

By the above rubric I do not mean to say that there are only two kinds of Buddhism in America. Rather, I propose that there have always been two distinct lines of development for Buddhism in America. One form of Buddhism places primary emphasis on sound, basic doctrines, shared by all Buddhists, and on solid religious practice (which may reflect sectarian doctrinal peculiarities). These groups are slow to develop, conservative in nature, and remarkably *stable* in growth, activity, and teaching. The other line of development includes those groups that seem to emerge shortly after radical social movements (such as the Beat Generation or the Drug Culture). They tend to garner the "fallout" of social upheaval. Stressing less the basic doctrine and painstaking practice, they usually base their attraction on the promise of something new, frequently centered on the personal charisma of a flamboyant leader. In other words, they replace the old social order, now in decay or disfavor, with a new one, replete with the same sort of trappings but transmuted into what is thought to be a more profoundly "relevant" religious foundation.

By nature flashy, opaquely exotic, and "hip," these movements gain much attention in the press but are inherently unstable. Some of these groups do endure, but only after the pandemonium has passed and they have adopted a more solid working basis. It is usually only these flashy groups that generate significant public interest and are noticed in the press. Yet because of their chaotic nature, they are perceived with ambivalence at best, and more often than not, are regarded as clearly undesirable. Thus, *all* of Buddhism—even the "quiet" and honest Buddhism—is misunderstood and/or rejected outright in the curious public's eye. The misunderstanding filters its way down to scholars, leading to their inappropriately facile dismissal of a religious tradition with several hundred thousand adherents in America.

There have always been two Buddhisms on the American scene, and the prospects for the future tend toward continuance of this tradition (or perhaps the appearance of yet a third Buddhism resulting from some new cultural mixture). We must, then, learn to discriminate between the various forms and their validity. As Robert Michaelson notes:

> Today on a hundred different fronts men and women are experimenting with new means in their search for soul. The experiments that will prob-

ably prove most long lasting in influence will be those that can, on the one hand, stimulate or elicit the power of spiritually transforming experience and faith and, on the other hand, channel that power into disciplined action. What is needed is a combination that holds in creative tension a number of seeming opposites; spontaneity and control, spirituality and practicality, ecstasy and action, grace and morality, virtue and power, individuality and community. This kind of combination has not been common in American history in the past century.[11]

PART TWO

The Flowering of Buddhism in America: Horses Run on Wheels

The spiritual supermarket is a funny place. No one who hasn't checked it out from wall to wall can write about it completely. No one who has done so and found some kind of spiritual technique that works for them seems to want to write about it except to lay their trip on other people.

—Robert Greenfield[1]

Even the notion of "dropping out" is an important American tradition—neither the United States itself nor its populous suburbs would exist were this not so.

—Philip Slater[2]

One day in the latter part of May 1976, I was leaving the office of Professor Masatoshi Nagatomi in the Yenching Institute at Harvard University, and as I stepped out onto Divinity Avenue to head in the direction of Widener Library, I met a rather ordinary-looking young man who questioned me about my business in the Yenching Institute. When I explained to him that Professor Nagatomi and I were working on a manuscript entitled "A Survey of Vinaya Literature" that we intended to publish, he became very intrigued and asked, "Are you into Buddhism?" When I replied in the affirmative, he said that he was too. Curiously though, as our conversation later revealed, my affirmative response indicated two things to him: first, that since the manuscript title mentioned was on a fairly difficult (and to most, unexciting) topic in Buddhism, I was *only* a scholar, and second, since a scholar's opinions on practical matters could not be trusted at all, he was not going to take our conversation too seriously. Of course his two assumptions did not surface until later, and quite unaware that he had made them at all, I pursued the matter of what his statement of involvement with Buddhism meant. My young informant noted that he had come to Harvard as an aspiring and idealistic student, hoping to reap the intellectual fruits of a great university. Sometime during his first year at Harvard he fell in love, got involved with drugs, became suspicious of the academic life, and "dropped out" (although he could not remember the exact order of the first three events). His dropping out marked the beginning of a spiritual odyssey of sorts, which he described in great detail. His initial involvements were with Transcendental Meditation (which he dismissed quickly as being too commercial) and the Divine Light Mission (which he dismissed not so quickly, but with much hostility —a hostility he refused to explain). He then explored in succession a variety of Zen groups, one Tibetan Buddhist group, Japanese Pure Land (Jōdo Shinshū), and Theravāda. "Exploration" meant, to this young fellow, to visit a group, try out their practices, and see if it had any immediate effect on his anxiety-filled life. In pursuing his quest, he never left the East Coast, and completed his search in just under one year. When questioned as to why he said he was still "into Buddhism" after such a dismally disappointing "exploration," he remarked that he had finally found "True Buddhism." He explained that two weeks ago, when his life was still a battleground of turmoil and despair, a friend invited him to attend a gathering of people who all professed faith in Nichiren Shōshū. While he hesitated at first, the friend persuaded him to try it out; after all, what did he have to lose? The transformation was immediate. As soon as he began to chant Nam Myōhō Renge Kyō regularly, his estranged lover (who had deserted him earlier) returned, he lost his interest in drugs, and met a professor who once again convinced him to return to his academic pursuits. How could he dispute, according to his testimony, this incontestable proof of the efficacy of Nichiren Shōshū? Further, he invited me to chant with him, and when I politely declined, he told me that if I wanted to remain "messed up" forever, chasing information *about* Buddhism, that was my own business. And as surprisingly as he had appeared, he darted down a side path and was gone.

My concern in this section is not so much *how* this young man could get interested in so many different Buddhist groups, or even *why,* for I suspect that the answers to these questions emerge from a consideration of the material presented in the first section. Here I am concerned with two further issues: *who are these groups* and *what do they do?*

Certainly both the criteria for selection for study and the specific groups to be considered are problematic issues. They are problematic

because any number of valid criteria might be considered in the
selection-making process, a difficulty compounded by the hundreds of Buddhist groups currently active. In selecting the individual groups to be studied in this section, I have first of all tried to be representative. Consequently, at least one group from each of the Japanese, Tibetan, Chinese, and South Asian traditions of Buddhism has been included. Further, in clear recognition of the high attrition rate of some groups, I have taken care to consider only those groups that appear to be generally stable while pursuing continued growth and popularity. Finally, I have elected to consider groups that are illustrative of major Buddhist movements in America. Applying the above features of selectivity, I have elected to include, from the Japanese tradition, groups representing three sectarian concerns: Buddhist Churches of America for the Jōdo Shinshū sect, Nichiren Shōshū of America for the Nichiren sect, and the San Francisco Zen Center and Shasta Abbey for the Zen sect. From the Tibetan tradition, I have included the Tibetan Nyingma Meditation Center for the rNying-ma sect and Vajradhatu and Nalanda Foundation for the bKa-rgyud sect. From the Chinese tradition, I have included the Sino-American Buddhist Association, and from the tradition of Buddhism in South Asia, I have included the Buddhist Vihara Society. The groups are presented in the chronological order of their appearance on the American scene.

In determining the mode of presentation, I have developed a series of categories that I have applied to each group. These categories, when applied to the individual groups, attempt to reveal not only the data pertinent to the organization, but also the manner in which some of the issues mentioned in the first section are concretely manifested. While there are ten basic categories (sectarian affiliation, history, facilities and structure, branches and affiliated groups, key members and/or personnel, membership, key and/or special doctrines, rituals-services-practices, future plans, and publications), it will at once become obvious that not all categories apply to all groups. Consequently, rather than rigidly adhering to this schemata, I will utilize it as a basic guideline, making omissions where appropriate. Further, any individual category may be weighted more or less heavily as the case in point dictates. Finally, I will end the discussion of each group with a concluding section, offering my own interpretive impressions.

CHAPTER 5

Buddhist Churches of America

I wish to extend greetings to the 75th Anniversary Commemorative Conference of the Buddhist Churches of America and to express my most sincere wish on this historic occasion for the continued flowering of your faith throughout the United States as you seek the Buddha presence.

It is in the finest American tradition for our citizens to look within their own inner being for spiritual guidance. Americans of the Buddhist faith are a valued element of that heritage. Citizens of all faiths may draw inspiration from your devotion to the Buddha.

May this occasion be a memorable milestone for the Buddhist Churches of America. I wish to assure you of my goodwill and reverent respect.

Gerald R. Ford
President of the United States[1]

SECTARIAN AFFILIATION

Buddhist Churches of America is the western hemisphere representative of the western branch of the Japanese Jōdo Shinshū tradition.[2] Although it functions as a predominantly independent organization, the home temple in Kyoto still considers it a "district" of Hompa Hongwanji (i.e., Jōdo Shinshū, western branch), requiring that Buddhist Churches of America make financial contributions to the home temple and follow its guideline, while offering no support in return.

HISTORY

The history of Buddhist Churches of America begins with the arrival in San Francisco on July 6, 1898, of two informal missionaries sent on a fact-finding tour by Hompa Hongwanji (in Kyoto).[3] The results of their report, coupled with the efforts of the Japanese immigrants who resisted the conversion attempts of American evangelists (perhaps embodied in the figure of Nisaburo Hirano, who actually traveled to the home temple in Kyoto to argue for a permanent clergy to serve the faithful immigrants), culminated in the arrival of Reverend Shuei Sonoda and Reverend Kakuryo Nishijima in San Francisco on September 1, 1899, to establish the Buddhist Mission of North America (as it was then called). These two "official" missionaries were the first Buddhist clergy to enter America.

The immigrants to whom Reverends Sonoda and Nishijima ministered could not, for the most part, speak the native tongue of their new culture and had been educated in Asian rather than European fashion. The two missionaries enjoyed much success in organizing these immigrant Buddhist families. They even organized a group for non-Japanese patrons, called The Diamond Sangha of America (which published a bulletin known as the "Light of Dharma"). Nevertheless, in spite of their modest efforts to inform Americans about the nature of Buddhism in general and Jōdo Shinshū in particular, an attitude of racism predominated. Just as legislation in the late 1880s excluded the Chinese from entry to America, attention now turned to the Japanese immigrants who were regarded as alien and non-Christian. As an expression of animosity, Japanese immigrants were not allowed by the government to become naturalized citizens of the United States, and in many western states they were not allowed to become individual landowners. The flaw in the governmental policy, despite the Japanese Immigration Exclusion Act of 1924, was the constitutional guarantee of religious freedom. Consequently, the Japanese Buddhists were able to purchase land for their temples, and by 1931 thirty-three main temples (and many branches) had been established. It may also be noted that with this large increase in the number of main temples, a larger English-speaking clergy was required. Thus, in 1930, under the guidance of Bishop Kenju Masuyama, a training center known as Wakoryo was opened in Kyoto to meet this need. Wakoryo provided the initial impetus for such a training center in America, which will be discussed later.

The Japanese air attack on Pearl Harbor in 1941 very nearly dealt a death blow to the Buddhist Mission of North America, as it was almost exclusively populated by members of Japanese ancestry. Most Japanese Buddhist ministers on American soil were arrested immediately, as Buddhism was confused with nationalistic Shinto and consequently with the Japanese military effort. In response, the Buddhist Mission of North America issued the following bulletin:

The suddenness and the unwarranted and inhumane attack upon these United States of America leaves us, the Buddhists in America, with but one decision: the condemnation of that attack. . . . The loyalty to the United States which we have pledged at all times must now be placed into instant action for the defense of the United States of America.[4]

In spite of their statement of loyalty, in February 1942, over 100,000 Japanese in America were uprooted from their homes on the West Coast and placed in internment camps, with over half of these persons being Buddhists and two-thirds being American born.[5] It was also in 1942 that the Buddhist Mission of North America officially changed its name to Buddhist Churches of America.

When the war concluded and the West Coast was once again available for Japanese residents, many Buddhists returned to their homes, necessitating a renewed and integral role for the many Buddhist churches. On the other hand, many Japanese who had left the West during the war years simply remained in their new residences in the Midwest and East. As a result of this latter trend, Buddhist Churches of America expanded into these areas to meet the needs of its followers. The need for an enlarged clergy was becoming acute in the postwar period and resulted, in 1948, in the establishment of a monthly study class for prospective ministers at the home of Mrs. Shinobu Matsuura. In 1951 the program was moved to the Berkeley Buddhist Temple and renamed the Buddhist Study Center. Its guidance was taken over by Reverend Kanmo Imamura. By 1958 the parent organization decided to establish a training center for ministers in the United States and have formal instruction offered in *English*. This program was implemented by Reverend Imamura at the Buddhist Study Center and was eventually taken over by Reverend Masami Fujitani. In October 1966 a building was acquired on Haste Street in Berkeley. The full potential of this program is now being realized. As it continued to meet the needs of its constituency, Buddhist Churches of America struggled through the decade of the 1960s; in August 1974 it celebrated its seventy-fifth anniversary.

FACILITIES AND STRUCTURE

Since 1937 the National Headquarters of Buddhist Churches of America has occupied a building at 1710 Octavia Street in San Francisco, which, according to Emma Layman, "looks like an elementary school, except for the stupa on top of the building enshrining the holy relics of the Buddha."[6] This building houses the various administrative offices of the organization. Administration of the organization is conducted by the Office of the Bishop, the Executive Secretary, the Youth Department, the Sunday School Department, the English Secretary, the Japanese Secretary, and the Bookstore Personnel. Further, there is a fifty-one member Board of Directors which serves as the governing body of Buddhist Churches of America. The Board of Directors includes the Bishop, Honorary Chairman, Chairman of the Ministerial Association, nine Directors-at-Large (elected at the annual National Council meeting), twenty-four District Representatives, eight Minister-Directors, four Representatives of Affiliated Organizations, and the three immediate Past Presidents of the Buddhist Churches of America Board of Directors. The Octavia Street Building also houses the Buddhist Bookstore, which is perhaps the most well-stocked, thorough, and up to date of its kind in America.

Regarding the appearance of the various churches associated with Buddhist Churches of America, these buildings usually fall into one of two categories. The older churches are usually housed in buildings that were acquired at various times by the organization from various sources, and thus tend to reflect more the original use of the building than its current one. The more recently acquired churches are often clearly reflective of their function, with some being patterned after Japanese temples. Emma Layman, who has apparently visited many more of these facilities than has this author, summarizes her impressions in an extremely useful descriptive fashion:

> In contrast to the varied exteriors, the American Buddhist churches are remarkably uniform on the inside. The main hall of the temple (*hondo*) is similar to a Christian church in terms of its division into nave and chancel, with the chancel area sometimes being separated into a choir and sanctuary. In the nave are pews or chairs, occupied by the congregation (some churches provide kneeling pads). At the front of the nave, on one side of the altar, there is usually a piano or an electronic organ; on the other side is a pulpit. Sometimes there is, in addition, a lectern, usually on the same side as the piano or organ. In the center front area there is likely to be a large incense burner on a stand, used by the congregation in presenting incense.
>
> A visitor wandering into a BCA church in Los Angeles, New York, or Chicago might feel that he was entering a Christian church rather than a Buddhist temple, until he noticed the altar, which is unmistakably Buddhist and Japanese. Some of the altars are extremely elaborate, others quite simple. Generally speaking, older members seem to favor an elaborate altar, younger members favor simplicity.
>
> The central position on the altar is occupied by a gold figure of Amida Buddha. (In some churches there may be substituted a painting of Amida or a scroll bearing the Japanese characters "Namu Amida Butsu.") The Buddha is seen standing, with his right hand held up in a gesture of reassurance and his left hand lowered in a gesture of conferring blessings on all.
>
> On the right of Amida, as one faces the altar, there is commonly a scroll bearing the image of Saint Shinran, and on the left a scroll bearing the picture of one of the chief abbots descended from Shinran. There may be other scrolls or figures on the altar, commemorating various leaders in the history of Jodo Shinshu. Of the images or scrolls in the altar area,

however, only Amida Buddha is an object of worship. Other figures are
placed on the altar, not to be worshipped but as a gesture of respect and thanksgiving for the contributions they may have made to the teachings.

As on other Buddhist altars, candles symbolize enlightenment, flowers express impermanence, and the burning of incense symbolizes the act of purification before worship, or before going out into the world after worship. Food is placed on the altar in symbolic praise and thanksgiving for Amida's eternal guidance. In front of the altar there are usually placed copies of the sutras and there is a kneeling pad for the use of the minister. On each side of the altar are percussion instruments—gongs, bells, *mokugyo* (wooden fish), and drums—used to designate parts of the service and to punctuate chants. There are also chairs for the priests or ministers. Of the above, only the chairs would not be found in a Japanese temple and in Japan the chancel and nave would be covered with tatami mats. In America, both are usually carpeted.

In designating the figure of Amida Buddha as the object of worship, it should be noted that when worshippers bow in reverence before the statue, they are not praying to Amida but are revering the wisdom and compassion of Amida, which the statue symbolizes.

All BCA churches have offices, Sunday School rooms, rest rooms, and space analogous to the parish hall in a Christian church. There is usually a kitchen and in the larger churches there may be extra chapels, meeting rooms for different groups, and rooms for special projects.[7]

BRANCHES AND AFFILIATED GROUPS

Buddhist Churches of America encompasses sixty independent churches and forty branches. These churches are divided into eight geographic districts. Each district is represented on the Board of Directors by its Minister-Director (chosen by the ministers in each respective district) and three representatives (chosen by the District Council in each respective district). The districts are delineated as follows:

1. *Southern District:* Arizona, Gardena, Guadalupe, Los Angeles, Orange County, Oxnard, Pasadena, San Diego, San Luis Obispo, Santa Barbara, Senshin, West Los Angeles
2. *Central District:* Dinuba, Fowler, Fresno, Hanford, Parlier, Reedley, Visalia, Bakersfield, Delano
3. *Coast District:* Monterrey, Mountain View, Salinas, San Jose, Watsonville
4. *Bay District:* Alameda, Berkeley, Enmanji, Marin, Oakland, Palo Alto, San Francisco, San Mateo, South Alameda
5. *Northern District:* Florin, Lodi, Marysville, Placer, Sacramento, Stockton, Walnut Grove
6. *Northwest District:* Idaho-Oregon, Oregon, Seattle, Spokane, Tacoma, White River, Yakima
7. *Mountain District:* Ogden, Salt Lake City, Tri-State Denver

8. *Eastern District:* Cleveland, Midwest Chicago, New York, Seabrook, Detroit, Twin Cities, Washington, D.C.

These districts and churches are served by the Buddhist Churches of America Ministerial Association, currently consisting of eighty ministers. The Ministerial Association holds meetings biannually and is represented on the Board of Directors by the (elected) Chairman of the Ministerial Association.

Buddhist Churches of America has two major educational centers: the American Buddhist Academy and the Institute of Buddhist Studies. The former center, located on Riverside Drive in New York City, serves the organization in providing preministerial training and functions as the educational arm of the New York Buddhist Church. The latter center had a very humble beginning in the mid-1930s, but in recent years has expanded considerably. Although it too was originally intended to provide preministerial training, it now has a graduate program leading to the degree of Master of Arts in Buddhist Studies. Its programs also meet all the prerequisites for ordination in Shin Buddhism. It not only has a growing library and full range of courses (including language training, history, philosophy, and the like, at varying levels of intensity and sophistication), but also a growing faculty that by 1973–74 included over twenty members. Further, some of the faculty members were visiting scholars of the highest standing, such as Masatoshi Nagatomi of Harvard University. The Institute of Buddhist Studies offers an intriguing philosophy of education, which is cited below in its entirety, due to the fact that in the mid-1970s many other Buddhist groups began offering programs utilizing a similar approach. In this sense it may be regarded as prototypic of Buddhist education in America.

The Institute's Philosophy of Education

1. Education is a process of mutual growth, so that ultimately there is neither student nor teacher. He who is at one moment in the teaching position is, at another moment, learning from his pupil. The faculty of the Institute, accordingly, does not reveal hidden wisdom to the student body; rather, together they seek the truth. In this search, education is a growth in wisdom and compassion.
2. Education is the exercise of mutual respect; grounded in the teachings of non-ego and Emptiness, mutual respect is the acknowledgement of the innate integrity of all sentient beings. Education exists only when student and teacher alike accept each other as they are and respect each other for what they are.
3. Education is a reformation, and it exists only when a change has come about in one's behavior and attitudes. True education are those changes that increase one's practice of wisdom and compassion.
4. Education is for eternity. It is a long process, bringing the ignorant, ordinary man from his state of suffering and frustration to the state of an Enlightened Being, free from greed, hatred, and delusion. What is learned in one state in this process may not appear as behavior until

some much later time; thus, the success or failure of the educational process cannot be measured in terms of today or tomorrow.[8]

Buddhist Churches of America also sponsors the Bureau of Buddhist Education, consisting of a Sunday School Department, a Youth Department, an Adult Department, and a Music Department. In addition, the Bureau includes a publishing house and several publications (which we will consider later), the aforementioned Buddhist Bookstore, an Audio-Visual Library, and a Speakers Program. Of these groups, the most interesting to me is the Sunday School. Although each church has functional autonomy with regard to the particular materials utilized, the material sponsored by the National Headquarters is, as Emma Layman notes, relied on to some degree. Professor Layman mentions a particular reliance on Ensei H. Nekoda's *A Guide to Creative Teaching in the Sunday School* (published by the Buddhist Churches of America Sunday School Department).[9] Further, she cites two categories, regarding the purpose of Sunday School, from the pamphlet:

Ultimate Objectives
1. To help children discover their true selves.
2. To help children realize that they live in Amida's wisdom and compassion.
3. To guide children to live intimately with Amida Buddha in his wisdom and compassion.
4. To teach children rebirth in Amida's Pure Land as the final objective.

Immediate Objectives
5. To teach children the Mahāyāna spirit.
6. To develop children's character along the Buddhistic spirit of love, compassion and wisdom.
7. To teach children to lead a life of gratitude.
8. To apply the best teaching methods to make Buddhism meaningful to children.
9. To develop the children's sense of appreciation for their Buddhist heritage.
10. To work in harmony with the home and the school to help children become well-rounded, wholesome individuals.[10]

Sunday School classes, it should be mentioned, are conducted in English.

There are several major affiliated organizations of Buddhist Churches of America. These include: The Buddhist Women's Association, the Adult Buddhist Association, the Young Buddhist Association, and the Sunday School Teachers Association.

KEY MEMBERS AND/OR PERSONNEL

The most significant figure in the administrative structure of Buddhist Churches of America is the Bishop, a position currently occupied by Kenyru T. Tsuji. In addition to Bishop Tsuji, we have the various administrators of the organization, the Board of Directors, and the eighty ministers comprising the Ministerial Association. Unlike other Buddhist groups in America, Buddhist Churches of America has never focused on the charismatic figure at the top of the institutional hierarchy, nor has it emphasized a "guru-oriented" relationship between minister and congregation members (in keeping with the tenets of Jōdo Shinshū). Thus, the organization has been very capable of functioning smoothly irrespective of the *particular* members of its governing body.

MEMBERSHIP

Although Emma Layman notes that "total membership is assessed at forty thousand,"[11] Buddhist Churches of America maintains that its organization has 100,000 members. Membership seems to be determined by those making financial contributions on a continuing basis rather than those necessarily professing Buddhism. Although statistics are not furnished, the majority of Buddhist Churches of America members seem to be of Japanese families, but American born. There is a very small following of Caucasians, but this group consists for the most part of people interested in Buddhism or of men with Japanese-American wives.

Since 1962, Buddhist Churches of America has had a Sustaining Membership Program intended to eliminate any reliance on borrowing or soliciting funds and to provide its members with an opportunity to engage in dāna or the act of "giving" for their religion. Sustaining members are required to contribute $25 yearly to the fund. In the twelve-year period between 1962 and 1974, $312,000 was raised and over 1,700 members participated in the program (there are 1,233 members currently supporting the fund). There was a steady rise in the number of members from 1962 to 1966, then a decline for two consecutive years, and an increase in every year since 1968. Monies from this program have been utilized for such purposes as to assist in the loan payments on the National Headquarters, to aid the Bishop's Buddhist Churches of America Expansion Program Fund, and to augment the Building and Expansion Fund.

KEY AND/OR SPECIAL DOCTRINES

The doctrines of Buddhist Churches of America are all in accord with the official position of the Western branch of Jōdo Shinshū. For those readers who are interested in a succinct statement of these doctrines for America, Reverend Haruo Yamaoka's *The Teaching and Practice of Jōdō Shinshu* may be referred to. This pamphlet, by the minister of the Stockton Buddhist Temple, was published by Buddhist Churches of America in 1974.

RITUALS, SERVICES, AND PRACTICES

Services in Buddhist Churches of America can be divided into two categories: ordinary services and special services. The ordinary services are usually held on Sundays and are conducted by the minister, who wears regular black robes rather than ceremonial dress. There is always an adult service conducted in Japanese (and attended by the issei and nisei members of the congregation), and sometimes an English service for the other members of the congregation (some nisei, sansei, and non-Japanese). Liturgical volumes are published by Buddhist Churches of America in Japanese and English. The services usually proceed as follows:

1. Organ prelude
2. Temple bell (minister)
3. Offering incense (chairman)[12]
4. Meditation (congregation)
5. Aspiration (chairman)
6. Gatha (congregation)
7. Homage, Threefold Refuge (minister and congregation)
8. Invocation (chairman)
9. Creed (congregation)

We rely upon Tathagata Amitabha with our whole heart for the Enlightenment in the world to come, abstaining from all sundry practices and teachings, and giving up the trust in our powerless self.

We believe that the assurance of our rebirth through his salvation comes at the very moment we put our faith in Him, and we call the name, Namu Amida Butsu, in happiness and thankfulness for his mercy.

We also acknowledge gratefully the benign benevolence of our founder and the succeeding Masters who have led us to believe in this profound teaching, and we do now endeavor to follow throughout our lives the Way laid down for us.

10. Chanting of the sutra (congregation)
11. Responsive reading (chairman and congregation)
12. Sermon (minister)
13. Offertory
14. Meditation (congregation)
15. Benediction and nembutsu (all)
16. Postlude[13]

This format is intended to provide a general picture only and does not include the variations that necessarily appear in the services of specific churches.

There are eleven special services recognized by Buddhist Churches of America:

1. *New Year's Day Service:* This service is called Shusho E in Japanese, and is the first service of the year. In America it is observed on the morning of New Year's Day, but in Japan, it is observed for seven days. It provides a chance for members to reflect on the past while committing themselves to lead a proper life in the coming year. In Japan, it originally was observed as a blessing to the emperor and as a hope for world peace and a successful harvest.

2. *Ho-on-ko:* This service, intended to honor the sect's founder (Shinran Shonin), was begun by the third abbot of the Hongwanji Church (who happened to be Shinran's grandson). It has been observed annually since. Members are reminded to be grateful for Shinran's contribution, and to follow his path. The western branch of Jōdo Shinshū observes this holiday on January 16, while the eastern branch observes it in November.

3. *Nirvana Day:* Called Nehan E in Japanese, this holiday honors the parinirvāṇa of the Buddha Śākyamuni. It is observed on February 15 and, like other holidays, provides an opportunity for reflection and change.

4. *Spring Higan:* Etymologically, "higan" is linked to the Sanskrit term pāramitā. Pāramitā means literally "going to the other shore," which is identified with Amida's Pure Land. The rite was first observed in 1043 and now offers respect to the dead. It is observed in Japan for one week, starting on March 18 or 19.

5. *Hanamatsuri:* Literally translated as "flower festival," this holiday is celebrated on April 8 to mark the birth of Buddha Śākyamuni. It reminds all members to strive to attain Buddhahood.

6. *Gotan E:* This holiday commemorates the birthday of Shinran Shonin (May 21). Observance of this holiday allows members to recall Shinran's life and offer gratitude. Some churches refer to this festival as Fujimatsuri or the Wisteria Day Festival.

7. *Bon:* Etymologically, "bon" relates to the Sanskrit term ullambana. First observed in China in 538, it is held between July 15 and August 15. The story from which the holiday derives concerns Maudgalyāyana's attempt to rescue his mother from the realm of the hungry ghosts (pretas) by an act of giving (dāna) to the other monks. Participants traditionally make floral offerings and light incense at the burial sites of their relatives as well as light candles to show the spirits of their ancestors the way to their homes. They conclude this holiday, which mixes solemnity and joy, by floating paper lanterns, lit by candles and bearing a cargo of food, out to sea to the resting places of the spirits of their ancestors.

8. *Buddhist Churches of America Founding Day:* Observed on September 1, this holiday honors the arrival of Reverends Sonoda and Nishijima in San Francisco. This is the only holiday of the sect originating in America.

9. *Autumn Higan:* Observed for one week beginning either

September 20 or 21, the holiday is arranged in such a manner that the autumn equinox falls on the middle day of the week. The holiday seems to be more Japanese than Buddhist, but in Buddhist context stresses crossing to the farther shore of nirvāṇa.

10. *Bodhi Day:* Observed on December 8, this holiday honors Buddha's attaining enlightenment. Since the holiday falls in December, members conclude the year with a reaffirmation of their faith.

11. *Year End Service:* Called Joya E in Japanese, in this service the temple bells are rung 108 times in hopes of wiping out the 108 human passions. It is observed on New Year's Eve and is a time for gratitude and reflection.

More information on these services can be obtained from Reverend George E. Shibata's pamphlet *The Buddhist Holidays* published in 1974 by Buddhist Churches of America.

FUTURE PLANS

Since the National Headquarters was completed in 1971, Buddhist Churches of America now plans to compose a written history of the sect in America.[14] They would further like to sponsor a translation project that would render a number of sūtras into both English and modern Japanese. With membership now leveling off, they face the problem of trying to find some mode of bolstering membership rolls, and this is compounded by the division in their congregation. As the issei members of the congregation die, Buddhist Churches of America cannot seem to decide whether to follow the general wishes of the nisei members and Americanize more fully, or honor the wishes of the clergy (and many young members) and reassert their Japanese heritage. Plans to train more ministers fluent in English continue. And, of course, general expansion is stressed.

PUBLICATIONS

All of the Buddhist Churches of America publications fall under the umbrellalike covering of the Buddhist Churches of America Publishing House. This organization has attempted to provide more books on Buddhism in general and Jōdo Shinshū in particular for its members. In addition to pamphlets on history, doctrine, practice, and the like (some of which have been cited previously), the congregation publishes *Wheel of Dharma*, a monthly newsletter in English, *Horin*, a monthly publication in Japanese, and *The American Buddhist*, its most serious publication, written in English, sold through subscriptions, and primarily educational in nature and scope. Occasionally miscellaneous volumes are published, such as the *Buddhist*

Churches of America 75th Anniversary Commemoration Volume. All of these publications, as well as a host of religious articles and books on Buddhism in its various aspects, are sold in the Buddhist Bookstore (previously mentioned).

CONCLUDING REMARKS

Although statistics are virtually impossible to obtain, it can be stated with reasonable safety that Buddhist Churches of America has the largest Oriental-American membership of any Buddhist group in this country. This situation may well be its greatest asset *and* its greatest liability. On the positive side, a constituency that is almost exclusively Japanese insures that almost all members of the organization share a common Buddhist heritage and ethnic background. Such a situation *could* provide an extremely significant sense of congregational solidarity in the culturally and religiously pluralistic society that America has become. In order to reap this benefit, however, Buddhist Churches of America will need to insure that it does not degenerate into religious or cultural separatism, especially now that a substantial portion of its membership knows no other culture but that of America. If Buddhist Churches of America were to approach the "boundary situation" that Paul Tillich spoke of so often with enthusiasm and vitality, its benefits would likely yield creative growth. In so doing, however, it might be sacrificing growth among the non-Oriental populace, and herein lies its greatest potential liability. Such a procedure limits Buddhist Churches of America to, at best, a stable numerical membership.

It is seemingly paradoxical that it is the youngest members of Buddhist Churches of America who are most caught up in the movement to fully reestablish their Japanese culture in America. Nevertheless, their nisei fathers and mothers are faced with an awesome predicament: to expand the Jōdo Shinshū tradition to a wider arena, including all Americans, and to bring the acculturation process to its completion subjects the niseis to the risk of widening the already extensive gap with their own children. Although religious orientation has always been one way of inculcating ethnic identity, Buddhist Churches of America realizes that it may well be a luxury that they cannot afford if they are to continue to grow and prosper in America. Unfortunately, an alternative mode that yields satisfactory results has not been found. Consequently, the national organization finds itself in the curious predicament of having been present on American soil longer than any other Buddhist group and having acculturated the least.

The acculturation problem is further compounded by the religious practices of the group. Most church services are performed in Japanese, with English services appearing as an accommodation that only a few of the larger churches offer. At a time when the Catholic Mass is performed in English and Hebrew is rapidly disappearing from the services of many Reformed Jewish synogogues, it may be appropriate for Buddhist Churches of America to consider the potential efficacy of offering Pure Land services exclusively in English, with no loss of ritual purity or integrity, power, or beauty. In so doing, the organization would offer a wider spectrum of appeal in its liturgical aspect. Further, many of the younger members of the congregation might become interested in the general concern for meditation that has been prevalent during the past ten years. Rather than losing a portion of its membership to other forms of religious practice, it might well be argued that there are several modes of meditation, with sūtra chanting or recitation of the nembutsu being equally as valid as the other forms. Thus it could be stated that *within* the context of Amida's saving grace (tariki, or "other-power"), personal growth and the cultivation of "self-power" (or jiriki) are fully manifest. In this fashion too, the sacred dimension could be more completely integrated with the secular.

A quick glance at the geographic dispersal of the Buddhist Churches of America movement reveals at once that the South and Midwest are not cultivated at all. In fact, Chicago is considered in the Eastern District. Further, the East is only poorly represented by church affiliates. If Buddhist Churches of America is to remain a vital organization, even if only for Japanese-American communities, expansion into unrepresented or poorly represented areas will need to be a high priority. The difficulty of this expansion is exacerbated by the number of clergymen required for such growth. In this regard, it might be possible to step up the activities of the Institute of Buddhist Studies to meet the increased need for ministers, while including in the ministerial programs Americans other than those of Japanese heritage. This kind of policy, in addition to meeting specific goals of the organization, would serve as a positive and explicit statement of the intent of Buddhist Churches of America to divest itself of the image of being *purely* and *solely* a Japanese movement for Japanese-Americans. Just as Buddhism in Japan did not achieve its greatness, importance, and pervasiveness on the basis of its link with the Chinese Buddhist tradition, so in America the significance of the Shin faith cannot be measured only in terms of its reliance on Japanese Buddhist culture. While the Pure Land tradition has a long history in Asia that dates back through Chinese and Indian cultures, Hōnen and Shinran shaped it into something distinct and valuable for Japan, and in each succeeding generation it became more fully Japanese. Its success in America seems dependent on the same circumstance. In addition, due to the apparent similarities with Western religious traditions, Shin Buddhism has perhaps the best chance of all Buddhist traditions for becoming masterfully transnational.

CHAPTER 6

Nichiren Shoshu of America

I want to wish the Nichiren Shoshu Pre-Bicentennial Convention every success. The program, the setting, the surroundings could not be more impressive.

Your celebration is a fitting and inspiring prelude to next year's Bicentennial, and Hawaii's position as the Nation's youngest state is an apt reminder that our Nation is historically young, vigorous, with so much to make the future bright.

Congratulations, and have a wonderful Pre-Bicentennial.

Sincerely,
Nelson A. Rockefeller
Vice President of the United States[1]

SECTARIAN AFFILIATION

Nichiren Shoshu of America, as it is usually referred to, was originally part of Nichiren Shōshū Sōkagakkai. The reference to Sōkagakkai, however, was deleted so as not to imply any of the political overtones that the parent organization has in its native Japan. Nevertheless, the organization is Sōkagakkai in nature, and more will be said on this point later. The official name of the organization is the Nichiren Shoshu Academy, and the organization now has members in the United States, Puerto Rico, Virgin Isles, and Guam.

The origins of this "new religion" in Japan date back to 1928, when its founder, Tsunesaburo Makiguchi joined the Nichiren sect of Buddhism. Two years later (on November 8, 1930), he started the Value Creation Education Society or Sōka Kyoiku Gakki, with the assistance of his young disciple Josei Toda (1900–1958). The organization grew, and by 1937 Makiguchi was officially named president of the Value Creation Education Society. A magazine known as *Creation of Value* was begun by the organization, but by May 1942 the government ordered the fledgling group to cease publication. In July of the following year, presumably for refusing to take part in the nationalistic Shinto worship ceremonies, Makiguchi and twenty other leaders of the organization were arrested. All but Makiguchi and Toda disavowed their involvement and were released. Makiguchi and Toda, however, were retained. This resulted in Makiguchi's death in prison on November 18, 1944. When Toda was paroled in July of the following year, he began to rebuild the now floundering organization.

After six years of strenuous effort, Josei Toda was installed, on May 3, 1951, and as the second official president of Nichiren Shōshū Sōkagakkai, renamed the organization Value Creation Society. In his inauguration, he vowed to increase the membership to 750,000 families within seven years and to reconstruct the Head Temple, Daisekiji. Toda's membership goal was reached before the conclusion of 1957. Toda died in 1958, and a third president was not selected until 1960.

On May 3, 1960, Josei Toda's closest disciple, Daisaku Ikeda, was inaugurated as the third president of Nichiren Shōshū Sōkagakkai. During the same year, he visited the United States, becoming the first official of this group to do so. This event was followed in 1961 by the first official pilgrimage to Japan by American affiliates, as eighteen pilgrims traveled to the foot of Mt. Fuji to visit the Head Temple.

The American history of this organization began to develop more fully in 1963, when the Los Angeles headquarters of Sokagakkai was established by Daisaku Ikeda's close disciple Masayasa Sadanaga. This influential figure changed his name to George Williams in 1972 as a means of more fully emphasizing the American nature of the organization. The first United States convention was held during 1963 in Chicago, with 1,500 delegates attending. By 1964, when the organization began to publish its newspaper (*World Tribune*), there were a total of thirteen Nichiren Shoshu chapters. Utilizing their aggressive approach to gaining conversions, in 1965 the *World Tribune* reported that 1,000 conversions per month were being effected. Also in 1965, the national convention was held in Los Angeles with 2,300 participants.

As Nichiren Shoshu progressed into the second half of its first decade on American soil, the American conversion rate became number one in the world in terms of conversions per member. The first temple was opened in Los Angeles in 1967, with two more to follow (in Hawaii and Washington, D.C.). Nichiren Shoshu began to offer a series of cultural events, featuring its newly formed Fife and Drum Corps and Brass Band, as a means of attracting the public's eye and gaining converts. These popular concerts, at reasonable prices, were the first attempts at a technique known as "min-on," which has remained popular. In 1968, Masayasa Sadanaga (soon to be called George Williams) offered his first seminar on Nichiren Shoshu of America at a college campus (UCLA), and these seminars have remained one of his most active pursuits. Between 1968 and 1973, Williams presented more than eighty of these seminars at different colleges and universities. The year 1968 also marked the opening of the American Joint Headquarters in Santa Monica, where it still remains, and the national convention in Hawaii. By the close of the decade, Americans were holding positions of authority at all levels of the administrative framework, and all meetings (except for the chanting of the Daimoku and the practice of Gongyo) were held in English.

In the current decade, Nichiren Shoshu has continued to become more fully American than ever before. The organization's meeting halls, formerly called "kaikans," were renamed "Community Centers," and these were established in more than a dozen major cities. In his presidential address of 1972, President Ikeda established his prospective timetable for the development of Nichiren Shoshu. Robert Ellwood summarizes the salient features of this important speech:

> He saw the years 2001–2050 as a period when, with the help of Nichiren Shoshu's growth, a "peace formidable enough to prevent the annihilation of the human race" must be built. Particularly, he hoped, these would be years of happiness for Asia, which has suffered so much in the twentieth century. Then, the years from 2051–2100, marking the hundredth anniversary of the Sho-Hondo, can be the years in which Nichiren's philosophy is recognized as "the contemporary expression of the times." Then, in the period 2101–2150, he said he would "like to see the indestructible foundation of a permanent peace completed." And in 2151–2200, "every aspect of Kosen-rufu will hopefully be brought to completion."[2]

The implications of this statement are stirring, and Ellwood offers what I believe is a most accurate interpretation of the group's position today:

> Certainly Nichiren Shoshu is an anomaly among spiritual movements in the world. While many others, especially other forms of Buddhism, are stagnant and backward-looking, it is growing, casts about it a very modern image, and talks of a splendid future.[3]

When the new temple at the foot of Mt. Fuji was dedicated in 1972, no less than 18,000 Americans made a pilgrimage to Japan for this momentous event. Continuing to implement their plans for world peace, the organization hosted in mid-decade the first World Peace Conference in Guam, run under the auspices of a new organization known as the International Buddhist League.

FACILITIES AND STRUCTURE

Since 1968, the national headquarters of Nichiren Shoshu has been located in Santa Monica, California. From this center all the activities of the organization are coordinated under the watchful eye of George Williams. Patterned on the administrative structure of the Sokagakkai parent group in Japan, Nichiren Shoshu offers a carefully implemented line of authority that has the doubly important function of assuring the smooth running of the organization while providing the framework in which the future leaders of the movement can be indoctrinated and trained.

The chief administrator of Nichiren Shoshu of America is the General Director. Immediately under the General Director are three Executive Directors, each one designated to oversee a particular geographic territory. The territories are quite simply noted as Eastern, Mid West, Western, and Pacific. Each territory is further divided into areas (there have been sixteen areas as of 1974), and each area has a headquarters and a director. The areas are further subdivided into communities (usually four or five per area). Each community has several chapters, each chapter comprising five to ten districts. The districts are further separated into five to ten groups. Each organization division has an appropriate chief administrator.

Mirroring this general organizational pattern, at each level there are four basic working divisions or "peer groups," consisting of a men's division, women's division, young men's division, and young women's division. This latter schematization is critically important, for immediately upon joining the organization, one is assigned to a particular peer group, which functions "mainly in the intercommunication and mobilization of the membership."[4] There are supervisory personnel at each level group, district, chapter, community, and area) in the peer group structure. Since each person who brings a member into the organization becomes the "teacher" of that member, a vertical hierarchy is established on a pyramidal basis. Such a system requires careful checks and balances, which are accomplished by an abundance of meetings (both administrative and religious).

In addition to the above structure, Nichiren Shoshu of America now has three temples on American soil. There are the temple in Los Angeles (actually in Etiwanda, California), opened in 1967, and two other temples, established in 1972: Honseiji Temple in Honolulu, Hawaii, and Myosenji Temple in Washington, D.C.

Nichiren Shoshu of America also operates an impressive Study

Department. This arm of the organization serves the double purpose of indoctrinating members and training the future leaders of the organization. It does this by offering a series of examinations beginning on the junior high level and ascending through Bachelor's and Master's degrees in Buddhism. For these two degrees, the aspirant presents a dissertation "which demonstrates his understanding of Nichiren philosophy and its applicability to modern life."[5] By 1970, 3,000 persons (in sixty-five examination centers) had taken these tests.

Finally, Nichiren Shoshu of America sponsors NSA Productions, which aims at a cultural revolution through the presentation of musical groups, theater groups, and the like.

BRANCHES AND AFFILIATED GROUPS

From its rather humble beginnings in 1960, with only 13 chapters in 1964 and 114 by 1969, Nichiren Shoshu reported 258 chapters by 1974. Major centers are located in Boston, Chicago, West Los Angeles, Dallas, Denver, Hawaii (Honolulu and Maui), Mexico, East Los Angeles, New York, North Hollywood, Panama, Philadelphia, Phoenix, Portland, San Diego, San Francisco, Santa Ana, Santa Monica, Seattle, Toronto, Washington, D.C., Malibu, and San Pablo. Perhaps the best way to delineate the scope and breadth of the movement is to include a map prepared by the organization.

KEY MEMBERS AND/OR PERSONNEL

The chief administrator of the organization (on the international level) is Daisaku Ikeda. In addition to serving as president of Sōkagakkai, he is the chief layman in Nichiren Shoshu. Thus he makes policy decisions for *both* organizations.

Immediately under President Ikeda, on the American scene, is George M. Williams. He was born in Seoul, Korea, in 1930, as Masayasa Sadanaga. His Japanese parents returned to Japan in 1945, and eight years later he entered Sōkagakkai with his mother. The following year he received the Bachelor of Arts degree in law from Meiji University in Tokyo and emigrated to America in 1957. During the next five years, Masayasa Sadanaga pursued graduate studies in the United States. Between 1957 and 1958 he studied political science at UCLA. In 1958 he studied government and politics at George Washington University, and in 1962 he received an M.A. in political science from the University of Maryland. When President Ikeda visited the United States in 1960, his young and sincere disciple Sadanaga welcomed him, and thus began his own rise to authority in the organization.

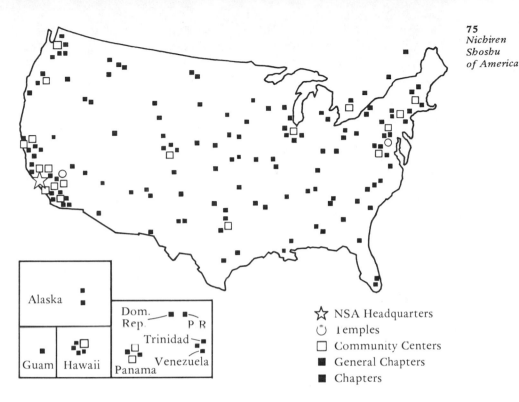

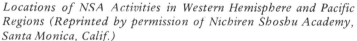

☆ NSA Headquarters
◌ Temples
☐ Community Centers
■ General Chapters
■ Chapters

*Locations of NSA Activities in Western Hemisphere and Pacific
Regions (Reprinted by permission of Nichiren Shoshu Academy,
Santa Monica, Calif.)*

In 1963 Sadanaga became a professor of Buddhism in the Nichiren
Shoshu Academy and began to serve as editor/publisher of *World
Tribune,* the Nichiren Shoshu newspaper. Further, he became General
Bureau Chief (for North America) for the Japanese-based Seikyo
Press. In 1964 he toured South America, Australia, India, and Southeast Asia with President Ikeda, and in 1965 they toured Europe. Also
in 1965, Sadanaga became Chief and Supervisor of the Europe-
America Headquarters. This position was upgraded to Joint Headquarters Chief for Nichiren Shoshu of America in 1967. From 1968
to 1973, Sadanaga embarked on a series of college seminars on over
eighty different campuses. Emma Layman nicely summarizes the
main points stressed by him in these presentations:

1. The meaning of True Buddhism is true humanism
2. Nichiren Shoshu follows the stream of the Buddhist tradition which
   began in India 3,000 years ago
3. Our daily life is governed by the Law of Cause and Effect
4. In True Buddhism of today, practice is more important than theory
5. Human revolution is the essential ingredient missing in our society
6. Through our individual human revolution, we can effect change in the
   entire world
7. Let's work together to create a society truly "of the people, by the
   people, for the people"[6]

Along the way, in 1972, Sadanaga changed his name to George M. Williams to give the American organization a more "American" leader. In 1969, he became General Executive for Nichiren Shoshu of America, rising to General Director the following year.

MEMBERSHIP

Pursuing its goal of world peace, Nichiren Shoshu of America was, by the mid-1960s, gaining converts at the rate of about 1,000 per month, but these were predominantly from within the Oriental-American communities. Consequently, in the latter half of the decade, the organization pursued non-Orientals through the shakubuku technique, with such success that by 1969 the conversion rate had increased to over 7,500 new members per month (well over 90 percent of these were non-Orientals). In its January 9, 1970, issue, *Life Magazine* noted that 200,000 Americans had joined Nichiren Shoshu. Nichiren Shoshu Academy, with chapters in North, Central, and South America, the Caribbean, and Oceania, now claims 250,000 members, with no separate breakdown offered for the United States.

Nichiren Shoshu is one of the few organizations to provide membership statistics for our examination. In 1970, we find that 25 percent of the membership was concentrated in Southern California, with the bulk of the rest centered in large American cities.[7] Whereas on the West Coast, Japanese members were equal in number to the non-Orientals, elsewhere there were many more non-Oriental members. With regard to *age,* we find the following breakdown:

·	20 or under	17%
·	21–30	40%
·	31–40	19%
·	41–50	15%
·	51–60	6%
·	61 or older	3%

With regard to gender, 59 percent were female and 41 percent were male. Marital status shows 47 percent were married, 40 percent single, 9 percent divorced, and 4 percent widows or widowers. As compared to 1960, when 96 percent of all members were Oriental, and 1965, when 77 percent were Oriental, by 1970 we find 41 percent Caucasian, 30 percent Oriental, 12 percent black, 13 percent Latin American, and 4 percent other groups. It is significant to note that this group attracts more blacks and Latin Americans than does any other Buddhist organization. With regard to religious orientation, there were 30 percent Catholic, 30 percent Protestant, 25 percent Buddhist, 6 percent Jewish, 5 percent atheist, and 4 percent other affiliation. Most of the Protestant members (40%) were Baptist. With regard to employment, we find the following division:

- · Housewife   27%
- · Student   19%
- · Clerical   10%
- · Professional   10%
- · Blue collar   9%
- · Technical   8%
- · Unskilled   6%
- · Executive   4%
- · Other   7%

In trying to understand the significance of these statistics, Robert Ellwood has generalized that "the real sociological strength of Sokagakkai lies in the tightness of its neighborhood groups, in which there is continual contact, jobs to be done, and mutual help."[8] Emma Layman, from another perspective, also notes that the hostility of the parent organization to other religious groups is moderated in America, as it is cognizant of its own foreign position in a Judaeo-Christian culture. Further, she notes that propagation activities center on four basic areas: (1) community service activities by members, (2) lectures and seminars on university campuses, (3) member testimonials of the efficacy of Nichiren Shoshu, and (4) individual members pursuing shakubuku.[9]

KEY AND/OR SPECIAL DOCTRINES

In accordance with the traditional doctrines of the Nichiren Shoshu sect of Buddhism, Nichiren Shoshu of America places reverent emphasis on the Lotus-sūtra. Doctrinally, the group makes no statements other than an emphasis on the various practices and a reliance on Nichiren's teachings of causality. Ellwood points out that the major thrust of Nichiren Shoshu is for harmony, expressed in four "key phrases":

1. *Esho funi:* subject and object are not two
2. *Inga guji:* simultaneous cause and effect
3. *Shikishin funi:* body and mind are not two
4. *Obutsu myogo:* king and Buddha (or society and religion), a single unity.[10]

In other words, the groups works towards the resolution of all opposites. Since the group is thoroughly secular in its orientation, the harmony that is sought applies to *this* world, yielding an unbounding happiness for its members.

RITUALS, SERVICES, AND PRACTICES

The practices of Nichiren Shoshu are twofold: Gongyo and Daimoku. Gongyo involves reciting the liturgy of Nichiren Shoshu five times in the morning and three times in the evening. The liturgy includes part of the second and all of the sixteenth chapter of the Lotus-sūtra. The chanting is performed entirely in Japanese, in a clear voice, with concentration focused on the Gohonzon (the central portion of the home altar, containing a rectangular paper scroll inscribed with the Japanese characters of the names of the Buddhas and Bodhisattvas in the Lotus-sūtra). For the individual, the Gohonzon represents his own Buddha-nature, clear and pure. The practice of Gongyo is followed by the chanting of the well-known Daimoku. Incumbent on all followers of "True Buddhism," this mantric formula of Nam Myoho Renge Kyo is the highest practical expression of the law of simultaneous cause and effect, resulting in the attainment of harmony with the universe for its reciters.

The benefits resulting from the practice of chanting are often material, demonstrating both the secular orientation of the organization and the efficacy of the chanting. At the various meetings, personal testimony is quite important, with members reporting on specific fruits that have resulted from their chanting. One young man, whom I had invited to lecture my introductory class in Buddhism on his personal involvement with Nichiren Shoshu, immediately began to cite examples of its benefits. Prior to commencing the practice, he was a poor student, unable to find part-time work and desperately in need of money to repair his automobile. As soon as he began the practice, his mother sent him two hundred dollars to repair his car, he got a job managing a Pizza Hut restaurant, and he eventually raised his grades. He was unequivocally convinced that each of these gains resulted from chanting the Daimoku. I should add too, for a balanced picture, that he did not know when Buddha lived, what the Four Noble Truths were, or when Nichiren lived. And he did not care! The Daimoku *worked* for him. In reflecting on the Nichiren Shoshu practice, one noted scholar has reflected:

> For Nichiren Shoshu, all of this is tied to the central experience: that its practice of chanting is a liberating, releasing, and identity-giving thing. The practice cleans out everything within the person which separates him from his environment and his own true nature and which blocks creativity. It makes him, like a Buddhist bodhisattva, able to act *spontaneously* from the ground of his being.[11]

FUTURE PLANS

The future plans for Nichiren Shoshu of America are clear and simple. The organization will continue to work for world peace in consonance with President Ikeda's 1972 presidential address. Further, it hopes to increase conversions so as to realize the goals of the organization. In practical terms, this means expansion at all levels of the administrative structure.

PUBLICATIONS

Nichiren Shoshu offers three primary publications and a host of pamphlets. The *World Tribune* started in 1964 on a bimonthly basis and by 1974 was published three times a week with 60,000 subscribers. Its newspaper format makes it light reading, informing its members of the latest news within the organization. The *NSA Quarterly* is a more substantial publication, begun in 1973. It advertises itself as a journal expressing Nichiren philosophy as seen through the eyes of President Ikeda. Recent issues have focused on major American cities, such as Boston and New York, as a means of demonstrating the American flavor that now pervades Nichiren Shoshu of America. The *Seikyo Times* offers the same sort of format as *World Tribune.* For a nonmember, the pamphlets are quite helpful. They focus on what is Nichiren, what its practices involve, and the like. All publications of the organization are slick and professional.

CONCLUDING REMARKS

In his important book *The Eagle and the Rising Sun,* Robert Ellwood notes eleven points concerning the Western appearance of groups representing the "new religions" of Japan. These include (in brief):

1. The New Religions are founded by strong, charismatic shamanistic figures.
2. All the New Religions emphasize belief in one God, or in the unity of the divine nature.
3. The New Religions all show evidence of syncretism; ideas and philosophies from East and West have been taken, in a time of radical cultural confrontation, and combined into new mixes.
4. The New Religions anticipate a New Age of earthly joy coming through immanent divine action and foreshadowed in the experience of the founder and the communal life.
5. Closely tied to this hope is the role of the sacred center.
6. Pilgrimage to the sacred centers is always an important feature of the New Religions.
7. The New Religions have tight and thorough organization, generally.
8. A fundamental message of all the New Religions is that an individual makes his own world, his health or sickness, prosperity or poverty, joy or despair, through his mental attitude.

9. The New Religions put emphasis on physical healing. But physical healing seems to be increasingly deemphasized as time goes on.

10. In communication, the New Religions tend to use the rhetoric of enthusiasm and testimony rather than argument.

11. The final characteristic is that each has one *simple process* for releasing the inner power and thereby dispelling the guilt, finitude, and frustrations of a cramped life in which joyous mind does not reign supreme over circumstances.[12]

An explication of several of these points reveals much about the success of Nichiren Shoshu of America. From the 1960s onward, as we saw in the first section of this book, the largest gains for Buddhism have come from those falling under the sway of a powerfully charismatic figure. President Ikeda and George Williams can certainly be seen in this light. It is a double-edged sword, however, causing one American scholar of Buddhism to suggest recently that perhaps the youth of our country need protection from some of these authoritarian personalities.[13] Nevertheless, their rhetoric is convincingly persuasive. The syncretistic endeavor of Nichiren Shoshu is a markedly clever tactic. More than any other Buddhist group in America, Nichiren Shoshu emphasizes *American* culture. Talk about Japan is discouraged, enabling its members to firm the underpinnings of their own cultural heritage. The highest expression of this can be seen in the overwhelming concern for America's Bicentennial among Nichiren Shoshu officials. As early as 1969 the theme of the national convention was "The Spirit of 1776." A recent issue of the *NSA Quarterly* was devoted completely to the Bicentennial. George Williams was quoted in the *World Tribune* (on August 15, 1969) as saying, "Only Nichiren Shoshu can actualize our forefathers' dream of a perfect democracy." Williams's background in government and politics, coupled with his fervent commitment to Nichiren Shoshu, makes him a most clever advocate of the American nature of the organization.

The concern for the "good life" on the part of Nichiren Shoshu, as symbolized by the vital, vibrant community, is an attractive antidote to the pervasive disharmony in American life. Unlike other Buddhist groups, which are struggling with a means for inculcating Buddhist values in the context of the First Noble Truth, Nichiren Shoshu says joy is possible—right now. Further, it regulates much more than just the time spent in religious observance (although it does that quite well too, with endless meetings and mobilizing for practice), by promoting a ceaseless chain of cultural and recreational events for its members. Such activities are precisely what Rosabeth Kanter means when she reflects on the necessities of commitment. Whether we approve of its community life or not, Nichiren Shoshu is suffering less identity crisis than are its other Buddhist brothers on American soil. And of course this is tied to the notion of sacred center. Ellwood refers to sacred center in terms of lavish buildings and centers that "are more than buildings and temples."[14] Nonetheless, in the light of

our discussion in the first part of this book, Nichiren Shoshu offers a
sacred center that is overwhelmingly American. I say this not simply
because the American flag flies over all Nichiren Shoshu buildings
in this country, but rather because the leaders and members of the
organization seem to offer this not *merely* as a perfunctory gesture
of respect, but with a real understanding of what the American flag
symbolizes. In understanding the advantages of having established a
sacred center that is in America and *of* America, Nichiren Shoshu is
able to tap into the creative power inherent in that center. And of
course we should not overlook the fact that pilgrimage to the sacred
center is now available for all Americans. The locus of the religion is
not somewhere else, halfway around the world (even if it is accessible by jet). An American member can renew his or her faith *here.*

One of the greatest handicaps to the Buddhist movement in
America has been its organizational carelessness, or perhaps we
should say, general lack of concern for the issue altogether. In the
complex society that is America, it is naïve to assume that things will
somehow just "fall into place." Nevertheless, that is what most Buddhist groups assume. Nichiren Shoshu, on the other hand, has been
careful to build a sound organizational basis for its activities. It has
also learned that there is great psychological benefit to be reaped
from involving many of its members in the administrative process. In
this way, a real sense of belonging is fostered and a real sense of
creating policy seems available to all members. In other words,
Nichiren Shoshu has implemented a hierarchy that is both functional
and agreeable. In appealing to the individual to influence his own
world, Nichiren Shoshu not only reminds its adherents of Buddha's
understanding of the law of karma, but it also speaks to a populace
that has, for a long time, been conditioned to the "rugged individualism" that America claims to offer. If the disciple claims that things
have "gotten out of hand," and this is no longer possible in a technological, pluralistic society, Nichiren Shoshu says, "try it!" And to
dispel the disciple of his doubts, the testimony of other followers is
presented as a combative measure.

Certainly not the least of Nichiren Shoshu's attractive points is its
overwhelming simplicity. The follower does not have to engage in
any meditative process that is difficult, mystical, or esoteric. He does
not have to go to church regularly or participate in all sorts of festi-
vals and holidays that he probably does not understand. All he has to
do is practice Gongyo and chant the Daimoku, and everything will
happen automatically. There is no sitting meditation, nor are there
faith or religious services. In a situation where inflation runs rampant,
profit margins abound, and the man in the street is the victim of the
faceless conglomerate, what could seem more attractive? Ellwood
himself notes that the

> . . . movement is doing a mighty task in the resocialization of people who
> were formerly alienated, lost in meaninglessness, or just "mixed up,"

giving them a positive self-image and an acceptance of American society. They have come to have an affirmative attitude toward their work, the capitalistic system, neatness, respect for parents, the American past.[15]

It is in this light that Nichiren Shoshu appeals more than any other Buddhist organization in America to minority groups. Further, it appeals to people of all ages. Fully one-third of its members are in the 31–50 age range, and only one-fifth of its members are students.

In discussing the psychological concerns relative to Nichiren Shoshu, Emma Layman notes that reinforcement and behavior modification are utilized by the organization (praise, group acceptance, increased status, and the like). Further, she notes that Nichiren Shoshu's idea of "human revolution" is quite similar to Abraham Maslow's self-actualization, and that Maslow "viewed self-actualization as a prerequisite to the attainment of social actualization."[16] She is, of course, both perceptive and quite right here. Nichiren Shoshu, however, is not without problems. While Buddhism has always had a tradition of supreme tolerance and inoffensiveness, Nichiren Shoshu has taken an attitude of open hostility, albeit somewhat suppressed in America, towards other religious groups—even Buddhist groups. If we accept Streng's notion that religion is a mode of ultimate transformation, then Nichiren Shoshu can be regarded as religious in that it appears to actualize such a possibility. However, as a living antithesis to ecumenism, with strong and often unpopular political involvements, it may well prove popular but isolated from its own heritage in Buddhism. Without a resolution of this latter problem, Nichiren Shoshu's achievements may well be short-lived.

CHAPTER 7

San Francisco Zen Center

The opening of the Gateless Gate through Nature to our own nature is the great Zen Gift to our age. I see in the founding of this Center such a disclosure of America as home. May it prosper and so, prosper us all in delight.

—Joseph Campbell[1]

SECTARIAN AFFILIATION

San Francisco Zen Center is affiliated with the Sōtō tradition of Zen Buddhism.

HISTORY

The history of San Francisco Zen Center is quite simple. On May 23, 1959, Shunryu Suzuki Rōshi arrived in San Francisco to become chief priest for the Japanese-American community at Sokoji Temple on Bush Street. At first he practiced zazen by himself, but shortly thereafter a group of Americans began to gather to practice sitting meditation with him. Emerging from this group, San Francisco Zen Center opened in 1961 and was incorporated the following year. After the formal incorporation of San Francisco Zen Center, Suzuki Rōshi began looking for a site to open a country meditation center. In 1967 Tassajara Springs, nestled in the mountains near Carmel, California, was purchased. In the spring, this 100-year-old resort opened as Zen Mountain Center, Zenshinji Monastery.

In addition to the opening of smaller Zendos, under the tutelage of Suzuki Rōshi and operated by older students of the main Zen Center, the San Francisco group had, by 1969, outgrown the facilities at Sokoji Temple and moved to its current headquarters at 300 Page Street. It was only fitting that the Zendo in the new center was named "Great Bodhisattva Zendo" by Suzuki Rōshi. In the spring of 1972, Green Gulch Farm was purchased in Marin County, seventeen miles from the city center.

On November 21, 1971, Suzuki Rōshi's chief disciple, Richard Baker, was installed as his successor in the "Mountain Seat Ceremony," and less than two weeks later, Suzuki Rōshi died. Under the guidance of Richard Baker Rōshi, San Francisco Zen Center is currently pursuing its development more fully than ever before.

FACILITIES AND STRUCTURE

San Francisco Zen Center has three major facilities: the city center, Zen Mountain Center, and Green Gulch Farm. All lesser divisions of the organization will be considered in the section on branches and affiliated groups.

The city center occupies a fifty-room building on Page Street. The three-story structure provides living accommodations for approximately seventy students. During his lifetime, Suzuki Rōshi and his wife occupied quarters on the second floor. In addition to the Great Bodhisattva Zendo, the main feature of the building is the Memorial (Founder's) Hall, created in 1972. The Buddha-hall is a simple room, white-walled and bare, with tatami mats on the floor. It has a wooden altar bearing a plaque signifying Śākyamuni Buddha and a metal figure of Bodhidharma, the first patriarch of Ch'an. The Buddha-hall opens off the right side of the lobby, while the left side gives way to the Zen Center offices. The rear of the building houses the kitchen and dining room.

In the previous section of this book we noted that Buddhism in America was largely a city movement, and tried to outline some of the problems inherent in such an endeavor. San Francisco Zen Center knows only too well the perils cited, but faces the issue squarely:

> A city is obviously the expression of man's conflicting moods, impulses, desires, fears—its institutions an extension of our inner life. It is our violence, our greed, our self-denial—as well as a source of our deepest self-affirmation. In the city, unlike Tassajara, Zen students must face the test of alternatives to a regulated pace of life, and often have unresolved doubts about the restrictions of city practice.[2]

Zen Mountain Center occupies the former Tassajara Hot Springs resort. The resort, oldest in Monterey County, was partially completed by Chinese immigrants before the turn of the century, but prior to that time, it had been utilized by California Indians. It lies at the end of a long (twenty-mile) dirt road which ascends a 5,000-foot incline. Its surrounding area (tens of thousands of acres) is preserved as a National Forest and Wilderness Area to maintain its beauty and wildlife. Although purchased in 1967 for $300,000, the purchase was not completed until the spring of 1972. Most of the funds came in small amounts, consonant with Suzuki Rōshi's idea that the students should work together for the completion of the project, although prior to June 1968, one couple had donated in excess of $25,000. In the Zendo of this center too, to the left of the main altar, there is a Memorial (Founder's) Hall, built in 1972. Zen Mountain Center operates a "guest season" in late spring, summer, and early fall, when the weather usually accommodates the visitors.

The most recent venture of the organization is Green Gulch Farm, purchased in the spring of 1972. Fashioned out of seventy acres of bottom land in the foothills of Mount Tamalpais, it was intended to help meet the food needs of the community. It was a magnificent "find" for San Francisco Zen Center, having remarkable facilities that included (among other structures) a large house (with five bedrooms, two kitchens, a library, two sitting rooms, and an enclosed sauna and swimming pool), a small bunkhouse, a ranch house, a studio, an enormous barn, and numerous outbuildings. Green Gulch Farm operates on a schedule similar to Zen Mountain Center, and has recently given rise to Green Gulch Greengrocer (which will be discussed in the next section).

All three facilities are run by the main body of San Francisco Zen Center and its officers and are organized in such fashion as to provide students with a way of life consonant with Zen practice. It is significant to note that, with the exception of mortgage payments on the city center and Green Gulch Farm, the community is completely self-supporting. In addition, a property fund was created to ease the mortgage burden, and had, by 1974, raised $105,000.

BRANCHES AND AFFILIATED GROUPS

In addition to the facilities noted above, San Francisco Zen Center maintains seven other branches. The first of these is the Children's Center, located in San Francisco and begun in 1972. The following year Zen Center took over the Alaya Stitchery, and continues to use the organization to produce meditation cushions and mats. The most ambitious of the branches is the Shunryu Suzuki Study Center, established in 1973 under the direction of Claude Dalenberg. For the most part, the Study Center relies on its own community for instruction, but occasionally guest teachers are invited to participate. Class topics have a wide range of diversity, with courses from Abhidharma to Buddhist art and iconography having been offered.

Green Gulch Farm was enhanced, in 1974, by the opening of a cabinet shop, and the following year Green Gulch Greengrocer opened in San Francisco. This latter operation served as an "outlet store" for the produce grown at the farm and provided funds for the farm's growth and development. Consonant with their concern for the surrounding community, in 1975 the Neighborhood Foundation was established, primarily to help restore the Fillmore district of San Francisco to its previous beauty. Finally, when Shobo-an, or the True Dharma Temple Hermitage, was disassembled in Ohara (near Kyoto) in 1972 and given to Richard Baker Rōshi as a gift, it was reassembled in the foothills of the Sierra Nevada.

Several Zendos outside of San Francisco are currently affiliated with San Francisco Zen Center. Two of these, the Berkeley Zendo and the Mill Valley Zendo, are under the direction of Richard Baker Rōshi. The Haiku Zendo in Los Altos is under the direction of Kobun Chino Sensei, and the Monterey Zen Group is run by Dainin Katagiri Rōshi.

KEY MEMBERS AND/OR PERSONNEL

There are five key members who will be mentioned here, the first of these being, of course, Shunryu Suzuki Rōshi.[3] Son of a Sōtō Zen priest (and rōshi), Shunryu Suzuki was born in 1904 in Tsuchisawa, Kanagawa Prefecture. Rather than following the custom of becoming his father's disciple, he became, at age thirteen, the disciple of one of his father's students (Gyakuju So-on, also a rōshi). At age nineteen, his master sent him to the high school that was part of Komazawa University. He completed both high school and undergraduate school, eventually gaining his English teacher (a Mrs. Ransom) as a convert.

Following his career as an undergraduate, he traveled to Eiheiji and became a monk, where he stayed one year. Six months more at Sojiji followed, and he was then made priest at Zoun-in (the former temple of his teacher So-on, who had moved to a new temple). At this point Suzuki asked his master to send him to a foreign land, perhaps North America, but was turned down. Gyakuju So-on died when Suzuki was only thirty-one, and his young student took over his responsibilities at Rinso-in in Yaizu; as head of this major temple, he had two hundred temples under his sway. The following year, Suzuki married and, contrary to tradition, lived in the temple with his new wife. He also became a lifetime student of Kishizawa Rōshi, a well-known scholar on Dōgen.

In his published lectures, Suzuki strongly resisted the rising militarism of the war effort; he eventually used this published material to have his teaching license restored after the war. In 1951, his wife died, leaving him a widower with four children. He devoted himself

Shunryu Suzuki Rōshi (Photo by Boris Erwitt.)

to the restoration of Rinso-in, which was completed in 1957. In 1958 he married Mitsu Matsuno, a local kindergarten teacher, and later in the year accepted a three-year position as priest of Sokoji Temple in San Francisco. When his wife and youngest child (from his first marriage) were dispatched to America (two and a half years after Suzuki left) to facilitate his return, they stayed on. He requested another three-year leave of absence, and in 1968 his eldest son took over as priest of Rinso-in.

Following a weakening turn in his physical condition, Suzuki Rōshi visited Japan in late 1970. In the fall of 1971, when Suzuki Rōshi became quite ill, his disciple Richard Baker, who had been studying in Japan, was summoned home and installed as the new abbot of San Francisco Zen Center. Shunryu Suzuki Rōshi died around 3:00 A.M. on December 4, 1971. Two recollections of Shunryu Suzuki Rōshi, for this author, capture the essence of this humble Zen teacher better than all others. The first, cited in Huston Smith's preface to Suzuki Rōshi's *Zen Mind, Beginner's Mind,* quotes Richard Baker Rōshi's statement at his master's funeral:

> There is no easy way to be a teacher or a disciple, although it must be the greatest joy in his life. There is no easy way to come to a land without Buddhism and leave it having brought many disciples, priests, and laymen

well along the path and having changed the lives of thousands of persons throughout this country; no easy way to have started and nurtured a monastery, a city community, and practice centers in California and many other places in the United States. But this "no-easy-way," this extraordinary accomplishment, rested easily with him, for he gave us from his own true nature, our true nature. He left us as much as any man can leave, everything essential, the mind and heart of Buddha, the practice of Buddha, the teaching and life of Buddha. He is here in each one of us, if we want him.[4]

The second is a reflection of Elsie Mitchell of the Cambridge Buddhist Association, recalling the events of an October 1964 visit from Suzuki Rōshi:

> The following October the Cambridge Buddhist Association received a visit from the Venerable Shunryu Suzuki. Suzuki Roshi was in charge of a Buddhist temple, as well as a Zen center for Westerners, in San Francisco. He had been living in the United States for about six years and had learned English and gathered together a large group of people seriously interested in meditation. I had met him in San Francisco after one of my journeys to Japan and had been greatly impressed with his integrity, his goodness, and particularly his willingness to work out ways of traditional Buddhist practice really suitable for contemporary Westerners. He wrote that he would be arriving on a Wednesday night, and we planned to meet him at the airport.
>
> Tuesday afternoon we returned to Cambridge from Cape Cod, and several of us set to work housecleaning. That evening the library cum meditation room was in the process of being scrubbed down when the doorbell rang. My husband climbed down a ladder and opened the front door. Suzuki Roshi was on the door-step with a smile on his face. He was amused to find us amid preparations for his arrival. In spite of our protests, he immediately tied back his long kimono sleeves and insisted on joining in "all these preparations for the important day of my coming."[5]

It is clear from even a cursory reading that each of these statements offers appropriate tribute for Buddhism at its best in America, embodied in the quiet little figure of Shunryu Suzuki Rōshi. His students now have his lineage and are constantly reminded of the master who did everything fully, completely, and properly—whether it be living or dying.

Although Richard Baker Rōshi received formal transmission of the Dharma from Suzuki Rōshi while still in Japan (on December 4, 1970), the completing ceremony was enacted the following year (on November 21, 1971) in the Great Bodhisattva Zendo at the San Francisco Zen Center. The Mountain Seat Ceremony marked the installation of Richard Baker Rōshi as the new head of the center. Fortunately, one of the observers of the ceremony, Denis Lahey, who was a student at the Berkeley Zendo, captured his recollection of the event in a paper submitted to one of Robert Bellah's sociology classes at the University of California, Berkeley. This account was reprinted in the 1972 *Wind Bell,* and I include it here, in full, as it captures not only the importance of the event, but the sensitivity and feeling that charged the entire atmosphere of the Zen Center:

I arrived at the Zen Center on Page Street well before the time of the ceremony, but found that there was already a sizeable crowd. Every bit of space in the upstairs hall was filled with chairs. I was seated upstairs for a while, and could see that they had built a large raised platform at the end of the Buddha Hall to serve as the Mountain Seat. Incense and candles were much in evidence. Certain dignitaries began to arrive: Lama Kunga, Tulku of Thartse, from the Evam Choden Center in Berkeley; Abbot Hsuan Hua and his retinue from the Gold Mountain Temple in San Francisco, and other figures of the spiritual life in the Bay Area. Sasaki-roshi from Los Angeles and Mt. Baldy Monastery was there with two disciples. Soon the word was passed around that the meditation students should go downstairs to the Zendo (Meditation Hall), and wait there for the fourth station of the ceremony, when Richard Baker would enter the Zendo to offer incense and a gatha (Buddhist poem). We all did so, and soon the Zendo was full and people were lined up out in the hall in front of the door. For a few moments we watched people arriving for the ceremony entering by the lower street door, and then all became silent. Suddenly, far off upstairs sounded a deep bass note on a huge drum, followed by a bell which began to toll in the lower hall. The drumbeats continued, quite slowly at first, but following one another in an ever more rapid succession, until the drummer was beating out a long, thundering roll which reverberated all through the building, punctuated by the slow, rather doleful strokes of the bell.

Upstairs, the procession was arriving at the front door of the building, having come from Dainin Katagiri-roshi's house up the street. We could hear faintly the procession entering the Buddha Hall for the preliminary offerings. Every few moments came the jangling thud of the Master's staff on the ground. The staff is six feet long and of heavy wood, and the top end is hung with brass rings which rattle loudly when the staff is thumped on the ground. Presently, the procession left the Hall and drew near to the stairs to the lower levels. Through the noise of drum and bell, we could hear the eerie sound of the two small bells carried by the processioners. These are just a half-tone apart in pitch, and their effect, coupled with the steady drumbeats and the low, mellow gong in the hallway, was to make the hair on the back of my neck stand on end, as the procession descended the stairs and approached the Zendo. I believe the rest of the procession remained out of sight around a turn in the corridor, for finally, only Richard Baker himself appeared, walking slowly down the narrow hall in the semi-darkness, holding the fly-whisk of horsehair, and wearing a robe given to him by Suzuki-roshi of sky-blue and gold cloth, decorated with brightly colored phoenixes. All heads bowed as he passed and entered the Zendo, where he made an offering at the altar. He returned a moment later, and looking neither right nor left, he walked steadily back to join the rest of the processioners. We heard them going back upstairs, the solid bangings of the staff and the strange notes of the bells receding in the distance, until only the gong and the drum broke the stillness of the dimly-lit hallway.

Then we were summoned upstairs to the Buddha Hall. We filed in through the Zendo and out through its rear door, then up the stairs and into the main corridor. Walking slowly, we entered the Hall, passing the great drum, and filled up the wide expanse of tatami mats left in front of the Mountain Seat Altar. Visitors were seated in chairs all around the perimeter of the mats, while we sat on our heels, Japanese style. Meanwhile, the procession had gone upstairs to the next floor, to the room of the Master, Suzuki Shunryu-daiosho, the founder of Zen Center, whom Richard Baker was succeeding. Everyone who knew this man loved him, and I myself, though I had only met him once, regarded him with the deepest respect. I knew that he was quite ill at that time, but when he, at the head of the procession, entered the Hall, I was shocked to see him as frail and shrunken as the man who appeared, a ghost of the person whose immense vigor and spiritual strength had guided the Center through the first uncertain years of its existence. He entered, practically being carried by his son, but holding his staff firmly, and thumping it on the matting as he approached the Mountain Seat. He bowed at the altar, and was helped to a place to the right of the platform. Richard Baker entered then with the retinue, and seated himself in a laquered chair facing the Mountain Seat Altar. The great drum fell silent. We chanted in unison the Prajna Paramita Hridaya Sutra in English, and then, having offered prayers and incense in front of the Altar, Baker-roshi ascended the steps of the platform and stood, several feet above the onlookers, offering incense to the Buddhas and Bodhisattvas and the Patriarchs, to the benefactors of the Center, and, finally, to his own beloved teacher, Suzuki-roshi. He said:

This piece of incense
Which I have had for a long time
I offer with no-hand
To my Master, to my friend, Suzuki Shunryu daiosho
The founder of these temples.
There is no measure of what you have done.

Walking with you in the Buddha's gentle rain
Our robes are soaked through,
But on the lotus leaves
Not a drop remains.

Then Katagiri-roshi, acting for Suzuki-roshi, recited the brief authentication verse with a full-bodied shout, in true Zen fashion. For his sermon, Baker-roshi stated simply, "There is nothing to be said."

This was perfectly true. Then followed the so-called Dharma-questions, when the other priests seek to test the new Abbot's understanding. The following marvelous dialogue ensued between Baker-roshi and the priest from the Mill Valley Zendo:

(Bill Kwong) "Chief Priest!" (shouting)
(Baker-roshi) "Is it host or guest?"
(Bill Kwong) "Iiiie!" (shouting)
(Baker-roshi) "Show me your True Nature without shouting!"

Bill then simply bowed, and returned to his seat.

Following congratulatory telegrams and such, the ceremony was concluded. Suzuki-roshi was helped to his feet and moved to the front of the altar to make his bow. But when he turned to face the people, there was on his face an expression at once fierce and sad. His breath puffed mightily in his nostrils, and he looked as if he strove vigorously to speak, to say something, perhaps to exhort the disciples to be strong in their practice, or to follow Richard Baker with faith; no one can say. He faced the con-

gregation directly as if to speak and instead rolled his staff between his
hands sounding the rings twice, once looking to the left and once to the
right side of the hall. It was as though some physical shock had passed
through the hall; there was a collective intake of breath, and suddenly,
everywhere people were weeping openly. All those who had been close
to the Roshi now realized fully what it would mean to lose him, and were
overcome with a thoroughly human sorrow. As their Master falteringly
walked from the Hall, still marking each step with his staff, everyone
put his hands palm to palm before his face in the gesture known as gassho,
and bowed deeply. And that was all. Very simple and direct, the ceremony
had lasted little more than an hour.[6]

In addition to Richard Baker Rōshi, one of Suzuki Rōshi's closest
associates was Dainin Katagiri Rōshi. Having come from Japan in
1964, he assisted the Master much after 1969. He had wanted to
branch out and start his own group, but Suzuki-Rōshi and the stu-
dents at the Zen Center always convinced him to stay. Eventually,
he split his time so as to spend half of the year with San Francisco
Zen Center and half of the year with the Zen group in the Carmel-
Monterey area. Finally, he moved to Monterey and established a
Zendo in his home, but still maintained ties with San Francisco Zen
Center by leading the Winter Practice Period at Zen Mountain
Center in 1972. Katagiri Rōshi then moved to Minneapolis to open a
Zendo where many of his own students (and old Zen Center students)
now live.

Also important to note is Kobun Chino Sensei. Long associated
with Suzuki Rōshi, he still works as head of the Los Altos Zendo
and conducts a zazen group in Santa Cruz. He has taught courses
on Buddhism at various colleges, among them Stanford University.
Now and then he visits Zen Mountain Center.

Finally, the widow of Suzuki Rōshi must be mentioned. Ever
faithful, she has remained on at San Francisco Zen Center, where
she teaches the Japanese Tea Ceremony.

MEMBERSHIP

Although San Francisco Zen Center does not offer statistics concerning its membership, there are four basic categories of membership in the organization: General Member, Practicing Student,
Affiliate Member, and Annual Member.

General Member: General members participate regularly in the
activities of the center or maintain a relationship with the organization through regular support. After one month of regular practice
they can attain membership status. They are expected to make a
monthly contribution ($20 is the suggested figure). After three
months, they receive library privileges, a discount rate on purchases
from the bookstore, a reduced rate for sesshin (intensive practice

periods), and a subscription to *Wind Bell* (the periodical of the Zen
Center).

Practicing Student: For those who want to fully utilize the opportunities for practice available at Zen Center, after three months as
a General Member they may apply for this category of membership.
This form of membership includes regular contact with a meditation
teacher; for those members not already living at San Francisco Zen
Center, Zen Mountain Center, or Green Gulch Farm, a $25 fee is
required each month.

Affiliate Member: Affiliate membership is available to those
persons who practice at an affiliated Zendo of San Francisco Zen
Center. For a $5 monthly fee, they receive membership privileges
at Zen Center, and after three months, they receive the other benefits of General Membership.

Annual Member: Many potential members live too far from Zen
Center or an affiliated Zendo to attend functions with any regularity.
For those students who want to maintain some affiliation, annual
membership is available by making a yearly pledge ($35 is suggested).
For this fee, they receive a subscription to *Wind Bell* and notification
of activities at Zen Center.

KEY AND/OR SPECIAL DOCTRINES

San Francisco Zen Center, following the Sōtō Zen tradition,
maintains a doctrinal position wholly consonant with the parent
organization.

RITUALS, SERVICES, AND PRACTICES

Although Sōtō Zen involves the practice of shikantaza or "just
sitting," San Francisco Zen Center has attempted to harmonize its
Zen practice with its new American homeland. Perhaps the most
appropriate way to describe the basis of this new cultural expression
of Zen is to quote directly from the organization's own elucidation
of the practice:

> Although Zen practice begins with the simplest things, breathing, or how
> to sit most awakely on a chair or cushion, it brings us (you) to an experi-
> ence of totality, a realization and an assurance about who and what we
> are which eludes a verbal definition, but allows us to act with an equilib-
> rium and deep sense of meaningfulness. We find the world not different
> from the possibilities within us. This does not mean that the definition of
> the world is limited to ourselves, but rather that we experience and expand
> that definition to include the mutuality of ourselves and the world.
> The practice of Zen Buddhism is as free from limitations as possible.

And the conceptual teaching is aimed solely at freedom from concepts and limitations and even from Buddhism itself. This is why Zen practice is based on sitting still (zazen), free from dogma or a particular way of thinking, in order for us to experience ourselves before we think or act— one might say between thoughts and acts.

Sitting still without any definite plan, we begin to experience more than we know, more than the limitations of our plan or what we have thought in the past. We observe the comings and goings and formation of thoughts. We begin to experience the sources and springs of action just by sitting still for a regular length of time every day. Not learned patterns, but the basic functioning and natural order of body and mind are the guides of practice and the ground of everyday experience. Our experience of ourselves begins to approach the totality of what we are. (Unless we sit every day at a regular time, our practice is limited by the needs and occasions which permit us to sit at this or that time.)

This Zen practice of sitting still at a particular place for a particular length of time (20 to 40 minutes) confronts us with the limitations of time and space and the immediacy of who we are at each moment and place. In this sense the limitations of time and space are transcended because they become the very ground and possibility of our being. Man has difficulty when he is not fully grounded in this experience, and instead attaches unrealistically to one or another relative point of view, taking the relative as if it were absolute.

Buddhism does not assert what is the Truth. It directs people to understand and explore their own mind and feelings, for in trying to understand Reality it is more important to know the awareness itself through which we know everything, rather than to know only what the mind knows about. This Awareness includes knowing our mind, feelings, emotions, and the conditions of our physiology. It is sometimes called Big Mind. And when we experience the root-source of our thoughts, feelings-emotions without a particular object of thought or emotion, we discover in ourselves that the essential expression of this pure-awareness is a love-compassion-gratefulness-awe for the people and things of this world. Such an expression is independent of and underlies whether we like or dislike, approve or disapprove, accept or reject.

One of the most difficult things to explain intellectually is the presence of altars and Buddhas in a practice like this. One reason, of course, is that people like to have a focus for those deepest emotions and ideas which are not ever fully satisfied by the mundane world. An altar and Buddha provide a focus for this deeper side of man which refocuses these deeper feelings and ideas on man himself. The Buddha is strictly a reminder not only of the historical person who realized this practice, but also of the unconditioned nature of ourselves beyond thinking and acting as well as the unity or interdependency and relatedness of all things; both of these aspects are also called Buddha. But altars and Buddhas are not necessary; one's own location in time and space is enough.

This practice of sitting still, open to the possibilities within us, is called the Middle Way, not because it is between the extremes of subjective and objective, nihilism and materialism, emptiness and form, good and evil, love and hate, but because it includes and gives a unified meaning to these various extremes without falling into the limitations of emphasizing one or the other. In our present day world which is so torn by individual and national strife this practice is needed to restore individual and social coherence–spiritual unity to our personal and universal life. Moment by moment, out of the great changes going on around us, we must create some way for men to live.[7]

Regularity seems to be one of the watchwords for the practice offered by San Francisco Zen Center. In each of its major facilities, regularity of schedule is emphasized. At the main city center, there is zazen (and service) morning and evening, Monday through Friday, as well as on Saturday morning. Saturday morning also is utilized for a lecture and formal zazen instruction. There is a regular resident's schedule for work activities, and sesshins (one-day sitting periods) are held on the first Saturday of each month, except during the two months in which seven-day sesshins are held (which also begin on the first Saturday of that month). At Green Gulch Farm there is zazen (and service) morning and evening, Sunday through Friday (but the evening session on Friday is omitted). Lecture and zazen instruction are held on Sunday morning, with a regular work schedule established. Work is also open to nonresidents on all but Saturday. Sesshins are held on the third Saturday of each month except during the two months of seven-day sesshins (which also begin on the third Saturday of that month). At Zen Mountain Center, the schedule is divided into three intensive periods: the Fall Practice Period (from September 15 to December 15), the Spring Practice Period (from January 10 to April 10), and the Guest and Summer Practice Period (from May 1 to September 6).

FUTURE PLANS

The future plans of San Francisco Zen Center are simple and straightforward. It hopes to continue to bring a meaningful practice and way of life to Americans and seeks the resources and facilities necessary to do so. Ever striving for self-sufficiency, Zen Center, perhaps more sanely than other Buddhist groups, undertakes projects consonant with its still modest resources. It seems not so concerned with quick, enormous growth, but rather with slow, sure development that is well-grounded in Buddhist principles.

PUBLICATIONS

San Francisco Zen Center has never aggressively pursued the publication trail. It publishes a small but carefully prepared journal, *Wind Bell,* which provides updated information about the organization, news, and occasional lectures. The Zen Center, however, has arranged for the publication of three books: Suzuki Rōshi's *Zen Mind, Beginner's Mind,* now in paperback and an excellent and pragmatic guide to Zen life, as well as Edward Espe Brown's two volumes of the *Tassajara Bread Book* and *Tassajara Cooking*, each of which has attained a wide and well-deserved readership.

CONCLUDING REMARKS

San Francisco Zen Center is something of a paradox. Although the Zen tradition places much emphasis on working under the guidance and tutelage of a Master, which provides fertile ground for a transparent "cult of the rōshi" to develop, Zen Center has never fallen prey to such a phenomenon. It represents that curious blend of reverent respect for the Master, always exhibited when conversations include Suzuki Rōshi, and intense understanding that, in true Buddhist fashion, one sits alone on the meditation cushion. The fact that Zen Center students never degenerated into a mere worship of the Master is perhaps the highest tribute to Suzuki Rōshi's ability to both diagnose the malaise of many modern Buddhist groups and offer the proper antidote. Personal charisma, when properly applied, can be a potent device with which to motivate individuals. In the hands of Suzuki Rōshi and his able successor Richard Baker Rōshi, the quiet simplicity of living Zen, rather than simply talking about it, has been a powerful source to effect difficult goals. To pursue the goal that is also no-goal has become, for Zen Center, more than just a cute intellectual game that some Zen devotees play. Of course, this limits Zen Center to a less than spectacular profile in the Zen scene in America, but less than spectacular is precisely what it has chosen to be.

A low profile, by its very nature, relegates San Francisco Zen Center to the slow-growth category of Buddhist groups in America. Nevertheless, it is also a solid growth that is being achieved. Zen Center has been very careful to learn well what it means to practice Zen in America, and like most enterprises of this nature, maturity has come slowly and painfully, but with much awareness. Claude Dalenberg, a former president of Zen Center, has noted:

> Zen Center should be in harmony with American society, capable of existing on its own two feet in the middle of that society. Now that we're thrown into this neighborhood and subject to the pressures of living here, I hope we will be forced to grow up, to mature, and not continue to be dependent on Japanese surroundings.[8]

One advantage of San Francisco Zen Center in the quest for American identity is that its followers are mostly non-Orientals. Certainly that poses problems regarding the practice of Buddhism itself, but it provides a community that has a deep understanding of American culture. Active community life has been a chief concern of Zen Center since its inception. By fostering deep personal involvements in the community for all Zen Center members, the organization has suffered less identity crisis than other Buddhist groups. Further, the integrity of each task and role is emphasized, as consonant with Zen practice. In this fashion, not only is a sense of belonging inculcated, but also an appreciation for the relationship between Zen practice and life. Indeed, for Zen Center, practice *is* life, and as students come to realize directly that life *is* practice, the entire community is infused with vigor and vitality that might otherwise be absent.

As the holistic approach to life is integrated into daily activity, it becomes clear that Zen Center recognizes well that Buddhism in America is largely a city movement, but that wherever one might reside is sufficient for human wholeness. It might be speculated by some that Zen Mountain Center and Green Gulch Farm represent quiet "safety valves" or retreats at which Zen Center members withdraw to salve the evils of city life. Such a claim is obviously not the appropriate one in this case, as the country centers provide only a balance and not an escape. Peace in the country is no guarantee of a like condition in the city, so Zen Center exhorts its members to be at home with themselves. Fortunately, that state of mind is portable.

Precisely because it is well organized, self-sufficient, concerned with serious Buddhist practice and solid Buddhist principles, quite thoroughly American, and involved in promoting a Zen life that is both spontaneous and moral, in which its members become fully active in a society that they can affirm and alter, San Francisco Zen Center represents, to this researcher, an example of Buddhism in America at its best. I do not mean to say that it is *the best* Buddhist group in America, for such a claim would be meaningless. Nevertheless, it presents an ideal format that other Buddhist groups and communities might utilize in their own learning and maturing process.

CHAPTER 8

Buddhist Vihara Society

Success in meditation or anything worthwhile cannot be achieved overnight. It requires a long, disciplined and sometimes even painful process of practice. At each sitting in meditation you gain some result. You may put yourself to the test to see for yourself how successful you are. We can understand many things abstractly but not the truth of meditation until it is practised. It is not something to be talked about, but something to be experienced.

—Henepola Gunaratana[1]

SECTARIAN AFFILIATION

The Buddhist Vihara Society is affiliated with the Theravāda school of Buddhism, which is the last surviving school of all the early sects of Indian Buddhism (collectively called Hīnayāna by the Mahāyānists). Most Theravādins identify themselves with the Sthaviravādins of the first traditional schism in Buddhism and thus regard themselves as the true "elders" (the meaning of the word "thera" in Pāli or "sthavira" in Sanskrit) of the Buddhist tradition. André Bareau has already established the inadmissibility of this thesis, noting that the Theravādins developed from the Vibhajyavādin tradition which, although representing a branch of the Sthavira tradition, arose several hundred years after the initial schism between the Mahāsāṃghikas, and Sthaviras.[2] Further, the philosophical and disciplinary laxity of the Mahāsāṃghikas, long supposed by the Theravādins as establishment of their own orthodox position, has quite recently come under serious reconsideration, which may cast a new light on the position of the entire Sthavira tradition.[3]

HISTORY

In 1964, when the Most Venerable Madihe Pannaseeha Thera (the Maha Nayaka of Ceylon) visited the United States, he noticed a serious interest in Buddhism on the part of many Americans, but a complete absence of Theravāda groups, and thus the idea for a Theravāda group was born. The following year, on the suggestion of this esteemed monk, the Sasana Sevaka Society of Maharagama, Ceylon, sent an emissary, the Venerable Bope Vinita from Vajirarama Temple (in Colombo, Ceylon), to Washington. After Vinita's arrival in August 1965, he enlisted the assistance of the Ambassador of Ceylon (and his embassy staff), and on December 10, 1966, the Buddhist Vihara Society was founded with Vinita as its president.

In 1967, Vinita was succeeded in office by the Venerable Mahathera Dickwela Piyananda, who had recently arrived from Maliyadeva College in Kurunegala, Ceylon. Piyananda was later joined, in September 1968, by the Venerable Mahathera Henepola Gunaratana from the Buddhist Temple in Kuala Lumpur, Malaysia. Under the guidance of these two vigorous men, and with the help of the Sasana Sevaka Society, the government of Ceylon, and the royal government of Thailand, the Buddhist Vihara Society purchased a building at 5017 16th Street N.W. (previously owned by the royal government of Thailand) and moved to its new home on May 26, 1968. It still operates out of this building. Eventually, another monk, the Venerable Punnaji, was sent to offer further administrative assistance.

FACILITIES AND STRUCTURE

The building on 16th Street N.W., originally in use as a residence, has two floors, a basement, and an extensive garden. The basement houses the vihara bookstore and the meditation hall, while the first floor is occupied by the office of the Secretary of the organization and the shrine room, and the upper floor consists of the monks' quarters and the library.

The shrine room is exquisite, centering on a beautiful Buddha image in the meditation posture. Donated by Prabhath Wijesakara of Ceylon, this gilded figure stands a full five feet high. To the right of the main altar is a secondary altar and image, both presented by the Buddhist Association of Thailand. The entire shrine room is carpeted in a deep red color. In the library, which centers on a Kalmuck Mongolian altar, there is a complete set of the Pāli Tipiṭaka with the

Burmese Commentaries and Subcommentaries. In addition, the library has a significant and growing collection of books on all aspects of Buddhist philosophy, Buddhist practices, and the various Buddhist traditions in Asia. In the garden, the main focus is an eight-foot-tall figure of Ananda, in bronze, that was created by Tissa Ranasinghe of Ceylon for display at Expo '67 in Montreal and donated to the vihara by the government of Ceylon. The bookstore, while still modest in its selection, has in recent years been growing to meet the expanding number of publications on Buddhist topics. The entire facility was renovated in January 1976 by a group of volunteers.

BRANCHES AND AFFILIATED GROUPS

The Buddhist Vihara Society has no affiliated groups in the United States, but the monks have pursued, since the inception of the organization, a vigorous schedule of visiting educational institutions for lectures. They have also lectured at churches and various other institutions in the hope of educating Americans as to the nature of Buddhism, thus promoting a sense of mutual understanding. Further, close contact is maintained with the parent group of the organization in Ceylon: the Sasana Sevaka Society.

KEY MEMBERS AND/OR PERSONNEL

Key personnel include Piyananda Mahathera, Gunaratana Mahathera, and Punnaji Thera. These three venerable monks continue to be the backbone of the organization. My personal experience with Piyananda and his predecessor Bope Vinita reveals that each man is not only humble as well as knowledgeable, but also the living embodiment of Buddhist teaching. Piyananda still maintains the rules of Vinaya for Buddhist monks, certainly difficult in modern America, while Vinita was known to utilize the services of other individuals to carry money, since monks are not allowed to handle money. When Piyananda visited Pennsylvania State University several years ago, he accompanied several of us to dinner at an inn owned by the university (although he only drank orange juice, because monks do not partake of solid food after noon) and enthralled all of us with his sparkling eyes and quick wit.

The style of these three monks is exemplary of all of Theravāda. While the monks may well serve as meditation teachers for individual students, functioning as "spiritual friends" (or kalyāṇamitta in Pāli) in the best sense of the word, they have never emphasized their own personal charisma (which is significant) or meditational acumen. They are content to maintain their role as guide, sharing with their

students the fruits of many years of practice, as well as the knowledge and insights that have resulted.

MEMBERSHIP

As of March 1973, the Buddhist Vihara Society cited a membership
of 347 and a mailing list of around 1,200. Most members are Americans, with membership requiring *interest* in Buddhism rather than
personal affiliation. Life membership may be obtained for $150,
whereas annual membership is $15 ($5 for students). Since they have
no branches, the majority of their membership is restricted to the
Washington, D.C., area. At this point, their growth is rather minimal,
but constant.

KEY AND/OR SPECIAL DOCTRINES

The doctrinal position of the Buddhist Vihara Society is consonant
with the general position of Theravāda. Of particular interest is the
clear distinction they maintain, as in Asia, between monk and layman. Their position, maintaining that they hold the "true" lineage of
Buddha, is fostered by the fact that they wear the same-colored robes
(yellow) as the monks in Ceylon, Burma, Laos, Thailand, and Cam-
bodia, all of which are Theravāda countries. Stated simply, any man
who does not wear the yellow robe is not a monk. This rather sectarian position is mitigated somewhat by the fact that at one point a
Tibetan monk from a center in New Jersey lived at the vihara for almost four months, as well as a Japanese monk of the Nichiren Shu
sect, who held services for Japanese persons. Further confounding
the issue is the rather ecumenical position of allowing Buddhists of
other sects to practice at the vihara.

RITUALS, SERVICES, AND PRACTICES

The Buddhist Vihara Society conducts regular services for its membership on Sundays. The service usually consists of five major parts.
The first of these involves "devotions" or vandana. This is followed
by a sermon, and next is a break for refreshments. Then there is a
"Dhamma discussion," in which various points in the doctrine are
elucidated, and finally the service is concluded with meditation
(which, the monks inform me, is "strictly satipaṭṭhāna").

There are three major ritual celebrations observed by the organization. First is the Wesak Full Moon in May. In this holiday the group

simultaneously celebrates the birth, enlightenment, and death of Siddhārtha Gautama, the historical Buddha. Second is Olcott Day, which honors Henry S. Olcott, an American colonel (of Theosophical Society fame) who helped revive modern Buddhism in Ceylon. Finally there is the December Festival, which celebrates the founding of the Buddhist Vihara Society.

The organization also sponsors periodic Uposatha retreats. Uposatha (Poṣadha in Buddhist Sanskrit and Upavasatha in Vedic Sanskrit) is the twice-monthly fast day in which the Pātimokkha, or precepts for monks and nuns, is recited and monastic business transacted in Buddhist cultures. For the Washington organization, Uposatha retreats are one-day intensive periods which last from 8:30 A.M. to 5:00 P.M. and include pūja (or devotion), observing the eight precepts, walking and sitting meditation, lunch, dāna (or donation), meditation discussion, vandana, chanting, and a formal closing that involves the taking of the five layman's vows. In addition to these periodic intensive sessions, there is continual spiritual counseling and guidance by the monks, available on an appointment basis. The vihara also conducts a variety of classes in such topics as yoga, meditation, Sinhalese for children, and the like.

FUTURE PLANS

Future plans for the Buddhist Vihara Society include a wide variety of activities. The vihara would like to further its repairs on its facility, and expand as well. The society would also like to extend its policy of inviting Buddhist monks from other Buddhist traditions to come to the vihara for periods of time. Efforts are being made to improve the quality of the program in religious education, and as a corollary of the above attempt, more courses in languages such as Pāli, Sanskrit and Tibetan and on the various aspects of Theravāda (and the other traditions) are planned.

The Buddhist Vihara Society would also like to continue its slow but steady growth and improve Americans' understanding of the Buddhist tradition for the mutual compatability of the endeavors of both.

PUBLICATIONS

The organization publishes a bimonthly newsletter, the *Washington Buddhist,* which includes short articles on aspects of Buddhism, Buddhist-inspired poetry, news, text (or sutta) study, and vihara activities.

In addition to the newsletter, the vihara has embarked on a series of essays, known as the Vihara Papers, which emphasize the application of Buddhism (particularly Theravāda) to modern urban life and note Buddhism's role in bridging cultural divisions and human understanding. The first of these is Henepola Gunaratana's *Come and See,* which is an introductory Theravāda meditation manual (one-half of which discusses Buddhism's position on drugs).

CONCLUDING REMARKS

It is difficult to interpret the work of the Buddhist Vihara Society with any accuracy, for there seem to be very many contradictions in their activities. On the one hand, the society has never made a significant effort to acculturate effectively, while on the other hand, it expresses interest in bridging the cultural gap. It is to some degree concerned with growth, in terms of membership, yet it has never aggressively (or even mildly) pursued such an endeavor by seriously extending its sphere of influence. The organization has firm ties with its parent group in Ceylon and is located in a reasonably affluent international community (which includes a number of people from Theravāda countries), but still has some degree of difficulty keeping its facilities in proper repair. Its monks teach the satipaṭṭhāna system of meditation, much esteemed in Theravāda cultures (as well as respected by other Buddhist traditions), but they do not attract very many American or Oriental students. Why do these paradoxes exist?

My own suspicion for the cause of these paradoxes is that Theravāda in America, as in so many other places, promotes sectarian squabbles simply by its overwhelmingly apologetic attitude. One might be tempted to surmise that because satipaṭṭhāna is such a vigorous system of meditation, many are discouraged from attempting it, but when faced with the large numbers of Americans who have pursued the difficult Zen path with seriousness or the foundation practices in Tibetan Buddhism, the cause appears to have a different basis. Too, one may not argue that the monastic nature of Theravāda has discouraged many Americans from pursuing this path, for Shasta Abbey (which will be discussed later) is notably interested in the training of Zen priests, but has fared better. Even Gold Mountain Monastery (also to be discussed later), which has established its own valid ordination line for bhikṣus and bhikṣuṇīs, has demonstrated significantly more activity and public interest than the vihāra in Washington. Nor can we argue that the religious nature of the organization keeps it in disfavor, for virtually all of the groups to be presented in this section of the study have clearly religious natures. It may simply be that Theravāda does not excite the romantic sensibilities that are often the beginning points of interest for Americans. It suggests no ties with poetry, the wandering life, or similar concerns, each of which offers powerful attraction to many Americans.

Although it is unfortunate, it appears that the Buddhist Vihara
Society is limited by its own lack of vision. It apparently has never really conceived of itself as anything other than an oasis to serve the international community of diplomats in Washington. There is no question that Theravāda can be attractive and important for large numbers of Americans, for even a cursory study reveals that Jack Kornfield and Joseph Goldstein, codirectors of the Insight Meditation Society in Barre, Massachusetts, have made marvelous strides towards bringing the Theravāda way of life to this country. Should the Buddhist Vihara Society continue along its current path, there is every likelihood that it will remain stable in its position and function, which is at least admirable and valuable.

CHAPTER 9

Sino-American Buddhist Association (Gold Mountain Monastery)

I've given Buddhism another name. I don't call it Buddhism. What do I call it? I call it People-ism (the religion of the people). Why? Because people become Buddhas. It isn't that the Buddha becomes a person, but that people can become Buddhas. So Buddhism can be called People-ism.

—Hsüan Hua[1]

SECTARIAN AFFILIATION

According to the Sino-American Buddhist Association,[2] it has been stated on several occasions that it teaches the "orthodox Buddha-dharma." This means that, in spite of its teacher's recognition as a Ch'an Master (about which more will be said later), the association emphasizes: (1) the Ch'an or meditation school, (2) the Vinaya or discipline school, (3) the T'ien-t'ai or "teachings" school, (4) the Tantric or esoteric school, and (5) the Ching-t'u or Pure Land school. This somewhat eclectic approach is not at all unusual for Chinese Buddhist groups. It may surprise some readers to see an acknowledged Ch'an Master emphasizing Pure Land Buddhism, and in this regard, John Blofeld offers some timely remarks:

> In the West, it has long been erroneously supposed, even by some erudite Buddhist scholars, that the doctrines of the Pure Land Sect (Ching T'u Tsung in Chinese, Shin Shu in Japanese) run contrary to the general teaching of Buddhism and that there must therefore be disagreement between that sect and the followers of Ch'an (Zen) doctrines. The special significance to which I have alluded arises from the fact that *Dhyāna Master*

means Zen Master, and that our present author, Zen Master Hua, far from combating Pure Land notions, extols them! To Chinese or Japanese Buddhists this will come as no surprise at all, for almost all of them subscribe to the dictum pronounced by the late Chinese Buddhist leader, the Venerable T'ai Hsü, that the teachings of the Eight Sects of Mahāyāna Buddhism fit in with one another as easily as eight identical beads on the same rosary. Indeed, all through the history of Chinese Buddhism, Ch'an (Zen) Masters have spoken highly of the Pure Land doctrines and recommended them to their own followers as being the surest and simplest path to enlightenment.[3]

The Sino-American Buddhist Association is affiliated with the Buddhist Lecture Hall in Hong Kong and with Hsi-lo-yüan and Tz'u-hsing monasteries, both located in the Hong Kong area.

HISTORY

Long famous in Asia, by the late 1950s the Venerable Tripiṭaka Master Hsüan Hua had accumulated an active group of disciples in America. In 1959, they founded the San Francisco Buddhist Lecture Hall and repeatedly urged the Master to come to America. In early 1962, with a firm resolve to bring Buddhism to the West, the Master arrived in San Francisco. In an event foreshadowing the future of the organization, Hsüan Hua announced on Chinese New Year's Day in 1968: "This year the Dharma Flower will bloom in America—a five-petalled flower."[4]

During the spring of 1968, Hsüan Hua was invited to Seattle to hold a week-long meditation session. He refused to go, having a disciple instruct the group that San Francisco would fall prey to a serious earthquake if he left the city. Upon learning of the Master's reluctance to leave San Francisco, the group of students from Seattle journeyed instead to the Master's dwelling and held the meditation session there. The week was so successful that many of the group urged Hsüan Hua to hold another session during the summer. Eventually, plans were made for an extended meditation and "cultivation" session which lasted in excess of ninety days. A large number of those who participated in the summer program stayed in San Francisco, joining with members of the San Francisco Buddhist Lecture Hall (and others) to found the Sino-American Buddhist Association on December 1, 1968. Hsüan Hua was elected chairman of the organization, a Board of Directors was established, and the formal mission of the organization was set forth: to promote the growth of the "Buddhadharma" in the West. Along with specific plans to establish monasteries, temples, meditation centers, schools, and translation centers, the association also emphasized the need to provide a vehicle by which Westerners could cultivate the basic principles of the Dharma. In order formally to begin an American monastic saṃgha, five disciples traveled to Keelung, Taiwan, in 1969 to receive three full platforms of precepts: śrāmaṇera, bhikṣu, and bodhisattva. They returned as the first ordained persons in this lineage, intending to lead the "homeless life" in accord with the regulations set forth in the Vinaya.

Subsequent years have been extremely active for the Sino-American Buddhist Association. In January 1970, the Buddhist Text Translation Society was founded, and a journal, *Vajra Bodhi Sea,* offered its maiden issue. During the winter of 1970–71, in addition to moving from its location on Waverly Place to its new home on 15th Street, a fourteen-week meditation session was held. Also during 1971, four more disciples traveled to Taiwan to receive the full ordination platform. The last week of March 1971 marked the organization's formal commitment to the promotion of world peace, as it held the first "Mahamantra Marathon," with repetition of the Oṃ Maṇi Padme Hūṃ mantra for twenty-two and one-half hours daily during the entire week.

The year 1972 was momentous for the organization in that it held a 108-day complete precept platform at Gold Mountain Monastery. The proceedings commenced on June 7 and marked the first (and to this day only) ordination lineage in America that is in full accord with all the regulations prescribed in the Vinaya. Almost two years later, on July 21, 1974, the Bodhi Dhamma Center in Seattle became an official part of the Sino-American Buddhist Association, and nine days later the organization sponsored World Peace Day. This event was the conclusion of a 1,150-mile journey (culminating in Marblemount, Washington) on the part of a young American bhikṣu, Heng Ju, who walked the entire distance, bowing once for every three steps taken while praying for world peace. A month later, on August 21, 1974, a site for a new center was inaugurated by Hsüan Hua in Marblemount, Washington. The year 1974 also witnessed the establishment of the International Institute for Translation of Buddhist Texts.

By 1976, the organization was beginning to extend its horizons still farther, and dedicated Gold Wheel Temple in Los Angeles. Also in 1976, a World Wide Dharma Assembly was held to promote the translation of the Buddhist canon into all the languages of the world. The crowning glory of the year, however, was the beginning of the "City of Ten Thousand Buddhas," a community to be completed in the Ukiah Valley (in California). It is a multimillion-dollar project on 237 acres, designed to house seven thousand to ten thousand people. In 1977, Dharma Realm University was established in the city.

FACILITIES AND STRUCTURE

The Sino-American Buddhist Association has five major facilities: Gold Mountain Dhyāna Monastery, the City of Ten Thousand

Buddhas (including Dharma Realm University), the International Institute for the Translation of Buddhist Texts, an Elementary School, and an Educational Bureau.

Gold Mountain Dhyāna Monastery houses the headquarters and administrative offices of the association. The monastery now occupies an old building that had formerly been used as a factory. It was purchased in December 1970, and in January 1971 the association moved from its former location at T'ien-hou-miao on Waverly Place. The three-story building required extensive repairs in order to convert it from factory to monastery. Upāsaka I Kuo-jung (R.B. Epstein) relates an interesting story regarding the early stages of the repairs:

> Gold Mountain had quite a close call when the refurbishing of the building first began. An old girl friend of one of the Master's disciples, who was later to leave the home-life, followed him to the Association and also took refuge with the Master. Later she arrived when the construction work had just begun, and, informing the Master that she had nowhere to stay, requested permission to live in a large closet under the stairs on the first floor of the building. The Master, knowing that she was fond of drink and tobacco, explained to her that she could only stay if she agreed not to smoke or drink while she was living there. She agreed and said that she would move in in a few days.
>
> Nevertheless, that very night, unknown to anyone, she somehow snuck into the building and went to sleep in the closet under the stairs. Late that night, long after everyone had already retired and fallen asleep, the Master, who was then on the third floor of the building, smelled smoke and immediately went down to the second floor to awaken Dharma Master Heng-shou, who groggily went down to the first floor to investigate. He quickly became alert, however, when he found thick clouds of billowing black smoke filling the first floor. The source he found was the closet under the stairs and upon opening it he saw several foot flames leaping from a quilt covering the sleeping woman, who had been smoking in bed and was still in a drunken stupor. With the flames only a few inches from her head, he yelled, "Wake up, Wake up, you're going to be burned to death," and threw the burning quilt out into the open room just seconds before both the woman's hair and the wood of the stairway would have burst into flame.
>
> Dharma Master Shou then went back to talk to the culprit, ignoring the flames in the middle of the room, which were then getting precariously close to the ceiling rafters. Fortunately, the Master at that moment came downstairs to investigate and seeing the danger, instructed Dharma Master Shou to stop talking and immediately get water to put out the flames.
>
> At that time the building which has an internal wood framework, was filled with wooden building materials, and if it had ever once caught flame would have been entirely destroyed in a few minutes. Although there were other people sleeping in rooms on both the first and second floors of the building, only the Master on the third floor smelled the smoke and by his quick action averted a terrible calamity.
>
> After the close call, work on the monastery continued, almost all of it done by the members of the Association. Gold Mountain was formally opened and dedicated on May 20, 1972.[5]

A further renovation project was completed in 1975, which included more office space, new rooms, and remodeling of the rooms of the monks and lay Buddhists. Emma Layman furnishes a succinct but useful description of Gold Mountain:

> The building which houses the Sino-American Buddhist Association and Gold Mountain Dhyana Monastery is a large, square, red brick building with wooden trim painted yellow and red. The entrance opens onto an office area, which adjoins the Great Hall or Buddha Hall, said to be large enough to accommodate eight hundred persons at a lecture or meeting.
> The arrangement in the Buddha Hall is similar to that found in small Chinese monasteries, where the same hall may have to serve for chanting, sutra study, lectures, and meditation. There are tables about the room on which are placed copies of the liturgies. Cushions for kneeling and meditation are on the floor, facing the altar. These may be moved to the side for meditation. Enthroned on the altar are three, large, seated Buddhas. In the center is Sakyamuni Buddha, and he is flanked on the right and left respectively by Amitabha Buddha and Bhaishajyaguru Buddha (the Healing Buddha). Extending the length of the hall on each side is a bench, where devotees sit during lectures and for meditation. On the walls are pictures depicting the life of Sakyamuni Buddha. In addition to the Buddha Hall, there are in the building kitchen, refectory, guesthall, living quarters, areas for study and translation, and editorial offices for the association's monthly publication, *Vajra Bodhi Sea*.[6]

Gold Mountain Dhyāna Monastery welcomes any fully ordained Buddhist monk and, on occasion, lay Buddhists interested in pursuing a rigorous religious life are housed in the monastery. All who live in the monastery must strictly follow all rules and adhere to the daily schedule, which begins at 3:40 A.M., ends at 10:00 P.M., and includes morning recitation, meditation, sūtra study, language classes, recitations, and work. Since the Vinaya expressly forbids housing monks and nuns in the same residence, the nuns live elsewhere.

Due to their concern for bringing what they consider to be the "proper Dharma" to the West, the Sino-American Buddhist Association is now in the process of constructing a monastic complex known as the City of Ten Thousand Buddhas in the Ukiah Valley near Talmage, California (about a two-hour drive from San Francisco). The administrators had originally planned to begin the entire complex from scratch, but architectural and engineering estimates ($10,000,000) frustrated this endeavor. Consequently, they purchased a vacant institution designed to provide accommodations for seven thousand to ten thousand people. The institution was originally built by the government during the 1950s on 237 acres and has twenty-seven major and sixteen minor buildings.

The organization foresees a complete Buddhist community that will include a monastery, Buddhist old-age home, orphanage, Buddhist university, meditation center, hospital, home for delinquent children, kindergarten, elementary school, high school, research institute, and institute for the translation of Buddhist texts. It hopes to use this facility as a base from which to spread Buddhism throughout the

West. While the construction of such a complex would probably cost $50,000,000, the former owner sold the entire complex to the Sino-American Buddhist Association for $6,000,000. Of course, the purchase is heavily debt-financed. The organization estimates that an additional $3,000,000 will be needed to make all programs fully operational. The buildings comprise some 600,000 square feet of usable space and include an office building, hospital, auditorium and gymnasium, kitchen-commissary, maintenance shop, library, industrial shop and warehouse, garage and motor pool, and facilities for employee housing. The minor buildings are sixteen cottages, ranging in area from 350 square feet to 2,400 square feet. No completion date is given by the organization.

The International Institute for the Translation of Buddhist Texts began on October 14, 1974, in a building on Washington Street in San Francisco which was largely financed with the help of C.T. Shen, an upāsaka. The institute contains facilities for research and translation, as well as a growing library, Buddha Hall, and residential area (for nuns of the Sino-American Buddhist Association, guests, and research fellows of the institute). This institute is consonant with another of C.T. Shen's enterprises, the Institute for Advanced Study of World Religions, located in New York. The International Institute for the Translation of Buddhist Texts not only functions as a translation facility, but also as a training ground for translators.

The Gold Mountain Instilling Virtue Elementary School offers a bilingual program (Mandarin Chinese and English) which aims at providing a solid academic basis in a nonpressure environment. The elementary school is housed in the International Institute for the Translation of Buddhist Texts. The classes are team-taught by a native Mandarin speaker (with an M.A.) and a native English speaker (with a B.A.). In addition to emphasizing world peace and harmony, the school seeks to fully involve the parents in the education of their children.

The Educational Bureau of the Sino-American Buddhist Association is primarily responsible for running the language classes of the association. To date, Chinese (classical, modern, and Buddhist), Sanskrit, Tibetan, Japanese, French, German, Spanish, Portuguese, and advanced English have been taught. Special classes on such topics as the lives of the patriarchs and other famous monks have been taught by Hsüan Hua. This educational arm of the organization also runs a speaker's bureau, which sends, on request, specially trained members to various groups throughout the United States. Several members of the Bureau have lectured in East and Southeast Asia as well.

BRANCHES AND AFFILIATED GROUPS

The chief affiliate of the Sino-American Buddhist Association is the Bodhi-Dhamma Center in Seattle, Washington. Originally founded in 1970 by Upāsaka Takping Pong and his wife Gwendolyn, it was merged into the parent organization in July 1974. The center is now managed by a formal Board of Directors, of which at least two-thirds are fully ordained members of Hsüan Hua's saṃgha. Of course the Master himself is Chairman of the Board.

The organization has extended down the coast of California with the establishment of Gold Wheel Temple in Los Angeles during 1976.

KEY MEMBERS AND/OR PERSONNEL

The key member of the Sino-American Buddhist Association is Tripiṭaka Master Hsüan Hua, said to be the forty-fifth patriarch from Śākyamuni, the eighteenth patriarch in China, the ninth patriarch of the Wei Yang lineage, and the first Ch'an patriarch in America.

Hsüan Hua, who is also called An-tz'u and Tu-lun, was born in Northeast China in Sung-chiang Province, near the city of Harbin, in 1908. His father, Pai Fu-hai, was a farmer, and his mother was devoted to Amitābha Buddha throughout her life. The youngest of eight children, Hsüan Hua was born on the same night that his mother had a vivid dream of Amitābha. Hsüan Hua's first confrontation with death came at age eleven, when he saw a dead baby. He became concerned with how one might free oneself from the bonds of death and found an appropriate answer from a visitor to the village: namely, to cultivate the Way. Immediately inspired to pursue the mendicant's way of life, Hsüan Hua asked his mother's permission to become a monk, but she asked her son to postpone his venture until after his parents' death. Although he honored his mother's wish, he nevertheless took refuge three years later under the Master Ch'ang-chih.

Soon the young man entered private school (at age fifteen), at first being slow to learn, but eventually surpassing all his classmates. During his school years he began lecturing to some of the illiterate monks in the local monastery (on the Platform Sūtra of the Sixth Patriarch, the Vajracchedikā-sūtra, and the Sukhāvatīvyūha-sūtra), started a free school, and engaged in similar activities. Four years later, Hsüan Hua's mother died. Shortly after the burial ceremony, he went to Three Conditions Monastery and renounced worldly life, taking the vows of a śrāmaṇera or novice monk. Thereafter, he spent a three-year vigil at his mother's grave site, during which time he studied the sūtras, meditated, and performed many acts of healing. He also took on a series of eighteen rigorous personal vows. Needless to say, his fame was growing rapidly, and by the end of the three years, he had received over two thousand visitors. Upon the completion of his filial duties, he went into seclusion in a cave to pursue more advanced meditation practice.

Tripiṭaka Master Hsüan Hua (Photo by Boris Erwitt.)

After emerging from this intensive period of practice, Hsüan Hua returned to Three Conditions Monastery, where he helped expand the facilities and preach the Dharma. The year 1946 marked the beginning of Hsüan Hua's long pilgrimage to Nan-hua Monastery in Canton in order to pay his respects to Venerable Hsü-yün, a great Ch'an Master. The following year Hsüan Hua received full ordination as a bhikṣu at P'u-t'o Mountain, a famous pilgrimage site devoted to Avalokiteśvara. His pilgrimage was completed in 1948 with his arrival at the monastery of the great Ch'an Master who possessed the transmission of the five Ch'an lineages. Upon meeting the young monk, Hsü-yün transmitted the "mind seal," but waited for an auspicious moment to announce this event, ordering Hsüan Hua to take a teaching position at the Vinaya school in the meantime. Hsüan Hua, however, did compose a verse to mark the occasion:

> The Noble Yün saw me and said, "Thus it is."
> I saw the Noble Yün and verified, "Thus it is."
> The Noble Yün and I both thus,
> Universally vow that all beings also be thus.[7]

Several years passed with various travels and responsibilities. In 1951, the young Master built Hsi-lo Yüan Temple in Hong Kong. He spent 1952 and 1953 lecturing, and in 1954 built Tz'u-hsing Dhyāna Monastery near Hong Kong and founded the Buddhist Lecture Hall in Hong Kong. During 1957, Hsüan Hua made a brief visit to Burma. In 1959, he was requested to come to the United States by founders of the San Francisco Buddhist Lecture Hall. Unfortunately, Master Hsü-yün became gravely ill during that year, and Hsüan Hua declined the offer. Despite efforts to aid his recovery, Hsü-yün died, and Hsüan Hua left for Australia in November 1960 to investigate the prospects for bringing Buddhism to that continent.

In 1962, Hsüan Hua finally acceded to the wishes of the San Francisco Buddhist Lecture Hall and came to America. He originally took up residence in the Chinatown section of San Francisco, lecturing on the Sukhāvatīvyūha-sūtra. During September 1962, he began a thirty-five-day fast for world peace, setting the stage for the organization's continuing involvement with the peace movement. The following year he moved out of Chinatown, lecturing on various texts and beginning to attract a larger and ever increasing following. In 1967, Hsüan Hua moved back to Chinatown, occupying T'ien-hou Temple (the oldest Chinese temple in America), where the San Francisco Buddhist Lecture Hall was now located. Since 1972, the Master has been lecturing on the Avataṃsaka-sūtra, one of the most difficult but important of all Mahāyāna texts. Ever traveling, he spent half of 1973 in South America, seeking to implement Buddhist teaching in that continent. In 1974, he lectured in Hong Kong and Taiwan and in 1975, made an extended lecture tour and pilgrimage throughout Asia.

Regarding his mission in America, Hsüan Hua has said, "I have come to America to create Patriarchs, to create Buddhas, and to create Bodhisattvas."[8] It is clear that he intends to implement this project, and his plan for so doing, unlike all other Buddhist teachers in America, is to begin with a saṃgha of fully ordained monks and nuns. More than just bringing Chinese Ch'an to America, the Sino-American Buddhist Association has brought a Master who, despite the temptations to the contrary, lives fully in accord with all the requirements of the Vinaya, is so well versed in the scriptures that he has earned the title "Tripiṭaka Master," and is thought by many to be a living Buddha. There is no doubt that Hsüan Hua is the most traditional of all Buddhist teachers in America.

MEMBERSHIP

The saṃgha of the Sino-American Buddhist Association corresponds to the traditional fourfold assembly of monks (bhikṣus), nuns (bhikṣuṇīs), laymen (upāsakas), and laywomen (upāsikās). All monks and nuns go through a twofold initiation process. First is the ceremony of becoming a novice (males become śrāmaṇeras, females become śrāmaṇerīs) and taking the ten precepts. Second, one takes the full precepts of the Prātimokṣa: 250 rules for monks and 348 rules for nuns. All Chinese Buddhist monks and nuns are given the surname *shih*, which is the first character in the transliteration of Śākyamuni. Two other names are also given: the tonsure name, given by the monk who performs the novitiate ceremony, and a more personal name. All of Hsüan Hua's ordinands have *Heng* as their tonsure name. Originally, the first novices traveled to Taiwan to receive full ordination. Now there is a sufficient number of fully ordained monks and nuns to perform the entire precept platform in America. The first such ceremony ran for 108 days from June 7 to September 22, 1972; included in the proceedings, in addition to transmission of the novice and full initiations for monks and nuns, was the transmission of the Bodhisattva precepts and intensive instruction in the Vinaya. All monks and nuns wear the traditional Chinese robes and receive incense burns on the scalp in the initiation ceremony; many take additional vows. The spirit of discipline observed by the monks and nuns is expressed in the following poetic statement, composed by the Master:

> Freezing, we do not scheme.
> Starving to death, we do not beg.
> Dying of poverty, we ask for nothing.
> We accord with conditions, but do not change.
> We do not change and yet accord with conditions.
> These are our three great principles.
>
> We renounce our lives to do the Buddha's work.
> We shape our lives to create the ability.
> To make revolution in the Saṅgha Order.
> In our actions we understand the principles,
> So that our principles are revealed in our actions.
> We carry out the pulse of the Patriarch's heart-transmission.[9]

In the lay community, composed of both men and women, all have taken refuge under the Master and have agreed to observe the traditional five vows (some take the eight layman's vows and the Bodhisattva vows as well). All of Hsüan Hua's lay disciples receive a "Dharma" name which includes the character *Kuo*. The lay community includes members from all walks of life, all ages, and many nationalities.

In addition to the fourfold community, there are nine categories of membership in the Sino-American Buddhist Association, with each geared to a specific monetary contribution. Lifetime memberships are threefold: (1) Founding Patron ($100,000 or a special contribution), (2) Sponsor ($50,000 or more), and (3) Donor ($10,000 or more). Term memberships are also threefold: (1) Supporting Member ($1,000 or more—five years), (2) Sustaining Member

($500 or more—three years), and (3) Contributing Member ($300 or more—two years). Annual memberships are again threefold: (1) Active Member ($100—payable annually, monthly, or in ten installments), (2) Member ($50—payable annually, monthly, or in ten installments), and (3) Student Member ($25). Each member gains voting rights in the association (and the right to serve as an officer), membership in Gold Mountain Monastery (and the City of Ten Thousand Buddhas), free attendance at all events of the association (sūtra lectures, ceremonies, holiday celebrations, and the like), half-price reduction on publications, half-price attendance at meditation and recitation sessions, a free subscription to *Vajra Bodhi Sea*, updated information on events, and appropriate credentials.

KEY AND/OR SPECIAL DOCTRINES

As noted earlier, the approach of the Sino-American Buddhist Association is somewhat eclectic, emphasizing the five traditional schools: (1) Ch'an, (2) Vinaya, (3) T'ien-t'ai, (4) Tantric, and (5) Ching-t'u. Rather than focus on the specifics of each of these schools, which goes beyond the scope of this work, perhaps the most efficient way to express the diversity of the teachings of the association is to note the texts which had by early 1976 been fully expounded. These include: the Śūraṅgama-sūtra, Saddharmapuṇḍarīka-sūtra, Prajñāpāramitāhṛdaya-sūtra, Great Compassion Heart Dhāraṇī Sūtra, Platform Sūtra of the Sixth Patriarch, Sūtra of the Original Vows of Earth-Store Bodhisattva, Sukhāvatīvyūha-sūtra, and the Sūtra in Forty-Two Sections.

RITUALS, SERVICES, AND PRACTICES

The practices emphasized by the organization combine intensive meditation with serious sūtra study. Every year the association sponsors several meditation sessions, which have already become well known for their strictness and severity. Most last only a week or two, but others are much longer. The longest session held so far was the fourteen-week one held during the winter of 1970–71. All meditation sessions follow the same basic pattern. Alternate sitting and walking meditation is held from 2:30 A.M. until 12:00 midnight. The only meal of the day is taken at 11:00 A.M., and there are short breaks for various instructional talks. All regulations for Ch'an meditation hall observance are in effect.

Buddha recitation and mantra recitation weeks are also conducted by the organization; the Mahamantra Marathon (mentioned earlier) is an example of this kind of practice. The daily schedule of recitation sessions usually runs from 4:00 A.M. to 10:00 P.M., alternating vocal recitation with periods of sitting meditation, during which silent recitation and mindfulness may be cultivated.

During the summer, there is an annual lecture and cultivation session, inspired by the first such session held in 1968. These summer sessions vary in length from time to time, but recently the organization has been sponsoring two separate six-week programs. The schedule for the summer sessions usually follows a time sequence similar to the one outlined below:

- 4:00 A.M. Morning Recitation
- 5:00– 7:30 A.M. Meditation
- 7:30– 8:30 A.M. Review lecture
- 8:30– 9:30 A.M. Study Period
- 9:30–10:30 A.M. Meditation
- 10:30–11:00 A.M. Great Meal Offering
- 11:00 A.M. Lunch
- 12:00– 1:30 P.M. Repentance Ceremony
- 1:30 2:30 P.M. Meditation
- 2:30– 3:30 P.M. Sūtra lecture
- 3:30– 4:30 P.M. Meditation
- 4:30– 5:30 P.M. Language lessons
- 5:30– 6:30 P.M. Meditation
- 7:00– 9:00 P.M. Evening Recitation and sūtra lecture
- 9:00– 9:30 P.M. Repentance Ceremony
- 10:00 P.M. Lights out

The structure of these sessions is geared toward permanent rather than temporary change in the participants' lives, based on their prolonged contact with the Dharma as well as on their intensified understanding of Buddha's teaching. During the sessions, all participants must adhere to the five layman's vows and the rules of the monastery. Recently, the association expanded its offering of practice sessions to include two one-week programs held in the spring.

Sūtra explanation is also an integral part of the practice program facilitated by the organization. In this regard, sūtra lectures are given daily (and twice daily on some occasions). In addition, sūtra lectures are offered with regularity at the International Institute for the Translation of Buddhist Texts. The sūtra lecture program of the organization has been so effective that members have been invited to lecture in various locations, including Asia, making them the first *American* monks to be invited to elucidate Buddhist sūtras in such fashion.

In addition to the usual meditation and sūtra recitation practices, the Sino-American Buddhist Association celebrates a number of other Buddhist holidays. Needless to say, there is an annual observance of Buddha's birthday. However, the organization is well known for its sponsorship of a World Peace Day. A "liberating life" ceremony is also held, in which animals destined for slaughter are purchased and then released. The ceremony marks the introduction of this practice, long customary in the Buddhist cultures of Asia, to America.

FUTURE PLANS

New centers are, of course, in the offing for the organization. Gold Dragon Monastery, near Marblemount, Washington, is one of the planned projects, as well as a center in Reedsport, Oregon. It is hoped that work will continue on the City of Ten Thousand Buddhas and that each of the other centers affiliated with the parent organization will be able to expand its operations.

It is also likely that Hsüan Hua will continue scouting out new areas in which to propagate the Dharma and will continue to bring Americans into the saṃgha, both as monastics and lay persons.

PUBLICATIONS

One of the most important tasks of the Sino-American Buddhist Association is the translation of the entire Buddhist canon into English as well as the other major languages of the Western world. This is the primary task of the Buddhist Text Translation Society, the publishing arm of the organization. Established early in the history of the organization, the Buddhist Text Translation Society includes members of Hsüan Hua's saṃgha, scholars, professional writers and editors, and graphic designers, each of whom contributes to the finished publications offered.

Each translator is expected to have the appropriate technical expertise necessary to carry out the task of accurate translation. The translators must also follow eight basic rules:

1. A translator must free himself from the motives of personal fame or profit.
2. A translator must cultivate an attitude free from arrogance and conceit.
3. A translator must refrain from advertising himself and denigrating others.
4. A translator must not establish himself as the standard of correctness and suppress the work of others with his fault finding.
5. A translator must take the enlightened mind as his own mind.
6. A translator must use the wisdom of discrimination to determine true principles.
7. A translator must seek certification from worthy advisors.

8. Once his work is corrected and certified, a translator must endeavor to benefit all beings through the translated teachings by seeing his translations into print.[10]

The Buddhist Text Translation Society is composed of four standing committees: the Primary Translation Committee, the Revision Committee, the Editorial Committee, and the Certification Board. The chief translator has the primary responsibility for accurately rendering the translation into the primary language. All changes and revisions require the consultation of the chief translator of the text. The Revision Committee checks the entire text against the original, making suggestions to the chief translator. A revised copy is then sent to the Editorial Committee, which attempts to render the translation more readable without altering the meaning of the text. Any questions or uncertainties require the opinion of the chief translator. Finally, the Certification Board, with Hsüan Hua as head, considers the text and renders its judgment. If acceptable, the manuscript is then published. A list of the association's published works follows.

1. *The Sixth Patriarch's Dharma Jewel Platform Sūtra and Commentary:* a translation of the famous sūtra of Hui-nêng with a commentary by Hsüan Hua (translated from Chinese by Bhikṣuṇī Heng Yin), 1971
2. *Records of the Life of the Venerable Master Hsüan Hua:* Volume I of a three-volume set, this issue covers Hsüan Hua's life up to his reception of the Dharma transmission from Hsü-yün (compiled and translated by Bhikṣuṇī Heng Yin), 1973
3. *The Ten Dharmarealms Are Not beyond a Single Thought:* gāthās and a commentary by Hsüan Hua (translated from Chinese by Bhikṣuṇī Heng Ch'ih), 1973
4. *Pure Land and Ch'an Dharma Talks:* instructions given by Hsüan Hua during a two-week Buddha recitation session and a one-week meditation session in December 1972 (translated by Bhikṣuṇīs Heng Yin and Heng Ch'ih), 1974
5. *A General Explanation of the Vajra Prajñā Pāramitā Sūtra:* a translation of the basic text with a commentary by Hsüan Hua (translated from Chinese by Bhikṣuṇī Heng Ch'ih), 1974
6. *A General Explanation of "The Buddha Speaks of the Amitābha Sūtra":* a translation of the smaller Sukhāvatīvyūha-sūtra with a commentary by Hsüan Hua (text translated by Upāsaka I Kuo-jung; commentary translated by Bhikṣuṇī Heng Yin), 1974
7. *World Peace Gathering:* a collection of articles regarding the pilgrimage for world peace made by Bhikṣus Heng Ju and Heng Yo, 1974
8. *The Essentials of the Dharma Blossom Sutra:* Volume I of the Lotus Sūtra with a commentary by Hsüan Hua (translated from Chinese by Bhikṣu Heng Ch'ien), 1974

9. *A General Explanation of the Essentials of the Śrāmaṇera Vinaya and Rules of Deportment:* a translation of the text written by Master Lien Ch'ih in the Ming Dynasty with a commentary by Hsüan Hua (translated by Bhikṣuṇī Heng Yin and Upāsaka Kuo Chen), 1975

The society has also published a translation of the *Earth Store Bodhisattva Sūtra,* but I have not been able to secure a copy.

The association also publishes a journal, *Vajra Bodhi Sea,* and has done so on a monthly basis since its inception in April 1970. Each issue includes translations from sūtras, biographical sketches of various Dharma Masters, information concerning members of Hsüan Hua's saṃgha, articles, poetry, book reviews, a monthly Sanskrit lesson, an occasional recipe, and world Buddhist news.

CONCLUDING REMARKS

There is little doubt that with regard to religious practice and study, the Sino-American Buddhist Association is the most rigorous of all Buddhist groups in America. This fact alone destines the organization to a rather small saṃgha of devotees and practitioners and a high attrition rate for those people who initially participate in the organization's activities. Nonetheless, the organization is perhaps the most fiscally aggressive of all Buddhist groups in America, largely due to its commitment to the City of Ten Thousand Buddhas project. In this sense they are not unlike many Buddhist monastic groups in Asia that have, throughout their history, engaged in serious and expansive development programs. In this way, some monasteries became vast landowners, accruing significant wealth and stature. The key word in such endeavors seems to be *patronage,* and the membership categories of the organization reflect this in title and amount. The very first type of membership listed by the organization is called *Founding Patron* and requires a contribution of $100,000. It might be argued that the various membership fees of the organization are unrealistic, but in some matters, the association does not seem unrealistic at all. Consequently, in this regard, it is likely that they are only asking what the traffic will bear. Further, their association with C.T. Shen is a fortuitous one, as this devoted Buddhist has lavishly given of his personal funds to many worthy Buddhist projects in America.

On other issues, however, the organization does seem somewhat unrealistic. Hsüan Hua intends to implement in America what he considers to be the "orthodox Buddhadharma." To him this requires establishing a sizable monastic saṃgha. He demonstrates this concern by having gone to great pains (and taken much care) to establish a valid ordination lineage in America. His efforts were exemplified by the holding of complete precept platforms in 1972 and 1976. For Asian Buddhist communities this is certainly a valid endeavor, as Buddhist culture has always emphasized the monastic way of life. Examples of the importance of monastic life might be drawn from Tibet, which, prior to the communist invasion, could boast that one-sixth of its male population entered the monastery, and from China, which, by 1945, had more than 267,000 Buddhist temples and 738,000 monks and nuns.[11] In America, on the other hand, the monastic life is not now, and never has been, a viable option for large numbers of people. I do not mean to say that Hsüan Hua's endeavor is not valid and important. I simply mean that it does not take into account that American Buddhism is *primarily* a lay movement. Nor should we overlook the fact that Hsüan Hua has included the laity as an integral part of his saṃgha. However, for the Sino-American Buddhist Association, lay status implies a commitment to the same ideals that such a designation implies in Asia, namely, *both* the three refuges and the five layman's vows. Tacit and complete acceptance of the layman's vows *may* simply be impractical for Americans, or at best an unrealistic goal. When Hsüan Hua notes that he has come to America to create Patriarchs, Buddhas, and Bodhisattvas, it seems that he means individuals who conform to the Chinese typologies for these categories of persons, rather than allowing for the possibility of innovating American typologies.

Lest it appear that the Sino-American Buddhist Association has little to add to the Buddhist scene in America, it must also be noted that members of the organization pursue the most arduous course of study of any Buddhist group. To be sure, they focus on traditional texts, most often the Vinaya and the Sūtras, but in addressing this task thoroughly, they overcome one of the most serious limitations of Buddhists in this country: they learn about their tradition. And they learn it fully. Needless to say, this means learning to read difficult Buddhist languages, but members of Hsüan Hua's saṃgha approach this rigorous task with alacrity and devotion. At the Syracuse Conference on the Flowering of Buddhism in America, held in April 1977, one of the participants suggested that most American Buddhists do not really know very much about Buddhism. While he is generally correct, members of the Sino-American Buddhist Association must not be considered to be of this group, for they are getting a thorough grounding in basic Buddhist history, doctrine, and ethical theory. Further, in publishing translations of various texts, we are not only getting carefully done products of Buddhist scholarship, but also the commentary of an acknowledged Ch'an Master.

The Sino-American Buddhist Association thus consists of an incredibly dedicated group of men and women who are pursuing the Buddhist path with vigor under the guidance of an able teacher. However, like some other groups, an overwhelming emphasis is placed on the Master. In this case their trust is assuredly well placed.

Nevertheless, there may be significant problems when the Master, who is rapidly approaching age seventy, dies or becomes inactive due to advancing age. The organization will eventually be forced to stand on its own and make its own decisions concerning future enterprises. Hsüan Hua may well choose an American Dharma heir, and it will certainly be interesting to see what directions the Sino-American Buddhist Association will take in subsequent years. At present, we can only comment that the organization is the classic "mixed bag," not yet having made up its mind which continent houses its sacred space.

CHAPTER 10

Tibetan Nyingma Meditation Center

America is a country almost deliberately designed to benefit from the infusion of many cultures, and, right now, the incomparable splendor of Tibetan culture is going begging. We can have it for a mere million dollars.

—Alan Watts[1]

SECTARIAN AFFILIATION

The formal sectarian affiliation of the Tibetan Nyingma Meditation Center, organized by Tarthang Tulku, Rinpoche, is (as is obvious from the center's name) rNying-ma. In Tibet, perhaps more than in any other Buddhist culture, the sects were an expression of teaching lineages that pervaded all of Tibetan Buddhism. The rNying-ma sect is the most ancient of all the lineages, tracing its history back to the beginnings of the Buddhist tradition in Tibet (in the seventh and eighth centuries). Stephan Beyer goes as far as to note that "there can be little doubt that they in fact possess authentic Indian teachings lost among the other sects."[2]

HISTORY

Ever conscious of its own history, the organization has recently published two volumes (1975, 1977) known as *Annals of the Nyingma Lineage in America,* which were circulated as private documents and from which it is possible to outline the salient features of their short history on the American scene. Tarthang Tulku initially arrived in America in 1968, settling in Berkeley, California, on February 15, 1969. In so doing, he fulfilled the wish of his main guru, Khentze, Rinpoche. At the outset he was completely unknown, having brought with him only a collection of Vajrayāna texts (rare in their own right), the best wishes of his teacher, and his own primary resource: his training. The first tentative steps toward the establishment of the Tibetan Nyingma Meditation Center involved beginning on a small (and somewhat private) scale with a select group of students. To these first disciples, Tarthang Tulku began to impart the pragmatics of basic Buddhism. Next, he set out to expand his activities to the general populace, and herein was the difficulty in such an endeavor. With the exception of a few dGe-lugs-pa lamas of Kalmuck heritage who had been present in the United States since the early 1950s, there were no lamas present on American soil, and most Americans had no idea what a Tibetan lama *was,* let alone what he could offer in religious matters. Certainly cautious, Tarthang Tulku made many suggestions about the *possible* relevance Buddhism might have for Americans, trying to capture in the process Buddhism's flexibility and vitality without appearing "heavy-handed" in his style. By March 1969, the fledgling Tibetan Nyingma Meditation Center moved into its first home at 2522 Webster Street in Berkeley.

In 1970, the organization staged its first genuinely "public" activity: an exhibition of Tibetan art at the California College of Arts and Crafts. In December 1970, the first expressly religious practice was held in which a three-day sādhana celebrated the annual ceremony of Nyung Nay. Vows were taken, chanting and fasting ensued, and about forty students participated. The following year another sādhana was held, celebrating for two days the anniversary of the parinirvāṇa of Long-chen-pa. Forty-eight hours of chanting the Vajra Guru Mantra was practiced by the participants. Also in 1971, a Berkeley fraternity house was purchased as a new home for the growing organization, and a retreat house in Inverness, California, was loaned to the organization (it was later used for public seminars). The first publication of the organization, *Crystal Mirror,* a periodical, made its initial debut in 1971.

In November 1972, the Tibetan Nyingma Meditation Center received a visit from Dudjom, Rinpoche, the leader of the rNying-ma sect, in which he blessed the new center, gave various initiations, and offered private meditation instruction. The year 1972 also marked the American expansion of Dharma Publishing, an operation that had its roots in Tarthang Tulku's refugee days in India. Dharma Publishing, about which more will be said later, moved to a new location in Emeryville, California, and acquired an old printing press. By 1975, the enterprise had twenty-three full-time employees. A second exhibit of Tibetan art was held during December 16–30, 1972, at Lone Mountain College, an event graced by the presence of Dudjom, Rinpoche. During the spring of 1973, the organization began an educational facility, Nyingma Institute, and purchased a building in which to house the institute's activities. The first Human Development Training Program was held at the institute in June of the same year.

Since 1974, all branches of Tibetan Nyingma Meditation Center have pursued vigorous growth. In August 1974, the center was visited by Sakya Trinzin, head of the Sa-skya sect of Tibetan Buddhism. Later that year (October 15 and 16), Gyalwa Karmapa, head of the bKa-rgyud sect of Tibetan Buddhism visited the center and performed the famous Black Hat Ceremony.

FACILITIES AND STRUCTURE

The major facilities of the Tibetan Nyingma Meditation Center are the center itself, the Nyingma Institute, and the Nyingma Country Center (Odiyan).

The Tibetan Nyingma Meditation Center is housed, as noted earlier, in an old Berkeley fraternity house at 2425 Hillside, purchased in September 1971 for $72,000 (the $15,000 down payment was raised primarily by the students and a few patrons). Known as Padma Ling or "Lotus Ground," this facility is the hub of all center activities and has over one hundred students living or studying there.

The Nyingma Institute was founded in 1973 and occupies a building at 1815 Highland Place in Berkeley. It was originally established not as a religious center, but rather as a secular institute, in hopes of preserving the "old tradition" (rNyingma) of Tibetan Buddhism. Tarthang Tulku, as its founder and chief official, has intended the institute to be a place of study and inquiry, and its pattern so far shows no signs of deviation. Unlike many similar ventures by other Buddhist groups, the institute became self-sustaining during its first year, primarily because of the foresight that such operations must start small and then expand as funds dictate. During its first two years over 1,000 students participated in the programs of the institute, but now over 7,000 students have enrolled in the many courses (over 150 offered). A Master's degree in Nyingma studies is offered by the institute, involving two years of full-time study (totaling eighty units of credit). In pursuing this degree, the student must combine study of the Tibetan language, preparation for both a written and oral comprehensive examination, and the writing of a thesis with attendance for at least one week per quarter at an intensive meditation retreat. Consequently, the program is academic, personal, and exceedingly rigorous. Faculty for the courses in the institute have ranged from the staff of the institute itself to very outstanding scholars in the field of Buddhist studies, such as Yuichi Kajiyama (from Japan), David Seyfort Ruegg, and Herbert Guenther. Courses range from Buddhist languages and philosophy to Kum Nye relaxation to the

Human Development Training Program. This program, now entering its fifth year, has been widely acclaimed in (among other sources) the *New York Times, Psychology Today,* and *Newsweek.* Designed for psychologists, physicians, therapists, and educators, the program offers basic instruction in rNying-ma psychology through various techniques. The program has been enormously successful and has included some well-known mental health professionals. One early participant noted:

> Since the program is still in progress, what I can say during this sixth week can only be a tentative, sketchy statement about what is proving to be a powerful and significant learning experience for myself and most other participants.
>
> The potential uses of these teachings in the "helping professions" are manifold, for example: In the therapy of so-called "sick" persons, whose particular problems might be alleviated through both the analytic probing and relaxation-meditation techniques taught. Some of these relate to our existing Western methods, but many are very new. . . .
>
> The value of Tarthang Tulku Rinpoche himself as a unique personal "model" for our professional work cannot be overemphasized. His deep and rare learning, experience, "helping" skills, sensitivity to our needs, and constant emphasis on compassion as the sine qua non of our work I think has stimulated many participants to form a fuller vision of what is possible for human life and leadership. I personally consider it a great privilege to be learning at the feet of one of the few living great teachers of the ancient, sublime Nyingma line of religious and human knowledge, and I think that all other participants would join me in this feeling.[3]

Even when stripped of the personal admiration this individual feels for the Master, his account reveals a sense of both the integrity of the program and its value.

Nyingma Institute has also offered a Buddhist Philosophy Training Program. They are now offering a Western Nyingma Teachers Program to graduates of the Human Development Training Program and those others who have had five to eight years' experience in Tibetan Buddhist meditation. The institute also runs a bookstore and gift shop; and in 1976 it completed construction on a meditation garden, with a large prayer wheel, behind the institute. Finally, the institute is developing a sizable library, with extensive collections on Buddhism, religious studies, Tibetan culture, and psychology. The library acquired, in June 1974, a complete 168-volume set of the Tibetan Tripiṭaka, and is at present assembling a formidable collection of art treasures.

The Nyingma Country Center, formally called Odiyan (the birthplace of Padmasambhava), will fulfill Tarthang Tulku's wish to establish a Buddhist community in the United States that is totally self-sufficient and self-contained. The land to house Odiyan is located in Sonoma County, on 900 wooded acres that overlook the Pacific Ocean. The style of the community will combine Western architecture with the design of traditional temples in Tibet. The immediate goals for such a community seem to be prolific:

1. To establish a central academic university which will involve Western scientists, scholars, psychologists, and orientalists;
2. To provide the proper atmosphere for the translation of Tibetan texts, most of which have never been rendered into a Western language;
3. To maintain the tradition of Tibetan thangka painting by training Western artists in this difficult undertaking;
4. To develop a center in which extensive meditation retreats may be undertaken;
5. To establish, within the community, centers for retirement, the education of children, and medical attention;
6. To establish a self-sufficient farming community, including both gardens and livestock;
7. To bring faculty members such as Tibetan lamas, scholars, artists, translators, and craftsmen to the community, with their families, in order to transmit the lineage of Tibetan Buddhism to the American setting;
8. To provide appropriate facilities in which Tarthang Tulku may continue to prepare his long-term students for more profound teaching.

Further, such a community is intended to augment the degree programs of Nyingma Institute. The entire community will be innovative in its facilities, as well as ecologically sane, emphasizing solar and wind energy, recycling of waste materials, and the like. It is envisioned that it will be a perfect interface of Tibetan and American culture.

BRANCHES AND AFFILIATED GROUPS

The Tibetan Nyingma Meditation Center has two main sister organizations. The first of these is the Tibetan Relief Foundation. With the Chinese invasion of Tibet, over 100,000 Tibetans (10,000 of these being lamas and monks) fled to India, Sikkim, Nepal, and Bhutan, where they now live in relocation (or in other words, refugee) camps. Between 1971 and 1975, the center raised approximately $50,000 to provide the Tibetans in residence in these countries with some minimal help. Utilizing funds raised through the various art exhibits, handicraft sales (at the institute's bookstore), and similar ventures, the organization continues to provide assistance for all four schools of Tibetan Buddhism. Associated with this endeavor is the Pen Pal Program. Through this program, Americans support a Tibetan "pen pal" with donations of $5 to $10 per month. In addition, a benefit called "Science and Mysticism" recently raised $5,000 for the relief project.

The second major branch of the center is Dharma Publishing, which will be covered in detail in the section on publications.

Nyingma Institute has affiliates in three cities: Tempe and Tucson, Arizona, and Boulder, Colorado. The Tempe affiliate, known as the Phoenix Center, was founded in 1971. Both Arizona outposts offer seminars, workshops, and classes. The newest affiliate, in Boulder, offered meditation courses and plans to extend its course offerings on Nyingma studies. In 1977, it will offer its first summer program, similar to the Human Development Training Program, as well as a program to teach rNying-ma meditation and psychology techniques to sociologists.

A nonprofit business known as "The Bakery" is also affiliated with Nyingma Institute. It operates out of the institute's kitchen, raising funds for the Odiyan project by producing whole wheat breads for sale in the various health food stores throughout the Bay Area.

As the Tibetan Nyingma Meditation Center becomes more firmly established, it increasingly expands its sphere of influence by opening affiliated groups in major American cities. The center now has affiliates in New York; Washington, D.C.; Ann Arbor; Los Angeles; and Hawaii.

KEY MEMBERS AND/OR PERSONNEL

The most significant member of the organization is Tarthang Tulku, Rinpoche. Son of an incarnate lama who had abandoned a position of political rule in order to pursue the religious life, Tarthang Tulku belongs to the royal family of Sogpa, in the province of Golok (located in eastern Tibet, near Kham and Amdo). Early in his life (at age seven) he was identified as one of thirty incarnate lamas of the large and famous Tarthang Monastery. Consequently, he began his religious training in various Buddhist subjects, including scriptures, philosophy, language, and music.

At the age of fourteen, he began an intensive thirteen-year period of training in meditation and scholarship, which resulted in his studying with more than twenty well-known lamas of the rNying-ma, bKa-rgyud, Sa-skya, and dGe-lugs sects. His scholarly training included intensive work with the texts of Long-chen-pa, Rong-zom, 'Jig-med-ling-pa, Na-ri Pandit, Min-ling-ter-chen, Khentze, Mi-pham, and the various Terma masters. His practical training included initiations in Mahāyoga, Anuyoga, and Atiyoga.

In 1959, when the Communist Chinese invasion was at its height, Tarthang Tulku fled over the mountains through Bhutan and India to Sikkim. Here he continued his studies with his root-guru. Before the

death of his master, the young lama was instructed to bring the lineage of Tibetan Buddhism to the West, and with this in mind, he
returned to India. Not long thereafter, the Indian government,
anxious to learn from the many Tibetans who had taken up residence
in India, asked the Dalai Lama to send a learned man from each of
the four sects to the Sanskrit University in Benares. In this way,
many manuscripts originally in Sanskrit but now lost could be re-
established from the Tibetan translations. From the rNying-ma tradition, after consultation with Dudjom, Rinpoche, Tarthang Tulku
was sent. For the next six and one-half years, he served as a research
fellow and professor of Buddhist philosophy at the university. In
1964, when the Dalai Lama was asked to send a representative to the
World Religions Conference in Mysore, India, Tarthang Tulku was
again chosen. Shortly thereafter, he established Dharma Publishing,
wrote three books, and arranged for the publication of twenty
volumes of Tibetan Buddhist texts.

In 1968, fulfilling the wishes of his teacher, Tarthang Tulku
traveled to America, where he now lives with his wife (Nazli) and
four children. A man of much persistence, Tarthang Tulku has in less
than a decade aroused the respect and support of many scholars and
educators, as well as those pursuing the spiritual life. In addition, his
keen sense of the integrity of all traditions has enabled him to be "at
home" with representatives of all faiths. One fitting example might
be the following, cited from a letter appearing in *Annals of the
Nyingma Lineage in America:*

> I have known Tarthang Tulku for nearly four years, and I have come to
> respect and admire and hold him in high esteem. He, himself, is a credit to
> his community, and he lends stability in an unstable world. The Bishop of
> the Diocese of California (Episcopal) has worked with him in the field of
> art, and together they have produced a movie which received wide acclaim.
>
> The Nyingma Institute is a rock in the midst of heavy seas. In a way they
> are a lighthouse to which men can repair.
>
> Souls differ. Their approach is a much needed one. I consider him my
> spiritual brother.

This high praise, certainly more than just ecumenical esteem, was
offered by John J. Weaver, Archdeacon for Personnel in the Episcopal
Diocese of California.

Perhaps the most appropriate manner in which to close our brief
description of Tarthang Tulku is to quote directly from his most
recent book, *Gesture of Balance,* in which he comments on the role
of the "teacher" from his own perspective, a role which he more
than adequately personifies:

> A teacher who we can trust to guide us well should have experiential reali-
> zation of the teachings, fused with compassion. It is also important that he
> understand his students and really want to teach them, and that he be free
> from emotional or selfish motivations—for these can distort the relation-
> ship. In other words, he must know what he is doing.

A teacher must be balanced himself, so that he can give balance to his students. But many traditions tend to emphasize one aspect of training more than others. Often a teacher may not offer a well-rounded system of teachings—meditation may be emphasized without the necessary philosophical training, or scholarship may not be combined with sufficient practical experience to create balance. So it is important to consider whether or not a teacher places equal importance on both study and practice.

It is difficult to find a qualified teacher, and equally difficult to accept the responsibilities of being a good student. These do not mean simply to work hard, but also to be receptive, open, and devoted to the teacher. Such qualities are not particularly encouraged in our Western educational system, so they are thus sometimes hard to sustain.[4]

MEMBERSHIP

The Tibetan Nyingma Meditation Center does not publish statistics regarding its membership. Nevertheless, several points can be noted: while its students come from across the United States, about one-third are college graduates (and many are now university students), they present an age range of from twenty to sixty-five (most being in their early thirties), and most are gainfully employed.[5] The latter point is consistent with the lama's affirmation of societal responsibility, and he insists that they maintain jobs.

In the first brochure of the Tibetan Nyingma Meditation Center, it was noted that membership was divided between Practicing Students and General Membership. It further mentioned that Practicing Students were selected by personal interview with Tarthang Tulku. This general process is described in an early publication of the center:

> Structure does not necessarily mean bureaucracy; it can be an important aid for development. At the Center a certain customary process is followed by new students that provides a basis for re-orientation of mental attitudes and growth.
>
> The first step is inquiry, to look through books and talk with people about the nature of Tibetan Buddhism and the Center. It helps to have some background in the philosophy and practices, as it is a rich and complicated tradition. There is a questionnaire and a letter sent to prospective students describing more about its set-up and asking about background and goals. Next is to arrange an appointment with Rinpoche, Tarthang Tulku, on a Wednesday afternoon and discuss personally with him your interests.
>
> . . . All students are involved in the Bum Nga, five introductory practices to develop mind and body and coordinate the two. Each is done 100,000 times. A little later, students begin coming to the evening ceremonies and sutra readings held four times a month.[6]

Practicing Students were required to make a monthly pledge, fixed at a reasonable sum. General Membership was divided into five classes:

Friends, pledging ten dollars monthly; General Members, pledging ten dollars yearly; Donors, giving from one to five hundred dollars; Sponsors, giving five hundred to one thousand dollars; and Lifetime Members, pledging one thousand (or more) dollars.

KEY AND/OR SPECIAL DOCTRINES

The doctrines of the Tibetan Nyingma Meditation Center represent the traditional position of the rNying-ma school very faithfully. This means that there is much emphasis on the Mādhyamika school of Buddhist thought. Also, excellent courses, by well-qualified staff members, are offered with much regularity at the Nyingma Institute. In addition, since the rNying-ma tradition is so concerned with the healthy functioning of the mind, the Abhidharma tradition is also studied thoroughly, and this, too, is reflected in the offerings of Nyingma Institute. Due to the fact that much of the Buddhist philosophy and practice vital to the rNying-ma tradition has been so widely ignored or misunderstood in the West, Tarthang Tulku urges many students to gain the necessary language training in Tibetan and Sanskrit so as to be able to read the traditional texts properly in the original languages.

RITUALS, SERVICES, AND PRACTICES

The rituals, services, and practices of the Tibetan Nyingma Meditation Center can be categorized under five main headings: Bum Nga (or foundation practices), Pūja, Sūtra Chanting, Special Rituals, and Seminars-Workshops.

Having been part of the traditional training in the rNying-ma tradition for over one thousand years, the Bum Ngà practices provide a solid introduction to Buddhist practice. Each of five basic practices is repeated 100,000 times. The first of these is prostration. Each prostration includes not only the physical act itself, which is a profoundly humbling experience for most Westerners, but also the Refuge Vow (which entails going for Refuge to the Triple Gem of Buddha, Dharma, and Saṃgha), mantra recitation, and visualization. Tarthang Tulku has said, with regard to this practice, "Americans, especially young, are very lazy. They need to wake up. Prostrations are like a cold shower."[7] Next, the student repeats the Bodhisattva Vow 100,000 times. This vow, which varies from school to school, requires the practitioner to deny his or her own entry into complete, perfect enlightenment until every sentient being does so. Third comes a merit offering to the Buddhas and Bodhisattvas. Fourth, a visualization is completed; and finally, the student is prepared for the various initiations by meditation on Padmasambhava (Guru Rinpoche). These five foundation practices prepare the student for the more rigorous Vajrayāna training which follows. In Tibet, the traditional practice is concluded by a solitary retreat lasting in excess of three years. Despite the fact that none of Tarthang Tulku's students has as yet progressed to this point, many have completed the 100,000 prostrations, and several (by 1975) were ready to move beyond the Bum Nga practices.

Pūja, a ceremony of devotion and offering, is traditionally held on the tenth and twenty-fifth of each lunar month in the Tibetan calendar. Emma Layman offers a clear but succinct description of the center's pūja ceremony:

> Traditionally, the students bring an offering, such as food, flowers, candles, and incense. Dressed in meditation robes, they chant a liturgy consisting of Prayers to Guru Padmasambhava and the Nyingma lineage, followed by recitation of the Refuge, Bodhisattva Vow, meditation on the Guru, invocation of the Vajrasattva (one of the Five Jinas), offering, prayer for the blessing, and dedication of merit to all sentient beings. The ceremony is usually punctuated by drums, cymbals, and horns, and may be accompanied by various mudras. At the close of the ceremony each participant is served a portion of each offering which is believed to have been transformed into the "elixir of life."[8]

Sūtra chanting ceremonies are held on the new and full moon days in each lunar month in the Tibetan calendar. In these evening ceremonies, the students gather to chant traditional sūtras in Tibetan. The ceremony also includes repetition of the prayer to Guru Rinpoche, the Refuge Vow, and the Bodhisattva Vow. Mantra chanting and meditation follow the recitation. The sūtra chanting is felt to help summarize preliminary Buddhist teaching for the student and assist him in recognizing the various obstacles in walking the Buddhist path. The ceremony often concludes with a discussion by Tarthang Tulku.

Rituals punctuate the calendar year at the center. Two particularly meaningful examples are the Long-chen-pa Sādhana and the Nyung Nay ceremony. The former ritual, first held by the center in February 1971, celebrates the enlightenment of a renowned rNying-ma lama. It involves forty-eight hours of uninterrupted chanting of the Vajra Guru mantra. The Nyung Nay ceremony, first observed by the center in December 1970, involves three days of observation, with two of the days devoted to strict observance of monastic vows. This powerful purification ceremony is dedicated to the removal of the suffering of all beings. Other special observances include such practices as a three-day celebration of Buddha's parinirvāṇa and the like.

Seminars and workshops are usually sponsored through the Nyingma Institute. During the spring quarter in 1977, for example, Tarthang Tulku offered seminars on "Dreams, Wonderment, and Being," "Vajrayana: Keys to Emotional Balance," and "A New

Vision: Time, Space, and Knowledge." Such seminars generally run
from Friday evening to Sunday noon. Following each of the lama's seminars, week-long meditation retreats are offered for additional charge. Workshops are usually offered to accommodate the schedule of visiting scholars who happen to be in the area. Formally referred to as "Intensives and Tutorials," they are likely to cover anything from language training to training for therapists.

FUTURE PLANS

The future plans of the Tibetan Nyingma Meditation Center involve continued development of the rNying-ma path in America and commitment to complete the work on its most ambitious project: The Nyingma Country Center (Odiyan). Presumably, expansion will continue, with a firming up of the newest branches and affiliated groups. Since Tarthang Tulku has openly stated that he is not interested in making Americans into Tibetans, we can expect the growth of this organization to be somewhat slower than other groups that have little regard for the problems of cultural assimilation. Nevertheless, the growth appears to be significant.

PUBLICATIONS

Dharma Publishing is an outgrowth of the printing operation Tarthang Tulku established in India in 1963. The American operation began in 1969, when two of the lama's students began to learn the printing trade. Initially, they used a small handpress, eventually utilizing the facilities of a local firm. In 1972, Dharma Publishing moved its headquarters to Emeryville, California, and acquired a large Harris bookpress. Later, Dharma Publishing purchased a photo-setting computer; now it has complete facilities for book production. The staff has increased to over twenty persons, making the organization the most accomplished operation of its kind among Buddhist groups in America.

Dharma Publishing prints two journals. The first of these, *Crystal Mirror,* is the annual publication of the organization. It has so far published five volumes, including various translations, articles by noted scholars, articles by Tarthang Tulku, and the like. The second, *Gesar,* began publication in the spring of 1973 under the editorship of Jane Wilhelms. It took its name from the ancient King of Ling in eastern Tibet, who protected the Dharma during difficult times in Tibetan history. It includes short articles, poetry, and news about the various centers affiliated with the organization. The book publishing program has already offered over twenty titles, for the most part on the Tibetan tradition (for example, Herbert Guenther's three-volume translation of Long-chen-pa, *Kindly Bent to Ease Us,* Lama Anagarika Govinda's *Psycho-cosmic Symbolism of the Buddhist Stupa,* and Leslie Kawamura's translation *Golden Zephyr*), but also including Jiyu Kennett's *Zen is Eternal Life* (on Sōtō Zen), and Thich Thien-An's *Zen Philosophy, Zen Practice.* We can anticipate aggressive pursuit of a continued publication schedule on the part of the operation.

CONCLUDING REMARKS

Any evaluation of the Tibetan Nyingma Meditation Center must proceed from a consideration of the organization's sense of mission in America. In this context, the decision to come to America was made not in haste, but with Buddhist pragmatism and an awareness of the great mutual benefit that might result from such an effort. In the first place, the Tibetan Buddhist tradition is in great peril. Life in the various refugee centers in India, Sikkim, Bhutan, and Nepal is at best tenuous. These hosts have thoroughly insufficient facilities necessary for the task of providing a new homeland in which the Tibetan tradition might prosper. The line of incarnate lamas, long the cornerstone of the teaching lineages and so critical in Tibetan Buddhism, is in serious danger of extinction. Disease is rampant, educational facilities are inadequate, and so forth. One could go on indefinitely, as it were, noting the difficulties and problems faced by those men and women charged with the task of preserving the Tibetan Buddhist tradition and teachings.

The choice of America, as a potential new home for this tradition, was indeed not hastily made. America has a profound understanding of the aftermath of a genocidal war, having welcomed with open arms masses of Jews who fled Europe in the post-Holocaust period. It is likely that many Tibetans envision the same sort of courtesy for their exiled people—not out of pity, but rather out of a serious respect for human dignity and integrity. In other words, many Tibetans hope to see America at its best. Further, America is, of course, a land which constitutionally guarantees religious freedom. Consequently, little potential persecution was anticipated and virtually none has occurred. America offers much in the way of balanced education and advanced health care facilities, both needed and respected by the Tibetans. And here, too, one could go on and on.

However, for such an enterprise to be supported, reciprocal gains must be forthcoming. Certainly the Tibetan Buddhist tradition is not lacking in its offering to America. The Tibetan Buddhist tradition has made a profound study of the mind and its functioning—as profound as any culture in ancient or modern civilization. In this regard it offers much of value to the Western psychological tradition. Tibetan medicine, in its holistic approach to healing, presents potentially great benefits for assisting Western medicine in both the mode and actual treatment of disease. Tibetan culture and handicrafts offer America the opportunity to be the chief repository for some of the greatest artistic treasures in the world. Tibetan Buddhism, emerging from perhaps the most significantly "religious" culture in the world, presents a wholly new perspective for America at a difficult time in its religious history. Much of the above is rather obvious, but nevertheless a necessary prerequisite to our consideration of Tarthang Tulku and the Tibetan Nyingma Meditation Center.

Like the best of the Buddhist traditions now present on American soil, the Tibetan Nyingma Meditation Center offers a sense of sharing and an opportunity for recapturing human wholeness through mutual exploration, religious practice, and growth. There is no doubt that Tarthang Tulku has not abandoned his Tibetan identity. However, with a scholar's mind and a yogi's insight, he is managing to find a cultural amalgam that is both dignified and efficient. In order to do this, he must combine a clear understanding of economics with a fine ability to appraise temperament. Each of these is manifested in the direction that the Tibetan Nyingma Meditation Center has taken. The lama has built slowly. Rather than beginning Nyingma Institute, for example, with a great flourish, overwhelming publicity, and a huge deficit budget, he began modestly, only pursuing advancement in numbers and breadth of the program as the demand accommodated. Consequently, the organization has incurred fewer debts than many other Buddhist groups. Part of the organization's mission is to educate Americans in Tibetan Buddhism. Tarthang Tulku recognized that publication was a most expeditious way to do so, but rather than publish volumes with already established firms, allowing them to reap the profits, he established his own firm, allowing the profits to be poured back into the organization. Within eight years, the operation became sufficiently successful that it now publishes volumes by highly respected scholars (who might well have chosen other publishers for their volumes). Tarthang Tulku recognized early on that many Americans were disappointed in the impersonality of their religious quest, and offered, in traditional Tibetan fashion, a close and supportive personal involvement with his students. However, rather than portraying the role, adopted by some other Buddhist teachers, as simply "good friend and guide" to his disciples, Tarthang Tulku recognized that such an approach wins many students but yields questionable results. Consequently, he maintains his traditional role as "guru," never taking more students than he can accommodate. In addition, he has been careful not to allow a "cult of the guru" to develop around his personality, which inhibits any undermining of his effectiveness and value as a teacher. Further, like many Zen Masters, he is constantly concerned with the cultivation of his own religious life, which renders him effective on a continuing basis.

Regarding the practical training afforded by the Tibetan Nyingma Meditation Center, there is little divergence from the traditional practice in Tibet. In other words, beginning students are introduced to both the exoteric and esoteric practices of the tradition. By this procedure it might be claimed that the organization maintains cultural distance and promotes separatism. I suspect, however, that rather than adjust the basic training in order to make it appear more attractive and elementary, the organization retains the methodology and adjusts the explanation. Thus Vajrayāna practice is shown to answer American questions and religious dilemmas just as it did Tibetan ones. The context has changed, not the training. Further, it is not "easy" practice, and no amount of exhortation in flashy phrases and catch sayings will substitute for serious effort on the part of the student.

Tarthang Tulku understands well that Buddhism in America has been handicapped by its lack of community life. In addition, he clearly sees that Buddhism in this country has been primarily a lay movement, and likely will remain as such. As a result, like San Francisco Zen Center, his organization does not require monastic training for its students. Instead, it tries to provide a rich sense of communal belonging through its various activities. Odiyan, when it is completed, may well serve the Tibetan Nyingma Meditation Center just as Zen Mountain Center does San Francisco Zen Center. It will not be an escape to the country, but a balance to city life. And of course, like Zen Mountain Center, it will be totally self-sufficient. Students are not encouraged to flee the city, but rather, all the major centers are being established in metropolitan areas, which is cognizant admission that Buddhism in America is a city movement.

Like other successful Buddhist groups that we have examined in this section, the Tibetan Nyingma Meditation Center is building a solid future on basic Buddhist principles and solid practice. It is a tradition that allows each individual to find humanity in the simplest task and the most humble pursuit. And as each practitioner reaps the benefits of his training, the tradition grows—not by idle talk, but by example.

CHAPTER 11

Vajradhatu and Nalanda Foundation

Let me start the rather longish list of caveats, of warnings, of what Tibetan Buddhism and Tantrism cannot be, or should not be in this country, one of the few in the world where it could take root and flourish. First of all, although I hold an American passport and I vote, since I was not born here I can say that there is one cultural disease in this country, and that is what I call *hypertrophical eclecticism.* . . . Now, just because something is different from Mommy and Daddy, and different from Richard Nixon and Billy Graham, that alone doesn't make it good. Just because it has an Indian accent doesn't make it good. There have to be other criteria.

—Agehananda Bharati[1]

SECTARIAN AFFILIATION

Vajradhatu and Nalanda Foundation represent the two branches, the former being religious and the latter secular, of the organization of Chögyam Trungpa, Rinpoche, a Tibetan lama and ex-monk who was formally trained in the bKa-rgyud-pa tradition of Tibetan Buddhism. The strongest ties of the organization are maintained within this tradition, although not in any formal or required fashion, but Trungpa also maintains some association with the rNying-ma lineage, predominantly due to his training in this area as well.

HISTORY

To a large extent, the history of Vajradhatu and Nalanda Foundation is more appropriately dealt with in the various sections of this chapter devoted solely to these endeavors. Nevertheless, it is possible to outline the basic chronological sequence of the development of Trungpa's organization.

In 1969, several of Chögyam Trungpa's students from Samyê-Ling, his community in Scotland, came to America and founded Tail of the Tiger Meditation Center. This act prepared the way for the coming of the Master, and he arrived in America in 1970. From these humble beginnings, Trungpa has assembled a complex Buddhist community which now rivals any in America. At the outset, there was an air of close informality about the proceedings at Tail of the Tiger. However, in bringing his teaching to this country, Trungpa quickly realized that he must provide more opportunity for Americans to hear what he had to say, and consequently, he set about to offer a series of lectures and seminars in a fashion that would have tired anyone not possessing Trungpa's seemingly boundless energy and stamina.

By September 1971, the horizon began to expand as the Rocky Mountain Dharma Center near Fort Collins, Colorado, was established, and in the following year Karma Dzong was organized in Boulder, Colorado. Trungpa was particularly fond of Colorado and its mountains reminiscent of Tibet, but he divided his time between Tail of the Tiger and Karma Dzong and sped across the country to continue his perpetual series of lectures and seminars, usually held in major cities or in the city centers or Dharmadhatus that he began to establish. In June 1972, the Karma Dzong community began to solidify, with many of its members moving into a fourteen-bedroom townhouse that they obtained. Further acquisitions ensued in 1973, with the donation of a tract of land in the southern Rockies to be utilized for retreats. Also in 1973, his burgeoning community held its first "seminary," an eighty-day intensive period of meditation and study, held in Teton Village, Wyoming. Amid this rigorous schedule, Trungpa continued his prolific writing. Prior to his arrival in America, he had already published two volumes: *Born in Tibet* and *Meditation in Action.* In 1972, however, he published a volume of songs and poems, *Mudra,* and this was followed, in 1973, by *Cutting Through Spiritual Materialism,* perhaps his best-known work.

By 1974, things began to escalate significantly. Maitri, a therapeutic community, was established, and Padma Jong, an arts and crafts community in Mendocino County, California, was added to the fold. The year 1974 also marked the beginning of Trungpa's most ambitious project to date: the beginning of an institute known as Naropa, that was to present an alternative form of education, seeking to integrate intellectual learning with personal growth and development. Following the constructive chaos of Naropa's first summer, Trungpa received a visit in the fall of that year from Gyalwa Karmapa, the head of his sect. Karmapa embarked on a whirlwind cross-country tour, accompanied by his usual entourage, which was exceedingly meaningful for Trungpa's disciples. In spite of the fact that all the arrangements took their toll on Trungpa's health, he pushed ahead when his followers often felt he was near exhaustion. Much impressed by what he saw on his American visit, Karma renamed Tail of the Tiger as Karmê-Chöling and performed the famous black hat ceremony on several occasions.

The year 1975 provided a brief lull, as the organization solidified its various establishments. Naropa Institute held its second summer session, with plans for accreditation as a degree-granting university well underway and program plans progressing. The third Vajradhatu seminary was held, and Trungpa's fame continued to grow through these activities. Distribution of his taped lectures was becoming more widespread through the efforts of his recording staff. The numbers of personal lectures and seminars decreased somewhat, however, as Trungpa began to spend more time in Boulder.

In 1976, all the usual activities continued, but once again Gyalwa Karmapa visited America, and Trungpa published his newest book, *The Myth of Freedom.* Thoroughly exhausted after seven overwhelmingly busy and hectic years in America, and with much of his own work and religious practice to be attended to, Trungpa finally set forth, in March 1977, on a year-long retreat. Apparently he feels that his saṃgha is now ready to stand on its own two feet.

FACILITIES AND STRUCTURE

In his seven short years in America, Chögyam Trungpa has assembled perhaps the most impressive spiritual dynasty of any Buddhist in the West. As Robert Greenfield reports in *The Spiritual Supermarket,* one of Trungpa's students is noted to have said, "He was trained to be a king and he lost his kingdom. Now he's building another."[2] Trungpa has built his organization on pure energy, with the culmination of his efforts resulting in an organizational framework that might affectionately be called a "spiritual Alcoa Aluminum." Although it is atypical of Buddhist groups in America, Trungpa's North American Saṃgha clearly reveals the outcome of combining the organizational skills of a monastic abbot with the teaching flair of a Buddhist well versed in applying upāya or "skill-in-means" to everyday life. It represents one of the most intricate saṃghas currently operative among Buddhists in America.

Vajradhatu
Vajradhatu literally means "the realm of the indestructible" and represents the religious aspect of Chögyam Trungpa's saṃgha. It is the parent organization for many subgroups and thus serves as the coordinating unit for all religious activities. It is located in Boulder, Colorado, having recently occupied a facility renamed Dorje Dzong.

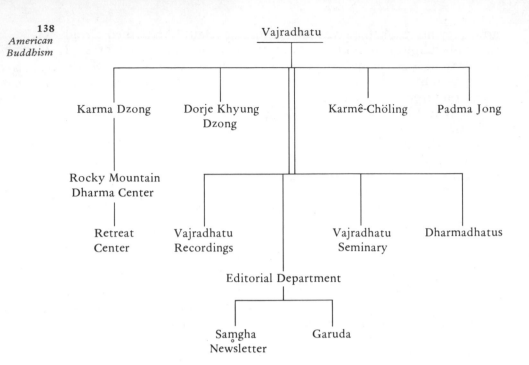

Organizational Structure of Vajradhatu

KARMÊ-CHÖLING. Karmê-Chöling is the chief meditative community of Chögyam Trungpa. Located on 530 acres in Barnet, Vermont, it was (as noted previously) the first center established in America by the group. Its resident community farms some of the land and engages in a rigorous daily schedule that combines work, study, and meditation. Several times each year, Trungpa holds public seminars that help to support the individual center and the parent unit. In addition, the center offers a number of Buddhist practice and study training sessions, lasting from a few days up to ten weeks and conducted by Trungpa or his senior staff. The center is open to visitors and provides facilities for solitary retreats. Further, it administers a Buddhist ministerial studies program (recognized by the Vermont State Department of Education), and is the site of a four-month period of training required of all students enrolled in the Naropa Institute B.A. program in psychology.

KARMA DZONG. Karma Dzong is the Boulder, Colorado, counterpart of Karmê-Chöling. Comprised of approximately 500 members, it is located within the general offices of Vajradhatu. It has a formal, brightly colored meditation hall with provisions for 500 meditators. It also has facilities for meetings and seminars. Most of its members have come to Boulder in order to be closer to their teacher and intensify their training under his guidance. Since Boulder is a reasonably urban area, Karma Dzong members are confronted with the problem of pursuing their religious life in the context of ordinary, daily activity. A full range of programs in study and meditation is offered, and like its sister center, Karmê-Chöling, it is the site of many seminars. Recently, members of the community have formed a Buddhist businessmen's league, reflecting the concerns of the work ethic Trungpa espouses. Some Karma Dzong members still live in the townhouse setting, although the site has changed.

ROCKY MOUNTAIN DHARMA CENTER. Also associated with Karma. Dzong is the Rocky Mountain Dharma Center in Livermore, Colorado, rising to an altitude of 8,000 feet in the northern Rockies. It has a small resident staff which tends to the 350 acres of land, much of which is reserved for meditation retreats. Several seminars have been held on this site, and it is currently under further development. Month-long group retreats, study programs, and short training programs are also conducted. In addition, the facility has a Retreat Center for solitary retreats, usually ranging in duration from several weeks to several months.

PADMA JONG. Padma Jong is an arts and crafts facility located in Dos Rios, California. Situated on 274 acres, this Mendocino County site doubles as a West Coast retreat center and is the center for many training sessions, month-long group retreats, and the like. The primary focus of Padma Jong has been to present a Buddhist approach to the various art forms.

DORJE KHYUNG DZONG. Received as a gift in 1973, Dorje Khyung Dzong rises to 9,000 feet in the Sange de Cristo mountain range of southern Colorado. It is located in the Huerfano Valley on a 240-acre tract of land. Since it is accessible only by jeep, it is used only for solitary retreats.

VAJRADHATU SEMINARY. Vajradhatu Seminary, held each fall beginning in 1973, offers Trungpa's students an opportunity for an eighty-day period of advanced study and practice. During each seminary, periods of intensive sitting meditation (often ten days) are alternated with periods of intensive study. The academic courses are taught by Trungpa's senior students, some of whom also teach at Naropa Institute. In addition to the advantages of the retreat setting, the highlight of each seminary is twofold: Trungpa gives his students their first introduction to the esoteric teachings of Vajrayāna Buddhism, and he offers a course taken by all seminary participants. It is here that Trungpa provides his most detailed and explicit elucidation of Buddhist teaching and practice.

DHARMADHATUS. Dharmadhatu literally means "realm of the Dharma." Dharmadhatus are city centers and thus will be discussed in the section on "Branches and Affiliated Groups."

VAJRADHATU RECORDINGS. Motivated by the double focus of spreading their teacher's doctrines and accruing income for the parent organization, Vajradhatu Recordings offers cassettes of Trungpa's seminars, lectures, and courses. The topic range of these recordings is quite diverse, including talks on such issues as the major figures in Trungpa's teaching lineage, basic Buddhist doctrines and practice, and Trungpa's courses from Naropa Institute. The tapes include not only his formal presentation (which usually last about one hour), but also the question and answer periods which follow. Some videotapes are available as well. Slowly, Vajradhatu Recordings is assembling a collection to match some of the better collections of this type (such as those available from *Psychology Today* or Esalen Institute).

EDITORIAL DEPARTMENT. The Editorial Department of Vajradhatu is primarily responsible for the two major publications of the organization: *Garuda,* a periodical with contributions from Trungpa, many of his advanced students, and many established scholars in various fields, and *Sangha Newsletter,* published biannually and providing general news concerning all aspects of Trungpa's organization. The editorial department is responsible for the professional character of all media issuing from the organization—and they are prolific.

Nalanda Foundation

Nalanda Foundation represents the secular aspect of Chögyam Trungpa's saṃgha. It is named after the famous university in India, which existed from around the fifth to the twelfth centuries A.D. During its period of greatest patronage (from the eighth to twelfth centuries), it was a primary Buddhist center that brought together scholars and practitioners alike.

MAITRI THERAPEUTIC COMMUNITY   The Maitri Therapeutic Community is a training center for "space awareness" which examines the interplay between sanity and neuroses. Founded on practices taken from Vajrayāna Buddhism by Trungpa, it was developed to its present state by the teacher, working in close conjunction with Marvin Casper and others. Located on a ninety-acre former farm in Connecticut (which was donated to Trungpa), Maitri, based on the Buddhist notion of true friendliness (or loving kindness), offers four- and nine-

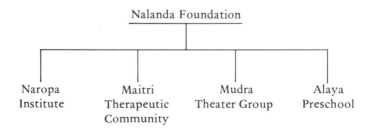

Organizational Structure of Nalanda Foundation

week programs. The program involves working with five rooms, each
of a different shape and color, in which a certain posture is maintained. This practice is felt to express different modes of relating to the world, and after initial exercises, the student focuses on the one or two expressions closest to his own psychological profile. Maitri believes that this practice integrates the way in which one approaches relationships and space. It is done in the context of loving kindness; consequently, one is able to take a warmer, more humorous approach to both sanity and neurosis. The daily routine at Maitri Therapeutic Community includes three hours of sitting meditation, three hours of "space awareness" practice, and further periods of work and study.

MUDRA THEATER GROUP. The Mudra Theater Group emerged from a play written by Chögyam Trungpa: *Prajna.* The play is based on Trungpa's interpretation of a famous Buddhist text: the *Heart-sūtra,* which is said to condense the whole of Mahāyāna Buddhist teaching into one page. The play had its debut at Naropa Institute in the summer of 1974, drawing somewhat less than rave reviews. The play has since been performed in several cities, and a summary of it is presented in *Loka,* edited by Rick Fields. Mudra Theater Group has branches in Boulder, New York, San Francisco, and Berkeley.

ALAYA PRESCHOOL. The preschool is the newest branch of Nalanda Foundation, having opened in January 1977. It is as yet not fully developed.

NAROPA INSTITUTE. According to Robert Greenfield, "the crown jewel of the empire is Naropa Institute, a Buddhist university at which some of the intellectual heavies of Western civilization have agreed to teach."[3] Although a bit dramatic, Mr. Greenfield is not far off. Founded as a reaction against traditional education in America, Naropa Institute seeks to combine the intellectual approach to study with the practice of a "nonverbal humanity," often meditation. Based on the example of the scholar-turned-yogi, Naropa (a greatly revered saint in Trungpa's teaching lineage), and on the balance stressed by Buddhism on the integration of study and practice, Naropa Institute opened its doors in the summer of 1974. During that summer, approximately eighteen hundred students attended the institute, followed by over a thousand in each of the next two summers. Obviously, with no outside funding and support, the financial circumstances are highly problematic. Nevertheless, the curriculum is overwhelming. Courses offered range from beginning and advanced programs in Buddhist languages to extremely solid and valuable training in all forms of dance. It is not at all unusual for a student to be enrolled in one course in Buddhist philosophy, one course in sensory awareness, and one course with Allen Ginsberg, to say nothing of the courses to be audited. Others have already written on the highlights of Naropa Institute in a popular fashion,[4] and it is not my intention to mirror their remarks. Rather, since the positive aspects of Naropa

Institute are both significant and important, it is necessary to elucidate the full range of their offering. It should further be noted that,
although not accredited as yet, the institute has implemented a series
of degree programs. In January 1976, a B.A. in Buddhist studies and
a B.F.A. in Buddhist art (thangka painting) were inaugurated, along
with certificate programs in dance, theater, and poetics, all of these
having been preceded by an M.A. in psychology, begun in June 1975.
Later, a B.A. program in Buddhist psychology was started (June
1976), along with an M.A. in Buddhist studies (January 1977) and an
M.F.A. in Buddhist art. The poetics program, particularly, has been
excellent; teachers have included members of the recently formed
Kerouac School of Disembodied Poets (with such notables as Allen
Ginsberg, Anne Waldman, Philip Whalen, Diane di Prima, and others).
In addition to the "ordinary" courses, the institute presents a series
of workshops and lectures, as well as a series of "intensives," in
which the students live, study, and meditate with each other and the
faculty. The intensive programs grew out of the now defunct
"module" experiment of 1975. In religious matters, the institute
claims to be thoroughly nonsectarian, with teachers of other Buddhist traditions being represented (Joseph Goldstein, who is trained
in Theravādin Vipassanā meditation, is a frequent faculty member, as
are several Zen rōshis).

Naropa Institute, representing the most ambitious enterprise as yet
undertaken by Trungpa, has the potential to provide the vehicle for
many Americans to pursue their academic and intellectual careers
while working towards the personal wholeness that has seemed so
elusive.

In delineating the various aspects of Trungpa's saṃgha, I have been
careful not to associate individuals with any administrative positions.
This situation is not by choice. The organization has been so fluid
that it is simply impossible to keep up with the various structural
changes. For example, in the summer of 1975, the administrative
staff of Naropa Institute was realigned. In the spring of 1977, it again
underwent major changes. Such has also been the case for Karmê-
Chöling, Karma Dzong, and other centers. The entire procedure
appears to be no accident, however. It is part of Trungpa's plan to
keep his students from becoming too comfortable and attached to
any one position. It also has the effect of infusing fresh talent into
different administrative roles, livening up the entire saṃgha. In addition, his senior students are developing multidimensional talents as a
result of this schedule of regular change.

BRANCHES AND AFFILIATED GROUPS

As noted previously, groups associated with Trungpa's organization are called Dharmadhatus. They are city centers where his stu-

dents can come together for the practice of sitting meditation as well as discussions of his teaching. In several cases, these centers provide actual dwelling places for groups of his students. During each year, Trungpa tries to visit each Dharmadhatu, offering a lecture or a seminar, which raises funds for the Dharmadhatu and for Vajradhatu. This has become an increasingly more unmanageable task, however, as the number of communities grows. There are currently about thirty Dharmadhatus in such major American cities as Boston, Chicago, Los Angeles, New York, San Francisco, and Washington, D.C. Some centers are in college towns like Ann Arbor, Michigan, or Bloomington, Indiana, and there are centers in major Canadian cities (for instance, Toronto). In late 1974, a Dharmadhatu conference was held in Boulder with over fifty Dharmadhatu representatives in attendance. Not only were "teaching packages" for centers discussed, but also such subjects as the intricacies of finances and fund raising. It is not unusual for Dharmadhatu members to attend Naropa Institute, the Vajradhatu seminary, training sessions at the various major centers, or similar programs, thus maintaining a sense of continuity within the organization.

KEY MEMBERS AND/OR PERSONNEL

Trungpa's Early Years

Chögyam Trungpa was born in February 1939 in the small village of Geje in northeastern Tibet. During the prior year, the supreme abbot of Surmang Monasteries (the tenth Trungpa Tulku) had died, and with his passing, the search began for his incarnation, to be enthroned as the eleventh Trungpa Tulku. To aid in the search for the incarnation, support was sought from Gyalwa Karmapa, the head of the bKa-rgyud sect of Tibetan Buddhism. While visiting Pepung Monastery in eastern Tibet, Gyalwa Karmapa was again prompted to offer assistance, this time through the entreaty of Jamgön Kongtrül, Rinpoche, a devoted disciple of the deceased tenth Trungpa Tulku. Shortly thereafter, Karmapa is said to have had a vision, which ultimately led to Chögyam Trungpa. After passing all the appropriate tests, he was enthroned, at the age of thirteen months, as the supreme abbot of Surmang Monasteries. Being under the age required to take monk's ordination vows, Trungpa was allowed only to take the vows of a layman (upāsaka).

At the age of three, the new Trungpa Tulku was taken to visit his mother's village, but shortly returned to Düdtsi-til Monastery to begin his formal training. This involved not only reading and writing in the Tibetan system, but also included his beginning studies of Buddhism in all its aspects and the meditational practices followed by his school. At age eight, he was given the novice (śramaṇera) ordination by Jamgön Kongtrül of Pepung, and at age eleven he took the Bodhisattva Vow, common to all Mahāyānists and Vajrayānists. Shortly thereafter, Trungpa began the preliminary practices of Vajrayāna

Buddhism (the general school to which his sect belonged), involving 100,000 full prostrations, 100,000 recitations of the Refuge formula, 100,000 recitations of the Vajrasattva mantra, 100,000 symbolic offerings, and 100,000 recitations of the mantra of Guru Yoga (the practice of union with the teacher). Incumbent on all Vajrayāna practitioners is extensive training under the tutelage of a guru who serves as the disciple's "spiritual friend" (kalyāṇamitra). In this regard, the Trungpa Tulku became a disciple of Jamgön Kongtrül of Sechen, and remained as such until his flight from Tibet. Throughout his teens, the young abbot of Surmang Monasteries continued his study and practice of Vajrayāna, but also fulfilled the obligations required of his ecclesiastical position.

The Holocaust and the Flight into Exile

By the mid-1950s, the political situation in Tibet was becoming quite desperate. With the Chinese Communists advancing in all directions, much concern was felt for both the future of Tibet and the future of Buddhism in the country. Although it was during this period that Trungpa passed his kyorpön examinations (equivalent to a doctorate) and also received the khenpo degree (master of studies), no solace could be taken in these significant achievements since the future of Surmang Monasteries was in serious jeopardy. Faced with a staggering burden for a teenager, Trungpa sought advice from Gyalwa Karmapa, Jamgön Kongtrül of Sechen, and an old friend, Dingo Chentze, Rinpoche. The ensuing replies offered no real advice. Gyalwa Karmapa provided no hints at the proper course of action, other than to continue in spiritual work. Dingo Chentze, Rinpoche, replied in poetry that mirrored Karmapa's response, and word was relayed that Jamgön Kongtrül of Sechen had been captured by the Communists.

By early 1959, with the Communists exceedingly anxious to capture high-ranking ecclesiastical officials, it was necessary to go into hiding, waging a touch-and-go battle with discovery by the Chinese. Shortly thereafter, the decision to flee was made, and with a small party, few provisions, and little but bare courage, the journey to India began. The details of this journey are related in a most stirring fashion in *Born in Tibet* and, needless to say, portray a high adventure in which the stakes were not simply the lives of a few young refugees, but rather the cultural and religious heritage of an entire country. By the time Trungpa and his party reached India in mid-January 1960, he was more than just a newly ordained monk (he took full monk's vows at age twenty) who had fled the Chinese Communists, for Trungpa (and the other incarnate lamas) represented an unbroken religious teaching lineage that had existed in a uniform pattern for over nine centuries.

Trungpa Leaves the East

The post-Holocaust experience for the Tibetan has largely focused around refugee communities in India, Sikkim, Nepal, and Bhutan (as noted in the previous chapter). During his stay in India, Trungpa continued his study and practice and, along with his friend Akong Tulku, was tutored in English by a marvelous English woman who had recently been ordained a nun in the Karma bKa-rgyud sect of Tibetan Buddhism. When a Spaulding scholarship afforded Trungpa an opportunity to study at Oxford, he left India and pursued studies in art, psychology, and comparative religion. In April 1967, Trungpa took over Johnstone House Contemplative Community in Scotland and founded Samyê-Ling, thus launching his career devoted to bringing Buddha's Dharma to the West. After a brief visit to India in 1969, Trungpa was injured in an automobile accident in May 1969, which led to a debilitating paralysis on the left side of his body. It was this injury, and a keen insight into Western culture, that led to Trungpa's taking off his monk's robes and returning to lay life. He hoped that stripping himself of the "exotic" features of Oriental tradition would enable him to deliver his message in a fashion more appropriate to the culture of his residence. After marrying in January 1970, he was led to America to reside at Tail of the Tiger Meditation Center.

Following the publication of *Born in Tibet* in 1966, Trungpa built a reputation as one of the most prolific writers on Buddhism to appear in the West. While recovering from his 1969 automobile accident, Trungpa published *Meditation in Action,* a book based on a series of taped talks presented at Samyê-Ling. *Meditation in Action* has proved most valuable for students of Buddhist meditation, in that the book addresses the significant questions regarding the applicability of meditation to daily living situations. It dispels the mystical aura that has surrounded Buddhist teachings in the West and describes four of the well-known perfections (pāramitās) of Mahāyāna Buddhism in psychological as well as religious terminology. Further, it is prototypic of all other Trungpa publications (with one exception) in that it presents in written form the oral teachings of this Tantric practitioner. The one exception to this rule of distilling books for publication from seminar and lecture tapes is *Mudra,* published in 1972. *Mudra* is a slender volume of scarcely one hundred pages, presenting many of the songs and poems of the teacher, all composed since 1959. Rather than presenting the Buddhist teachings in a formal manner, this volume is the exemplification of the manner in which the Buddhist ideals have come to permeate the thoughts and actions of Chögyam Trungpa.

Perhaps the most forceful of all Trungpa's books is *Cutting Through Spiritual Materialism,*[5] published in 1973. Edited by John Baker and Marvin Casper from a series of talks given in the fall of 1971 and the spring of 1972 at Karma Dzong, the book is "the author's attempt to outline (and hopefully combat) the 'numerous sidetracks which lead to a distorted, ego-centered version of spirituality,' which he coins as 'spiritual materialism.'"[6] Since Trungpa's own teaching lineage considers the Tantric practice of the Vajrayāna school of Buddhism to be the essence of Buddhist teaching, we might expect *Cutting Through Spiritual Materialism* to be a summary of these teachings and practices. A rather contrary picture emerges from the pages of the book. Trungpa clearly understands that before what he considers to be the pinnacle of Buddhist practice can be introduced to the American scene, a firm foundation must be laid for these teachings. Consequently, the book is filled with basic Buddhist doctrine. Often comparing the growth of Buddhism to the growth of flowers, the author comments on the importance of cultivating the soil, planting the seeds, and exercising care and caution in tending the young plants. Trungpa's latest book, *The Myth of Freedom,* further expands his teaching on the American scene, but covers much the same territory as his previous works.[7]

Trungpa has often been a contributor to *Garuda* and *Maitreya,* two journals published by Shambhala Publications, Incorporated. It also should be noted that Trungpa has been a frequent collaborator with other scholars. The year 1975 marked the publication of two works in this direction: *The Dawn of Tantra,* written with Professor Herbert V. Guenther, and *The Tibetan Book of the Dead,* with Francesca Fremantle. The former is the outgrowth of a seminar held in Berkeley, California, in 1972, with excerpts from a Trungpa seminar in San Francisco in 1973 and a Guenther lecture in Boulder in 1973. The latter volume integrates Trungpa's seminar on *The Tibetan Book of the Dead,* held at Tail of the Tiger in the summer of 1971, with Francesca Fremantle's new translation of the Tibetan text. We are likely to see Trungpa at his technical best if the non-Tantra portions of his Vajradhatu Seminary lectures are edited for publication. Unedited versions are currently circulating among his various communities, and although they are not free from a few technical errors, they present a more substantial statement of Buddhist doctrine than he has previously offered. They also present a side of the teacher that few of his students had anticipated: Trungpa as scholar.

Several years ago I began preparing materials for a course designed to study the similarities and differences between Shamanism and Tibetan Buddhism. In trying to consider my students' pleas for relevancy, I elected to focus on the then current counterculture hero Don Juan as the exemplification of modern Shamanism, and on Chögyam Trungpa as representative of the Tibetan situation. Being somewhat naïve and ambitious, I wrote to Trungpa, informing him of my plans and requesting that he visit the class to deliver a lecture or two. Shortly thereafter, I received a letter in which Trungpa thanked me for my interest and noted that he would come to lecture if I thought it important. Of course I immediately responded that it was indeed important, and anxiously awaited his reply regarding formalized arrangements. To be sure, no response came. Again I wrote, asking if perhaps my letter had been misplaced. Again I received no response. I have learned in the subsequent years that this is commonplace when one enters the domain of Chögyam Trungpa.

My first meeting with Chögyam Trungpa took place in mid-June 1974, shortly before the first session of Naropa Institute was scheduled to open. Like all faculty who were new to him, we were each afforded a formal introduction and a few moments of his time. Curiously enough, each new introduction seemed to bring with it a new interpretation of some aspect of his personality. For some faculty members, finding the head of the saṃgha with a cocktail in his hand was disappointing, as Buddhist laymen's vows prohibit the taking of intoxicants. For others, the sheer joy of meeting the accomplished Master was overwhelming. For all, he was impressive, although there appeared to be parity between positive and negative responses. It takes but a few moments of careful study to reveal that Trungpa is a composite of contradictions. At once he is powerful and perceptive with his rather opaque, dark eyes that reveal very little, while at the same time he conveys a sense of pliability, of softness, hardly consonant with his role as director of this growing empire.

The contradictions that circumscribe the life of Chögyam Trungpa pervade virtually all aspects of his routine and duties. Revolving around the dual poles of his role as guru in the Buddhist sense of spiritual friend and his instrumentation of the teachings, he is impossible to predict, likely to be inconsistent, always concerned with dispelling the expectations of his students, and playful as one would expect from a teacher hailed by his followers to be a fully realized Tantric siddha ("perfected one"). Since he represents for many of his students the embodiment of Buddha's Dharma (and for some of them, the only contact with Buddhism that they have had), he is treated with an awesome reverence. For overly deferential students, Trungpa picks away at the underpinnings of their portly respect with a biting sense of humor. For students who take his teachings too literally, he relies on the reductio ad absurdum dialectics of the famous Buddhist philosopher Nāgārjuna to dismantle their misunderstanding.

My own impressions of Trungpa, in spite of rather inauspicious beginnings, nevertheless remain reasonably positive. He presents a contagious and genuine warmth, offered freely and openly. He also makes no apologies for himself or any aspect of his behavior (which is not always exemplary). He makes no promises that he cannot fulfill and does his best to promote a strong sense of equanimity in his community. The community's self-reliance was severely tested when the master embarked on a year-long retreat beginning in March 1977. In his stead he empowered Thomas Rich (Ösel Tendzin) as "Vajra Regent," to act on his behalf during his absence.

MEMBERSHIP

No statistics are published concerning the size or growth rate of Trungpa's saṃgha, and no demographic materials are available. Nevertheless, it is possible to make some observations which speak to these matters. First of all, the saṃgha is growing quite rapidly. In the early days of his career in America, Trungpa traveled so intensely and lectured so often that these techniques brought in many disciples. Now, however, he travels and lectures less, but his books have circulated so widely that many of his disciples had their first contact with him through his many volumes and simply followed up on their positive response. It is not unusual for many who claim to be disciples of Trungpa, Rinpoche, to have never met their "teacher." There is an overwhelming diversity in the age and background of saṃgha members. They are, however, uniformly well educated, and he attracts a large number of professionals, particularly persons from academia. The sexes seem to be about evenly split. An inordinate number of his community members come from Jewish backgrounds, resulting in the slang phrase "Buddhish" (a contraction of Buddhist and Jewish) for identifying many disciples. There are few blacks or other minorities in the organization, but quite recently a black was appointed Executive Director of Karmê-Chöling. The Dharmadhatus serve as a breeding ground for new members, and in this regard their activities have proved thoroughly successful. Many of the Dharmadhatus offer quite complete programs for beginners. It is clear that the image to be projected on the part of community officials is one of professionalism, witnessed in both the style and dress of the various administrators. On the position of membership in general, Trungpa takes a hard line on the definition of what constitutes a Buddhist. This is captured in a passage from a recent Rick Fields article:

> Since virtually none of the members of Karma Dzong, the buddhist community in Boulder, was a born buddhist, the question of what it means to be "buddhist" is the subject of some discussion. The most popular interpretation in the new American sangha is that it means to *practice* buddhism, but Trungpa's instructions at one refuge ceremony were shockingly blunt: "When you go into the hospital," he said, "and they ask what your religion is, you sign "buddhist" on the dotted line."[8]

KEY AND/OR SPECIAL DOCTRINES

Although the major doctrines of Trungpa's teaching conform to the basic tenets of the bKa-rgyud school of Tibetan Buddhism, it must be said that his approach to their elucidation is thoroughly unorthodox. In other words, he transmutes traditional explications of the doctrine into language which a Western audience can easily understand, and this invariably means utilizing a vocabulary that is heavily laden with psychological terminology and American idioms. The approach is not unlike the notion of "matching concepts" (ko-i), which was employed as an explanatory device when Buddhism first moved from India to China and sought to match Buddhist ideas with similar concepts in Chinese thought. This approach reveals some pitfalls,

however. For example, Trungpa's exegesis of the constituents of the
human being is highly problematic. Traditionally, the human being is said to be composed of five aggregates or "skandhas": form (rūpa), feeling (vedanā), perception (saṃjñā), mental constituents (saṃskāras), and consciousness (vijñāna). Apart from Trungpa noting the five to be ignorance-form, feeling, perception-impulse, concept, and consciousness, which is unsupportable from a textual standpoint, he examines the origins of the aggregates in a most unusual fashion. Originally, he claims, there was completely open space. "We *are* this space, we are *one* with it, with vidya, intelligence and openness."[9] He then goes on to indicate the mode by which, through *self-consciousness*, the aggregates emerge from this so-called open space.

On the one hand, no Buddhist text identifies open space as the single item of ontological ultimacy. Several Buddhist schools note space (ākāśa) to be one of several unconditioned elements (asaṃskṛta dharmas), but only in conjunction with others, and the "others" vary from tradition to tradition. On the other hand, by identifying what we might loosely refer to as a first cause, he violates one of the most cardinal doctrines of Buddhism, namely, dependent origination (pratītya-samutpāda), which expressly states that Buddhism posits no first cause.

All of Trungpa's explanations are understandable in the light of his quest for presenting a psychological approach and explanation of the world and ourselves, but they are often textually unsound. We are thus faced with the perhaps irresolvable issue of how much latitude is allowed in transposing Buddhist doctrines to the American mind-set. The matter is further complicated when we consider that for Buddhism, the primary target of our effort is to eliminate our bondage to pain or suffering (duḥkha) by eliminating its cause: craving (tṛṣṇā), as well as its concomitant: grasping (upādāna). In a society dominated by dreams of acquisition and case on both the material and spiritual planes, this quest becomes exceedingly difficult to convey. For Trungpa, the matter is approached with a showman's flair for undermining the very substance of the quest: The antidote is hopelessness. Robert Greenfield cites an example from a seminar:

"What we haven't hit on here at all is the notion of hopelessness. Not at all! There is no hope. None whatsoever. We have no chance so long as we possess our body and our face, we have no way we can get liberated at all. Absolutely no hope. We are drowning in a deep pool of shit, an ocean of shit, bubbling and grey in color. Drowning all the time. True!" he says with emotion. "Hopeless! Absolutely hopeless."

"Who dreamed up God?" he asks rhetorically, without pausing for breath. "Who had the idea for enlightenment? Who proclaimed himself to be God on earth? The whole thing is full of shit, if I may use such a term. Full of dung. Scriptures, textbooks, magical displays are not going to help us. They only increase complete ignorance."

"That we haven't given up hope, that's our problem actually. No one has given up hope of attaining enlightenment or getting out of suffering. We are conned by all kinds of trips and spiritual suggestions, by our own ignorance and egos. . . ."

"I am afraid," he says, "that this is very boring. Buddhism is the only religion that doesn't promise anything. Only suggests we work with ourselves fundamentally. . . . Maybe we can have a discussion, if you don't feel too depressed."[10]

On the surface, apart from the colorful language, Trungpa seems to stress disavowal for the possibility of the goal: nirvāṇa. When I confronted Trungpa with just this issue, he clearly proclaimed his affirmation of the Third and Fourth Noble Truths, namely, that there is both a goal and a path to it. How then do we reconcile this apparent disparity? We can offer two suggestions, one textual and one practical (although there is considerable overlap). Buddhist texts, particularly of the Mahāyāna and Vajrayāna traditions, stress the employment, as a teaching device, of the notion of "skillful means" (upāya). For the Buddhist practitioner, attainment of intuitive wisdom (prajñā) alone is a rather empty attainment without the proper mode of applicability to the multifaceted aspects of one's life. Thus, skill-in-means becomes the critical factor for the teacher in transmitting the teachings. It requires that each teacher must be able to "size up the situation" and react accordingly. In this regard, Buddha is often compared to a physician who manifests remarkable skill in not only the diagnostic but also the prescriptive aspects of his craft. It would seem that Trungpa has diagnosed the illness properly: craving and grasping at the hope of gaining spiritual advancement, of gaining enlightenment. It is, of course, the standard, orthodox diagnosis. By characterizing and highlighting the symptoms of the disease in the most outlandish terminology possible, Trungpa feels that he helps undercut the basis of his students' misguided, even if noble, expectations. The paradoxical nature of his statements is resolved through the practical aspects of his prescription: meditation (about which we shall say more in the next section of this chapter).

In other regards, Trungpa is more orthodox. For example, he emphasizes strongly in his teachings the "Three Yāna Principle" of Tibetan Buddhism. In this notion, Hīnayāna refers to the "narrow path," Mahāyāna the "open path," and Vajrayāna the "unity of goal and path," with all of these terms being psychological metaphors. For the Vajrayānist, the two previous expressions of Buddhism represent, in addition to their historical, philosophical, and sociological roles, necessary psychological stages of preparation for the practice of Tantra. Thus Hīnayāna and Mahāyāna are doubly important, having integrity for their own contributions to the development of Buddhism in general, and for their status as a necessary precursor to Tantric practice. Many of Trungpa's students, in diverging from his orthodox teaching, focus only on the psychological aspects of these traditions, from Vajrayānist perspective, and conclude that since they are but preliminaries to Tantric practice, they must be inherently inferior traditions on all levels of inquiry. In addition to falling

into the trap of spiritual materialism, by mixing the proverbial apples
and oranges, they lose sight of the fact that history, philosophy, sociology, and psychology are complex categories even when ana- lyzed by experts. In the hands of novices, conclusions unwarranted by their teacher are evidenced, thus undermining any ecumenicism for their organization—or at least any that is not patronizingly offered.

When asked about the nature of his teachings, Trungpa often makes an analogy to the construction of a dwelling place. First the foundation is poured, then the home is built, and finally the roof is constructed over the dwelling, rendering it secure. He has established the foundation by teaching basic Buddhism to his disciples. He is, by his own estimate, currently building the home by having introduced many students to Tantric practice. He also comments that it is not important whether or not he is around for the final dedication. When asked about the misconceptions of his students, many of which arise from his unorthodox interpretations of Buddhist doctrine, he answers back in Tantric dialogue: "Well, I think some of them are working through it."

RITUALS, SERVICES, AND PRACTICES

The practices utilized by Chögyam Trungpa's organization are two- fold: On the one hand, an integrated program of meditation, work, and study is followed, and on the other, a series of ritual ceremonies are performed.

The beginning aspects of Trungpa's meditational system are quite similar to those of other Buddhist schools. It focuses on what is traditionally referred to as śamatha or "calming, quieting" practice. The technique involves spending several hours per day engaged in paying attention, while seated on the meditation cushion, to one's breath. According to Trungpa, this is a powerful technique for dis- pelling hopes of trances, mystical attainments and powers, and instant enlightenment. It causes the practitioner to confront the enormous amount of "mental clutter" that prohibits one from gain- ing the bare, precise attention necessary to proceed on the path. The daily meditational period is usually augmented by frequent involve- ment in extended sitting practice, aimed at allowing the meditator to confront the strictures of his or her own ego. Thus, as the meditator, conditioned by his or her own hopes of exotic attainments, con- stantly finds these expectations unfulfilled, the rationalized practice of "pretending to meditate" gradually gives rise to more substantial involvement. Extended sitting practice usually takes one of three forms: Nyinthuns, Dathuns, or retreats. Nyinthun is an all-day sitting practice, usually from early in the morning to mid-evening. Periods of sitting meditation are interspersed with periods of walking meditation, and breaks are taken to eat and do minimal work. A Dathun is simply a month-long series of Nyingthuns, but intensified not only by the longer duration of the practice, but by the added discipline of taking meals in silence in the meditation hall and maintaining a serious mind-set throughout. Dathuns are held only at the major contemplative centers, while Nyinthuns are held in all communities, including Dharmadhatus. Retreats are often conducted for periods of from several weeks up to several months. They are carried out in isolation, at appropriate facilities, with the added rigor that the removal of usual social intercourse creates.

Needless to say, some of Trungpa's students do indeed advance beyond the stage of basic śamatha practice, through the insight stage (vipaśyanā) that follows, and into Tantric practices. Most of the Tantric practice groups are now engaged in the foundation practices of fulfilling, 100,000 times each: full prostrations, recitation of the Three Jewels, recitation of the Vajrasattva mantra, symbolic offerings, and recitation of the mantra of Guru Yoga. A few students have completed the foundation practices and are ready for the more advanced Tantric teaching, about which little can be said. Since the saṃgha has grown so large, Trungpa is not now able to provide personal meditation instruction to all his students. Personal interviews are quite rare for most. Consequently, many of his senior students have been certified to teach beginning meditation practice.

Study for Trungpa's students is encouraged in several ways. Many students are urged to continue in school, and others are urged to pursue formal graduate study in accredited universities. Dharmadhatus often have their own study programs, and many students annually make the trek to Naropa Institute. Seminars are still offered, either by Trungpa or his senior students. This is combined with great emphasis on holding responsible jobs in society. The highest integration of these activities occurs at the annual Vajradhatu Seminary, where in 1976 there were eight hundred applications for one hundred positions. Training programs emphasizing meditation, study, or both, are regularly offered at all the major centers of the saṃgha.

Ritual ceremonies are stressed less by Chögyam Trungpa than by most other Buddhist teachers in America. He has stated many times that involvement with traditional Tibetan culture is too often a seducing influence on Americans, causing them to get lost in the exotica. Too often they attempt to become Tibetan, according to Trungpa. In some of his earliest seminars in America, he referred to the image of trying to wear Tibetan brocade on one's bluejeans, resulting in a patchwork that did not quite appear consistent. Nevertheless, two major ceremonies are retained: that of taking Refuge in the Three Jewels and the Bodhisattva Ceremony. Each of these is a beautiful occasion, mixing the solemnity and seriousness of formal commitment to Buddhism with great joy and humor. As with other events, Trungpa is almost always quite late to perform these rituals. For many, his lateness is a last opportunity for the prospective Bud-

dhist to reconsider this serious undertaking. For each ceremony, the
person receives a new "Dharma name" symbolic of his entry onto a new path, and these Dharma names are always Tibetan. Many of Trungpa's senior students have abandoned their English names altogether. Trungpa sees these two ceremonies as progressive stages on the path, with the taking of Refuge being quite preliminary. After taking Refuge, one can still change one's mind and disavow association with Buddhism, but the Bodhisattva Vow marks the stage of no turning back. Consequently, considerably less discretion is used in offering Refuge. It is standard practice for gifts to be offered to the teacher on these occasions, ranging from record albums to rather large donations. Since 1974, when Gyalwa Karmapa first visited America, performing the Black Hat Ceremony in several cities, Trungpa's students have been increasingly more aware of the complex ritual aspect of the Tibetan Buddhist tradition.

FUTURE PLANS

It is both easy and difficult to speculate on the future plans of Trungpa's organization. Obviously, solidification and expansion are prime concerns for the saṃgha. On the other hand, one never knows quite which direction the expansion will take, with new enterprises often resulting from spontaneous notions arising in Trungpa's fertile and creative mind. It does seem clear that he is allowing the organization to function more and more without reliance on him.

PUBLICATIONS

The organization itself does not publish very much, apart from the usual publicity brochures. They do, however, publish *Garuda* (in conjunction with Shambhala) and the *Sangha Newsletter*. They have in addition arranged for the publication of many other items. Two volumes of *Loka* (a journal from Naropa Institute) have been published by Anchor Books, and they handle all the various tapes that have been distributed, as well as having an almost completed film on the life of Milarepa.

Apart from *Born in Tibet*, published originally by Penguin, all of Trungpa's books are published by Shambhala Publications, Inc. The list is quite formidable, and includes: *Meditation in Action, Mudra, Cutting Through Spiritual Materialism, Visual Dharma, The Myth of Freedom, The Dawn of Tantra* (with Herbert Guenther), and *The Tibetan Book of the Dead* (with Francesca Fremantle).

We can anticipate future publications from Trungpa, Rinpoche, as well as the continuation of the organization's usual offerings.

CONCLUDING REMARKS

Perhaps the one single word that best describes the movement surrounding Chögyam Trungpa is *growth*. Trungpa and his organization realize that to make any significant impact on America, a substantial community is a prime requisite. And with the exception of the Nichiren Shōshū movement, Trungpa's saṃgha has grown faster than any other in this decade. Now, in the late 1970s, the organization is just beginning to learn that unrestricted growth presents as many problems as no growth at all.

While his array of students represent a living testimonial to the efficacy of Trungpa's teaching in America, they also distort it seriously, and along with it, one's image of Trungpa as well. During 1974, when I began to notice that many of his students attempted to copy his speech patterns, drinking habits, and even his sexual proclivities (which results in a boundless flow of rumors and gossip), I mentioned these problems to him and met with his usual response: "Well, I think some of them are working through it." He then referred to the old axiom applied to gurus: a guru is like a fire; if you remain too distant, there is not enough heat, while if you get too close, you get burned. This sort of response provides one with the impression that amid all the chaos, Chögyam Trungpa has, to some degree, lost touch with what is going on in his communities.

Trungpa is an acknowledged meditation master in both the bKa-rgyud and rNying-ma traditions of Tibetan Buddhism. Like all young lamas in these traditions, Trungpa was thoroughly schooled in all aspects of Buddhism. His scholarship, however, is the most difficult aspect of his training for his students to understand. Rather than focusing on the balance between study and practice sanctioned by Buddhism in general and their teacher in particular, his students are often victims of a serious misunderstanding that results in a transparent anti-intellectualism. Examples of the above could be cited continuously, but one significant one serves well to illustrate the point. At a recent conference on "The Flowering of Buddhism in America," held at Syracuse University on April 15–17, 1977, in response to audience questions about the nature of Trungpa's teaching and Tibetan Buddhism, the representatives of Vajradhatu and Nalanda Foundation consistently offered only one response: it was impossible to speak about Buddhism apart from sitting meditation. In other words, serious and well-intended questions *about* Buddhism were answered with evasive suggestions that the questioners would *only* find the solutions when they actually did sitting meditation. And while the representatives of Trungpa's saṃgha were impeccably dressed, spoke like mirror images of the master, and looked very insightful, they seemed to rely on what is rapidly becoming a commonplace practice among some Buddhist groups: when you do not have a satisfactory answer, plead the evils of conceptualized approaches. Only when the students of Chögyam Trungpa begin to find a proper balance between their study and practice of Buddhism, resulting in a community of practitioners who are at home with their new religious commitment, their role in society, and themselves, will we be able to say that Trungpa's teaching has been actualized.

In seeking to find a new cultural amalgam that represents the best of Tibetan Buddhism and American religiosity, Trungpa has sought to find the proper "blend" of rigorous meditation practice and meaningful explanatory devices. For many he has done just that. Others, however, have reacted without the sympathy he evokes from his disciples. Chögyam Trungpa's saṃgha has a potentially great future in America. It offers to many a reasonable way in which to accept the expectations of our society and culture, while cultivating their own religious growth in a meaningful fashion. It also has the potential to do serious harm to the Dharma in America through its inherent shortcomings. It will take at least another decade before an accurate accounting can be given in this case.

CHAPTER 12

Shasta Abbey

Leaving Japan for America,
Sea stretches out into sea, mountains into mountains.
Where is the center of the water?
Where is the destination of clouds?
I do not know!
My heart tells me there is a happy field in the American land.
I presume myself to be a follower of old Columbus.

—Soyen Shaku[1]

SECTARIAN AFFILIATION

Shasta Abbey is cast in the Sōtō tradition of Japanese Zen Buddhism, but is not now affiliated with it formally. In order to identify the origins of the organization without making undue confusions with the Japanese, the organization refers to itself as "The Reformed Sōtō Zen Church."[2]

HISTORY

Shasta Abbey is an outgrowth of the Zen Mission Society, begun in Japan as the "Foreign Guest Department" of Sōjiji Temple, one of the chief teaching temples of the Sōtō Zen tradition. The department had been established in 1963 by the Very Reverend Chisan Kōhō Zenji, Chief Abbot of Sōjiji Temple, with the intent of instructing

Western visitors in Zen. Jiyu Kennett, one of the abbot's chief disciples, was responsible for directing the activities of the Foreign Guest
Department. When Kōhō Zenji died in 1967, the operation was
moved to Umpukuji in Mie-ken, Kennett's temple. Since Jiyu Kennett was English by birth, it was her teacher's wish that she eventually
return to the West, and in 1969, she came to America with two
Western disciples. Originally, the Zen Mission Society in America was
located in San Francisco, but as it expanded in size it moved to Oakland. The initial locations were meant to be temporary, however, as
the organization intended to establish a monastery suitable for use as
a seminary to train Zen Buddhist priests. A proper site was located
near Mt. Shasta in northern California, and in November 1970, the
Zen Mission Society officially opened with Jiyu Kennett Rōshi as
abbess and director.

As noted above, the Zen Mission Society intended to serve as a
training monastery for Zen Buddhist priests. By March 1973, there
were twenty-five priests and priest trainees in residence, and ten on
leave of absence. There is a clear nondiscrimination policy at the
abbey with regard to race or gender, and all trainees are free to marry.
In fact, by the March 1973 date listed above, there were three married couples residing at the facility, with each member of each marriage being a member of the priesthood. Although primarily a
program for the priesthood, laymen are welcome for training periods
of three to six months.

The program of study and training undertaken by the residents of
the organization includes the traditional practice of zazen, services,
ceremonies, classes in Zen training, and work. Emphasizing that Buddhist experience must be applicable to everyday life, the monastery
attempts to inculcate this ideal in its functioning. Further, in acknowledging that most of its residents are from a Western background, the organization claims that all teaching and training is done
in this context. It also registers and qualifies its own priests, highlighting its independence from the Japanese tradition.

The Zen Mission Society continued to expand its facilities throughout the early 1970s and by 1973 included a Main Hall, several shrines,
a cloister, and gardens. This expansion has been and still is an on-
going process. In 1974 the society dedicated its cemetery, the first
in the West to serve a specifically Buddhist community. The following year it opened Kannon Dell to provide facilities for married residents. In 1976, the organization officially changed its name to Shasta
Abbey.

Throughout its history, Shasta Abbey has been interested in opening branch communities; it has affiliates in the United States, Canada,
and England. Since 1970, it has published a journal, now known as
The Journal of Shasta Abbey, and pursues a vigorous program of lectures, periodic retreats, and the like, as well as its regular training
program. Further, Shasta Abbey has joined with other Buddhist centers in the West to found the North American Association of Bud-

dhist Seminaries and Monasteries. This organization not only disseminates information, but also serves in an accreditation capacity.

FACILITIES AND STRUCTURE

Shasta Abbey is located on sixteen acres of land in the Shasta-Trinity National Forest, at the foot of Black Butte Mountain. The major facilities include Shasta Abbey itself and the auxiliary Kannon Dell.

Shasta Abbey includes seventeen basic buildings. Three of these are dedicated as shrines. First, there is the Zendo. The Zendo serves to accommodate not only meditation, but also morning, evening, and vesper services, as well as formal meals and special ceremonies. The Zendo is the hub of the organization's activities. Second, there is the Founder's Shrine. This hall is dedicated to Kennett Rōshi's teacher, Chisan Kōhō Zenji, and is the site of a daily memorial service. Third, there is the Kannon Shrine. Dedicated to the Bodhisattva Avalokiteśvara, this building is utilized for weddings, memorials, and occasionally as an extra meditation hall. Five buildings serve functional purposes in the running and maintenance of Shasta Abbey: a sewing room, laundry, tool shed, store room, and library. The library boasts a 2,500 volume collection, including a complete set of the Taishō Tripiṭaka. Eight buildings are used as residences, but parts of the various buildings serve as a bakery, infirmary, crafts room, and a meeting and class room for laymen and junior monks. The final building to be described is second in size to the Zendo. In addition to functioning as the office, kitchen, and dining room, it serves as a common room and class room for the senior monks. A cloister connects all of the buildings. The cemetery occupies about two acres, and about one acre is reserved for gardening, as Shasta Abbey produces most of its own food during the summer months.

Kannon Dell is situated on twenty acres of land. Its lone building is the former Mt. Shasta railway station. The building was moved and renovated so as to provide residence for four married couples. It also has kitchen and bath facilities, as well as a nursery and school room. The organization hopes to be able to expand Kannon Dell as a housing facility, in the short term, as well as utilizing some of its land for farming. Long-range plans include a retirement community, nursing home, and other facilities consonant with a complete Buddhist community.

BRANCHES AND AFFILIATED GROUPS

Shasta Abbey has several branches. Three are in England: Throssel Hole Priory, the London Zen Priory, and the Mousehole Buddhist

Group. Throssel Hole Priory was dedicated in June 1972 and is a monastery in Northumberland, on eighteen acres of land. The London Zen Priory and the Mousehole Buddhist Group (in Cornwall) are less complete facilities. There are also two branches in the United States: the Berkeley Buddhist Priory and the Saginaw Zen Priory (in Cottage Grove, Oregon).

Groups holding regular meditation also meet in California (Santa Rosa, Santa Barbara, and Los Angeles) and Oregon (Ashland and Portland). Further, retreats are on occasion held in Canada (Vancouver and Toronto), Washington (Seattle), California (Santa Cruz and San Diego), Montana (Missoula), and England.

While the priories are more formal organizations, housing a qualified priest, all branches and affiliated groups are functionally autonomous. They remain in close contact with Shasta Abbey, but are in no way dependent on the parent organization.

KEY MEMBERS AND/OR PERSONNEL

The founder of Shasta Abbey is Jiyu Kennett Rōshi. She was born as Peggy Teresa Nancy Kennett on January 1, 1924, in St. Leonards-on-Sea, Sussex, England, to Buddhist parents. At age sixteen, under her father's influence, she entered the Theravāda saṃgha and proceeded to study with various monks from Southeast Asia who happened to be in London. Occasional visits from D.T. Suzuki facilitated her study of Zen. For many years she was a professional organist (1945–1958), eventually gaining a Bachelor of Music degree from

Jiyu Kennett Rōshi (Photo courtesy of Shasta Abbey.)

Durham University in 1961. During this period she became involved with the London Buddhist Society, and from 1958 to 1961 was a lecturer and member of the council.

In 1960, while on a world lecture tour, the Very Reverend Chisan Kōhō Zenji, Chief Abbot of Sōjiji Temple, heard of this remarkable young woman and paid her a visit, during which time he invited her to come to Japan as his personal disciple. Since she had abandoned Theravāda in 1952 and had for the past ten years been studying privately with Chinese and Japanese teachers in London, she decided to accept his offer, and traveled to the Orient late in 1961. On January 21, 1962, she was fully ordained as a priestess (in the Chinese Rinzai Zen tradition) in Malacca, Malaysia. Three months later she went to Japan. On April 14, 1962, she was received as a priestess into the Sōtō Zen tradition (at Dai Hon Zan Sōjiji, in Yokohama) as a personal disciple of the Chief Abbot of Sōjiji Temple.

Immediately the young disciple ran into problems, primarily because she was both a foreigner and the first woman admitted to Sōjiji (or Eiheiji, the other main training temple in Sōtō Zen) since the fourteenth century. Nevertheless, she worked diligently, and on May 28, 1963, only a little over one year after her arrival, she received the Dharma Transmission from Kōhō Zenji, becoming one of his Dharma heirs. The following year she received the First Class Divinity degree from the headquarter's office of Sōtō Zen (on April 2), and in November of that year was given the rank of abbess, as well as her own temple, Umpukuji, in Mie-ken. Also during 1964, she served as Foreign Guestmaster and lecturer to foreign students at Sōjiji Temple, a post which she held until 1969, and began a three-year stint as Foreign Secretary of Sōjiji Temple.

Jiyu Kennett received the Sei degree (equivalent to the Doctor of Divinity degree) from the Sōtō Zen headquarter's office on March 29, 1966, and continued to study at Sōjiji Temple until the death of her teacher in 1967. In 1968, she was licensed as a full teacher, able to perform sanzen or spiritual direction. She is one of the few women in the history of Zen to attain this rank.

It was Kōhō Zenji's wish that Kennett Rōshi return to the West to spread Zen teaching, and this is beautifully expressed in his foreword to her book *Selling Water by the River:* ". . . the Zen of the West must be born of Western priests in Western countries and not be spread by Japanese who know nothing of Western ways and customs."[3] Thus, on June 1, 1969, Jiyu Kennett left Japan to sail to America, accompanied by two Western disciples. Since her arrival in San Francisco in November 1969, she has founded and directed Shasta Abbey, written *Selling Water by the River* (revised and republished as *Zen is Eternal Life*), founded *The Journal of Shasta Abbey,* begun several Buddhist groups, and worked diligently to fulfill the charge of her teacher. Further, she has lectured at several universities and seminars and been an exemplary guide for Americans pursuing the Zen path. Finally, she has been extremely careful not to allow herself to be glorified by her students in any way. This is clearly expressed in an article entitled "How to Be a Transpersonal Teacher Without Becoming a Guru."[4]

MEMBERSHIP

Shasta Abbey has never had a particularly large membership, primarily due to its seminary orientation and Jiyu Kennett's "no nonsense" approach to Zen practice. As of March 1973, there were twenty-five priests and priest trainees in residence at the monastery, with ten priest trainees on leave-of-absence. There were also eight lay trainees. In subsequent years, the figures have about doubled. Nevertheless, if figures for its branches were tabulated, and the number of people who have become laymen (formally or informally) through the efforts of Shasta Abbey were included, the figures would be considerably higher. In other words, the organization has had small but solid growth.

Four separate classes of membership have developed over the years, each depending on the individual's degree of commitment. First, there are *Corresponding Members.* These members do not live at Shasta Abbey, but keep in contact and receive the journal. Many corresponding members have taken lay ordination and come to weekend retreats or week-long sesshins. Jūkai, or the lay ordination, is the single most important set of ceremonies for a Zen lay person. It is held every spring, and involves four principal ceremonies: Reading of the Kyojūkaimon (which involves taking the three pure and ten great precepts), Sange (literally, the ceremony of confession, but expressing a full desire to look inward and confront oneself), Ketchimyaku (literally "blood lineage," indicating the passage of precepts from master to disciple), and Recognition (a ceremony demonstrating the respect of the Buddhas and Patriarchs for each disciple).

The second class of membership is that of *Lay Members.* Lay members are those who have actually lived at Shasta Abbey, usually for three to six months, during which time they engage in serious training, following all rules of the organization. In the Lay Training Program there are four training periods yearly, with each lasting two to three months and ending with a week-long sesshin. A typical daily schedule for the training program would be as follows:

- ·   5:00 A.M.   Rising Bell
- ·   5:20 A.M.   Meditation
- ·   6:00 A.M.   Morning Service
- ·   6:45 A.M.   Community work period
- ·   7:30 A.M.   Individual clean-up
- ·   8:00 A.M.   Breakfast
- ·   8:30 A.M.   Community Tea

- 9:00 A.M.   Lecture/study
- 11:00 A.M.   Work
- 12:00 noon   Meditation
- 1:00 P.M.   Lunch
- 2:00 P.M.   Work
- 3:30 P.M.   Evening Service and meditation
- 4:00 P.M.   Work/private direction
- 5:00 P.M.   Meditation
- 6:00 P.M.   Dinner
- 6:30 P.M.   Rest/bath/study
- 7:30 P.M.   Meditation
- 8:45 P.M.   Vespers
- 9:10 P.M.   Retire[5]

The third category of membership is *Priest Trainee*. Priest Trainees have decided to make a full commitment to religious life by taking formal ordination into the order, shaving their heads, wearing the robes of the order, and taking Kennett Rōshi as their teacher. The priest trainees live under strict discipline and up until the ceremony of Transmission, may leave the priesthood. Shasta Abbey describes the training program this way:

> At the Abbey, academic or intellectual study is always taken within the context of monastic training. The subjects studied include Zen and Buddhist scriptures, Buddhist history, ceremonial, comparative religion, temple administration, and other subjects which can help a priest to better understand the nature of Zen training as they arise. A great emphasis is placed on private study and tutorials under the direction of Kennett Roshi who, with the assistance of senior priests, gives most of the instruction. The formal program takes a minimum of five years' full-time training. Before a person can apply for the program, he or she must be in residence at the Abbey as a lay student for at least one training term.[6]

The fourth category of membership is that of *Priest*. The priest is one who has made a complete commitment to his or her training and undergoes the formal ceremonies of Dharma Transmission and Denkoroku. These ceremonies link the disciple to the lineage dating back to Śākyamuni. After receiving Dharma Transmission, one cannot leave the priesthood, and it is felt that at this point one's training actually *begins*. Thus we see that membership in Shasta Abbey ranges all the way from casual interest to lifelong commitment.

KEY AND/OR SPECIAL DOCTRINES

Shasta Abbey claims that the simplest and best explanation of its position is the Shushōgi portion of Dōgen's *Shōbōgenzō* (an excellent statement of which appears in *Selling Water by the River*, pp. 129–

135). The organization emphasizes both a serious zazen practice and the attempt to make each action a meditation. Consequently, all trainees must cook, dig, clean, and perform all the tasks of ordinary existence. Shasta Abbey emphasizes bowing as integral, for in bowing one learns to see everything as Buddha. Shasta Abbey asserts, however, that neither Zen nor itself is utopian. Further, the organization feels that the attainment of kenshō (an enlightenment experience) is not particularly difficult and marks the real beginning of training. In other words, one should not get stuck anywhere, and this is precisely how Kennett Rōshi translates the final mantra in the Heart Sūtra: "O Buddha, going, going, going on beyond, and always going on beyond, always *becoming* Buddha. Hail! Hail! Hail!"[7] Thus the Zen Master is not one who simply gains enlightenment, but one who is continually rededicating himself or herself to the Zen of daily life.

Shasta Abbey makes no doctrinal innovations to Sōtō Zen. It has, however, attempted to bring itself in line with its American surroundings and culture. This is clearly expressed in the statement of Jitsudō Baran and Isan Sacco:

> Zen has come to America through Japan. In Japan, Zen adopted Japanese customs, discarding its Chinese forms. It must do the same in America. Many Westerners have gotten involved in the chopsticks, tatami mats, flower arrangements, green tea, etc., thinking them to be Zen. This is a terrible shame. The Japanese made use of their own forms to express meditation, and there is just as much Zen in golf or car driving or jogging. Copying Oriental customs is completely unnecessary. We must let Zen permeate our daily lives, not graft on a foreign artificial lifestyle. Remember the Buddha did not eat with chopsticks and never in his whole life chanted in Japanese. Enchantment and mystification with Japanese or Indian ways is detrimental to religious training.[8]

In this regard, American style dining has replaced eating on the floor, Gregorian chant forms have replaced chanting in Japanese, Western style ecclesiastical dress has replaced Japanese robes during excursions into society, and English-style tea has replaced formal Japanese tea ceremonies. In addition, Shasta Abbey feels that the more Western style of relationship between master and disciple is appropriate, without undermining the content and quality of that relationship.

RITUALS, SERVICES, AND PRACTICES

Shasta Abbey relies heavily on the practice of zazen or sitting in meditation. Generally, meditators sit two to three hours per day, facing the wall. During periods of strict training, the meditation practice is increased. Nevertheless, work and daily life are also emphasized as meditational endeavors as well. In 1976 the organization published a special issue of their journal (vol. 7, nos. 9–10) entirely devoted to

Zen meditation, and it is one of the finest and simplest expressions of Zen practice that appear in print in the West.

There is also scripture recitation in the morning after zazen and in the evening before zazen. In addition, there are several daily services worth noting. There is a Morning Service after zazen, in which the trainees do three bows, incense is offered by the celebrant (Kennett Rōshi), and the scriptures are intoned and recited. This is followed by three further bows, at which point all proceed to the Founder's Shrine, where more scriptures are recited and more bowing is done. There is also an Evening Service, in which scriptures are recited, as are the basic rules for zazen. There is also a Mealtime Ceremony, in which scriptures are recited while the food is being passed around, all intending to cultivate a sense of gratitude in the participants, for it is felt that without gratitude there is no Zen training. There is also a Meditation Hall Closing Ceremony recited on days in which the meditation hall is closed (on any day of the month in which there is a four or nine) and a nightly Vespers ceremony, as well as short ceremonies to be recited during activities such as shaving the head, putting on the kesa (robe), and so on. All these ceremonies are summarized in a fine little pamphlet entitled *Scriptures and Ceremonies,* published by the organization.

The daily schedule of Shasta Abbey is regular, and follows the pattern indicated below:

•	5:45 A.M.	Rising bell
•	6:15 A.M.	Zazen
•	7:00 A.M.	Morning Service
•	7:45 A.M.	Community Tea
•	8:15 A.M.	Breakfast
•	8:45 A.M.	Community clean-up
•	9:15 A.M.	Trainees' class led by Kennett Rōshi
•	11:00 A.M.	Community Tea
•	11:30 A.M.	Junior trainees' and laymen's class (led by Senior Priest)
•	1:00 P.M.	Lunch
•	1:30 P.M.	Rest
•	2:00 P.M.	Priests' class (others' work period)
•	3:00 P.M.	Community Tea
•	3:30 P.M.	Work period
•	5:00 P.M.	Zazen
•	6:00 P.M.	Dinner
•	6:30 P.M.	Choir practice
•	7:30 P.M.	Evening Service
•	7:45 P.M.	Zazen
•	8:30 P.M.	Tea
•	9:00 P.M.	Return to houses

The rising time is sometimes adjusted to meet the demands of the season and reflects the general physical health of the community.

Further, the only truly "exclusive" item on the agenda is the priests' class, reserved only for those who have received Transmission, and taught by Kennett Rōshi.

Three other aspects of the practical life of Shasta Abbey need mention. First, there is Toko-bet-sodo, a once-a-year strict training period, when no reading is permitted and zazen practice is greatly increased. The period usually lasts for three months. Second, there are week-long sesshins, held at the end of every training period. There are three of these training periods (none during the summer), and during the spring period, Jūkai is held. Concomitant to the sesshins, there is a yearly "Transmission of the Lamp" or Den-kō-ei, in which the records of the patriarchs (Denkoroku) are lectured on by Kennett Rōshi. Third, there are several holidays. These have been adapted to the West, with Buddha's birthday, for example, being celebrated on Christmas Day and called the "Holly Festival."

At the Abbey, trainees wear black robes following a sort of cassock pattern. Robes must be worn at all times except during work (when work clothing is simply more practical). During meditation and the various ceremonies, the traditional robe or kesa is worn (with the trainees wearing black and the priests wearing orange-gold). A small version of the kesa, called a raksu, is worn around the neck during the day, and each trainee has a bowing mat for use at the appropriate times. Once a week, on their day off, all trainees shave their heads.

FUTURE PLANS

Future plans of Shasta Abbey seem somewhat uncertain. Since interest in the organization is increasing, it hopes to be able to expand its facilities to accommodate those wishing to participate fully. As the population of children at the Abbey grows, it will be necessary to expand the school. From time to time, it is likely that branches will be established, and Kennett Rōshi will continue to give various lectures and seminars.

PUBLICATIONS

Since 1970, Shasta Abbey has published *The Journal of Shasta Abbey* on a monthly basis. This tidy little publication keeps subscribers up to date on the various activities of the organization, contains articles and the like, and since 1972, has been serializing Jiyu Kennett's *The Wild White Goose*, a diary of her training in Zen. In addition, the organization has published a variety of pamphlets, including *Becoming a Buddhist, Zen Meditation, Women and Buddhism, On War and Violence,* and *Scriptures and Ceremonies.* By and large, these pamphlets are of excellent quality and extremely useful.

Shasta Abbey is now issuing tapes of some of Jiyu Kennett's lectures and courses. These are of singularly fine quality and represent the best of all tapes being offered by Buddhist organizations. A tape of the scriptures and ceremonies is also available. Finally, there is Kennett Rōshi's book *Zen is Eternal Life* which formerly appeared as *Selling Water by the River*.

CONCLUDING REMARKS

It seems to this author that Kōhō Zenji was correct in noting that ". . . the Zen of the West must be born of Western priests in Western countries and not be spread by Japanese who know nothing of Western ways and customs." In this regard, Jiyu Kennett makes an excellent emissary for bringing authentic Zen teaching and practice to America. Having lived a good portion of her life in England, she is not only thoroughly conversant with Western customs, but also shares a fund of knowledge concerning Buddhism's growth in her native country. Nor is it an accident that she was the first woman admitted to either of the two main Sōtō training temples. It is my estimate that Kennett Rōshi is as fine and inspiring a Zen Master as there is in this country, if such a statement can be deemed appropriate. Nevertheless, all is not quite so rosy as it seems on the surface. To simply transmute Japanese Zen customs, such as the tea ceremony, to some Western counterpart will never suffice for genuine attempts at acculturation. And in this respect, Shasta Abbey has not made significant progress. Of course the motive is pure. Perhaps more than most Buddhist organizations, Shasta Abbey is committed to not distorting Buddhist practice in the shift to America. It does seem possible, however, to preserve the integrity of the practice while making a more concerted effort to accommodate the location. The problem is also compounded by the fact that Shasta Abbey, in the transformative, developmental process, has become clearly more British than American. Thus we have the curious state of affairs in which Japanese Zen, in trying to become American Zen, ultimately turns out to be British Zen (in style, custom, titles and ranks, and procedures).

Shasta Abbey encounters one of the same problems that the Sino-American Buddhist Association does. The abbey has a profound intent, attracts thoroughly serious and devoted participant members, and pursues a monastic style that is rather foreign to the mainstream of American religious life. To be sure, in acknowledging the potential marriage of priests and in sending them out to serve the various branch priories, Shasta Abbey does not stress the rejection of the "home life" as does the Sino-American Buddhist Organization. The life that Shasta Abbey rejects is one in which one truly fails to "live," whether by simple ignorance, inability to confront reality "as it is," or unwillingness to be serious about developing religious discipline. But in spite of the fact that Shasta Abbey has the courage and honesty to turn inward, to attempt to develop a genuine compassion for humanity, its approach relegates it to a minor position among Buddhist groups active in America. At a time when the Buddhist movement in America could indeed gain much from the rigor and seriousness of Shasta Abbey, it may well go for the most part unnoticed due to its small growth. I do not mean to say that the organization is not growing. Rather, I mean that by isolating itself in the mountains of northern California and doing little to promote its own cause, American Buddhists are robbed of the opportunity to learn from the marvelous teaching of Kennett Rōshi. Of the eight groups that we have examined in this section, Shasta Abbey is the only one to have its main center in a rural setting, and its minute size tends to demonstrate the contention that Buddhism in America is, after all, predominantly a city movement.

On matters of practice, however, the situation is quite different. Shasta Abbey has recognized well the necessity for serious and prolonged zazen practice coupled with hard work. The practice schedule for the organization is as rigorous as any Buddhist group in America, excepting the Sino-American Buddhist Association (which is certainly an extreme case of discipline). Further, in transposing the ceremonials into the English language, Shasta Abbey has understood the efficacy of providing services that the community fully understands, rather than simply intoning various sounds that escape comprehension. Vestiges of the Japanese customs, though, still remain. The most notable of these vestiges is the practice of bowing. It seems, in fact, that community members bow to almost everything imaginable. Perhaps a more American expression of humble respect may, in time, be found to replace the custom of bowing.

Anyone who attends one of Kennett Rōshi's lectures or hears a tape recording of her lectures or seminars will undoubtedly conclude that she understands human nature very well. They will also conclude that when she speaks of finding the "iron being" within, she knows with great precision the great joy and beauty such an endeavor reveals. In carefully regulating the conditions under which Dharma Transmission takes place, she at least bequeaths to America a small number of disciples who preserve her lineage with supreme integrity. As times and conditions change, and situations alter Shasta Abbey, perhaps the still small tree will yield a plentiful bounty of tasty fruit.

PART THREE

New Heaven and Earth: Dharma Comes to the Land of the Red Man

Ah no, I cannot tell you what it is, the new world.
I cannot tell you the mad, astounded rapture of its discovery.
I shall be mad with delight before I have done,
and whosoever comes after will find me in the new world
a madman in rapture.

—D.H. Lawrence[1]

In April 1977 I was invited to a conference on "The Flowering of Buddhism in America," held at Syracuse University. Like all short conferences, the agenda was packed and events proceeded at break-neck speed, with little opportunity for conversation or reflection. Nevertheless, during the lunch break on the first day of the confer-ence, I happened to overhear a conversation between two of the participants. Their chat began with the usual fare: how nice it was to see each other again, how splendid it was for Syracuse to sponsor such a conference, what a wide variety of opinions were represented, and so forth. Then, however, the tone and topic shifted measurably. One of the conversationalists began to speculate on the prospective future of Buddhism on the American scene, and his partner was quick to interject a few additional opinions. Despite a very animated discussion, the two were in complete agreement. Each was sure that Buddhism would enjoy a long and prosperous history in America. After all, Buddhism had been present in this country for over one hundred years, had grown by leaps and bounds since 1950, and was now branching off into a wide variety of ancillary activities that included universities, bookstores, restaurants, and the like. The two further commented that Buddhists of the various traditions and sects were not all that different anyway, and what they lacked in sameness, they made up for in sheer numbers and common commitment. To an outsider, and to many insiders as well, the conversation would invariably sound both optimistic and accurate. To this interested listener, their mutual congratulations reminded me of what Philip Slater refers to as the "Toilet Assumption—the notion that unwanted matter, unwanted difficulties, unwanted complexities and obstacles will disappear if they are removed from our immediate field of vision."[2] In somewhat less outrageous prose, Harvey Cox makes the same observation, unknowingly striking at the underpinnings of the above lunchtime analysis:

> Religious remedies to the ills of a culture take two basic forms: one tries to get at the underlying causes of the malady; the other provides a way for people to live in spite of the illness, usually by providing them with an alternative miniworld, sufficiently removed from the one outside so that its perils are kept away from the gate. The East turners have almost all chosen the second form.[3]

While Cox's conclusion may not hold for all of the "East turners," it does hold for the discussion recorded above.

As the lunch recess ended and the conference resumed, one of the journalists in attendance asked a panel participant how his family had adjusted to his new choice of religious tradition and endeavor. The panelist ignored the first portion of the question, but was explicit in noting that he certainly was not a Buddhist of the variety mentioned by the journalist, and that Buddhism was indeed not something of Buddha's creation. The panelist went on to explain that his major concern was significantly more involved with seeing and living than with naming and conceptualizing.

What a remarkable puzzle this presents to the scholar of American Buddhism. On the one hand, many American Buddhists argue that Buddhism has made magnificent strides in this country, with the future advancement of the tradition virtually assured (and history handily compelled to comply). On the other hand, some so-called American Buddhists argue that there is no such thing as Buddhism— except in the minds of ardent but woeful addicts of "public reality." And of course this latter position renders any adjectives affixed to Buddhism fictional as well. Irrespective of the accuracy or inaccuracy of either of the above cited expressions, it can be said that the former falls into the category referred to as "scenery" by Louis Nordstrom (the convener of the Syracuse conference), and the latter fits Professor Nordstrom's designation of "path." Further, Nordstrom hints strongly that studies focusing on the scenery of American Buddhism (such as Emma Layman's *Buddhism in America*) miss the target altogether, while studies concerning the path enhance the Buddhist mission in America. The following chapter attempts to trace a middle, tenuous course between these two extremes by placing the Buddhist movement in America squarely in the context of what Jacob Needleman referred to in his 1970 volume as the "New Religions," while at the same time offering some critical observations concerning Buddhism's prospective course in the coming years.

CHAPTER 13

In Pursuit of American Buddhism

People need not only to be seekers; they need to be finders. But, to use those words of child's play—which admittedly are not always merely words or sentiments confined to children or to play—need finders be keepers? To be spiritually satisfied, must we know that we have found *the* way—the one way, the only way, and the whole way?

—Robert Michaelsen[1]

Despite the fact that Jacob Needleman devotes two of the seven descriptive chapters in *The New Religions* to Buddhist groups, including them for survey as "new religions" poses two important questions (which apply equally to other imported religious groups in America). Of course, these questions are eminently conspicuous: What do we mean by *new*? And what do we mean by *religion*? Anyone even remotely associated with the study of religion, in virtually any of its aspects, at once recognizes that formal definitions of religion are both plentiful and problematic, and it is not my intention to introduce yet another (probably idiosyncratic) offering into an already overcrowded arena. Nevertheless, it is necessary to point out, as Robert Ellwood does, that it would be helpful to identify the majority of groups studied under the rubric of "new religions" as "not normatively Judaeo-Christian."[2] A consideration of the term *new* is far more interesting and fruitful. Obviously new has geographic specificity with regard to the American scene, since many of the traditions included as new religions (Buddhism notwithstanding) have long and glorious histories in Asia. Yet *how long* is new in an American setting? In this context, it does little good simply to fall back on the equally variable phrase *recent*. For many, new will indicate since 1960, especially because it was around this time that the groups in question began to make their American presence felt. Others, however, present a radically opposite approach:

> *New* means groups which have arisen or taken root in America within the last 150 years and are extant today. This time span, going back to the early nineteenth century, may seem overly long. But it is necessary to include in our general purview the beginnings of Swedenborgianism—actually eighteenth century—Spiritualism, New Thought, and Theosophy. These movements have all had continuing interaction to the present day with the cultural milieu of the types of groups we are studying. All are still of importance today. Groups which have arisen only in the last century and a half, of course, are very "new" in comparison with Judaism and Christianity, even though major American denominations and schools of both are no less recent.[3]

Although it initially appears somewhat bizarre to define *new* as 150 years—especially in a country that has only recently celebrated its bicentennial—it is this latter estimate that provides the historical perspective for considering the various new religions, including Buddhism, in their own right on the American scene. To settle for a more modest estimate of newness would, in this case, inadvertently rob Buddhism of the greater part of its formative gestation in America. However, it is certainly not necessary to define newness only with respect to chronological considerations.

With regard to the new religions, Barbara Hargrove has recently suggested that new may well refer to that which is "unusual" or "exotic." It may signal a reversal of trends or a new way of combining familiar elements. In other words, new may represent the *cultural transformation* of elements already present in the culture.[4] If we apply both of the above approaches to our consideration of Buddhism, we find that not only can we appreciate the integrity of Buddhist history in America (and of the parent tradition in Asia as well), but we can ascribe its recent emergence from obscurity in this country to the tumultuous cultural changes that have occurred in the last quarter century, all united under the genuinely innovative and alternative mode of religious expression offered by the Buddhist tradition.

THE PUBLIC'S FEAR OF BUDDHISM

Precisely because of its newness, innovation, and alternative of religious expression, Buddhism has suffered, with the other new religions, from an enormous amount of public suspicion. In a recent conference, Harvey Cox noted four themes exemplary of this skepticism.[5] The first is what Cox calls "the subversion myth." Here it is assumed that the religious movement poses a considerable threat to the civil order, leading to an erosion of the basic fabric of society.

It may also be postulated that some of the new religions may simply be religious "fronts" for subversive organizations. With regard to Buddhism, specifically, the outward manifestations of this myth range from the arrest of Japanese Americans during the Second World War to a veiled distrust of Asian-American Buddhists currently active in America. Cox's second theme presumes that when all the "window dressing" is stripped away, some sort of orgiastic behavior (either promiscuity or stringency) is transpiring in these new religions. To be sure, some of the popular literature on Tantric sexuality does little to dissuade people from a tacit indictment of Buddhism. Third, Cox talks of the "myth of dissimulation," wherein it is suggested that members of the various groups cannot be engaged in accurate and informative conversation, for they are coached to mislead the questioner. The persistent insistence on the part of many American Buddhists that the only valid answers to questions arise in meditation does little to allay public suspicion. And the curious but widespread habit of relying on Zen or Tantric dialogue takes an important religious practice totally out of context, rendering it meaningless. Finally, we have what Cox refers to as the "evil-eye notion," which supposes that anyone belonging to a movement is indeed not there on a voluntary basis. In spite of the fact that preliminary evidence indicates that nothing approaching the accusation actually occurs in the new religions, it is not difficult to foresee an American Zen priest or member of *any* American Buddhist group hustled off in a waiting "getaway car" to the deprogrammer's lair.

Cox is right in claiming that these themes express the public's fear of corporate and individual chaos, and he cites historical precedents as well. Professor Cox's analysis and sympathies leave him—and many of the rest of us—in a perplexing mess. On the one hand, our scholarly investigations clearly reveal that the majority of public suspicion regarding the new religions is simply false and uninformed. We are learning that, like Cox's investigation of the Boston area, our own studies reveal a turning to alternative religious traditions is often motivated by a search for friendship, immediacy, authority, and naturalness.[6] It is ironic that the turn East "is occurring just as many millions of Asians are involved in an epochal 'Turn West' toward Western science and technology, Western political systems, and Western cultural forms."[7] Some of us might even chuckle at Cox's citation of a friend's reference to Cambridge as "Benares-on-the-Charles." On the other hand, there are those of us who part company with Professor Cox when he concludes:

> Although America today *seems* uncommonly receptive to spiritual ideas and practices from the East, the truth is that we are not really receptive to them at all. True, no stone walls have been erected to keep the pagans out. No orders of Knights Templar have ridden forth to hurl back the infidels. The gates are open, and the citizens seem ready to listen. No wonder many Eastern teachers view America as fertile ground in which to sow their seeds.

But curiously it is precisely America's receptivity, its eagerness to hear, explore, and experience, that creates the most difficult barrier to our actually learning from Eastern spirituality. The very insatiable hunger for novelty, for intimacy, even for a kind of spirituality that motivates so many Americans to turn toward the East also virtually guarantees that the turn will ultimately fail.[8]

In spite of the difficult problems cited immediately above and throughout this study, (as well as some not previously cited, such as the lack of political input and impact on the part of the new religions), I believe that it is possible to propound that the future of the new religions in America, and particularly Buddhism, may not be nearly so bleak as Professor Cox supposes. And I do not infer this conclusion solely on the basis of religious freedom in America or a constant and eager supply of "East turners."

BUDDHISM AS A CULT

In searching for a mode by which we can present both a retrospective look at the materials offered in this volume as well as a consideration of Buddhism's future in America, Robert Ellwood's typology of the general characteristics of cults is extremely useful. Ellwood defines the word *cult* in the following way:

A *cult* is a group derived from the experience of one or a few individuals who are able to enter (or are fascinated by the possibility of entering) a superior, ecstatic state of consciousness in which contact and rapport with all reaches of a non-historical and impersonal universe are possible with the help of intermediaries (human and/or supernatural). In a cult an outer circle of members experience the presence of the sacred in these individuals, and seek to participate in their experience.[9]

With few exceptions, almost all Buddhist groups in America fit this general definition. Ellwood's typology postulates fifteen characteristics:

1. A founder who has had, or at least seems to know the secret of, non-temporal ecstatic experience.
2. An interpretation of the experience as possession of marvellous travel.
3. A band of supernormal helpers.
4. A desire to be "modern" and to use scientific language.
5. A reaction against orthodoxy.
6. Eclecticism and syncretism.
7. A monistic and impersonal ontology.
8. Optimism, success orientation, and a tendency to evolutionary views.
9. Emphasis on healing.
10. Use in many cases of magic techniques.
11. A simple but definite process of entry and initiation.

12. In some cases, the establishment of a sacred center.
13. Emphasis on psychic powers.
14. Tendency to attract isolated individuals rather than family groups.
15. Increasing emphasis on participation by all members in the ecstatic experience through group chanting, meditation, and so forth.[10]

Characteristics 2, 10, and 13 have little or no application to Buddhism in America and will be omitted from discussion. Each of the others will be dealt with in order.

The Charismatic Leader

Of the eight groups studied in this volume, at least six are headed by leaders of the type described in the typology. It might be possible also to include the leader of Nichiren Shōshū of America (George Williams) in this category, leaving only Buddhist Churches of America without a charismatic leader of the type described. I have opted for use of the word *leader* rather than *founder* here, for although each of the seven men considered is indeed the founder of the American variety of the tradition in question, none is the actual founder of the tradition as a whole. Setting aside considerations of the individuals involved, since those are entertained elsewhere in the book, we must question to what degree leaders of the type described assist the Buddhist endeavor in America. Needless to say, the issue of authenticity is of paramount importance for a fledgling religious organization. While the credentials and religious experience of the Buddhist teachers considered above are unquestionable, there are other Buddhist organizations in America whose leaders are not so exemplary. To be sure, it is difficult to estimate the percentage of qualified and nonqualified Buddhist teachers in America, especially since no criteria for so doing have been established. For Buddhism to make a meaningful contribution to American religious life, it is virtually imperative that the integrity of its various traditions be protected by teachers who bear the authentic seal of their lineage. In a tradition that depends so much on the fusion of intuitive wisdom with skill-in-means as the basis for accurate transmission of the tenets of the religion, it is thus essential for American Buddhists to establish certification procedures for its clergy and lay instructors. Implementation of such procedures obviously requires considerable infra-Buddhist communication and an ecumenical attitude that supersedes or cuts across sectarian barriers. I do not mean to say that individual identity must be compromised. Rather, I suggest a stance of cooperation and an atmosphere of mutual respect. The ramifications of such an endeavor might well have far-reaching effects, going considerably beyond the issue of teacher certification.

Two other features of the founder (or leader) as one "who has had, or at least seems to know the secret of, nontemporal ecstatic experience" are worthy of note. The first is the role of teacher as shamanic figure. Until quite recently, scholars tended to think of shamans in terms of the classic history-of-religions approach characterized by Mircea Eliade's *Shamanism.* In a brilliant new approach, however, Catherine L. Albanese has argued for consideration of a "shape-shifter" based on the example of Davy Crockett, the Trickster figure that appears in a number of aboriginal myths.[11] Professor Albanese maintains that "Crockett's shape-shifting revealed the mythic power of his identity: it displayed for Americans the inner coherence of a culture of history-makers while simultaneously snatching away history in the uncontrolled ecstasy of natural violence."[12] Further, she argues that "Crockett embodied 'not so much what the American people were, but more what they wanted to be— or did not dare to be.'"[13] We all of course know of Davy Crockett's reputed kinship with both the animals that inhabited the wilds and the wilderness itself. This kinship suggested to Professor Albanese that Crockett had mastered their secrets. I would argue that the same case might be made for many of the Buddhist leaders now operative on the American scene. Indeed, many Americans have been attracted to Buddhism precisely because the charismatic leader of some group or other demonstrated, in troubled times, just what Americans *might be.* In addition, when we observe the kinship that many American Buddhist leaders have established with the city and its inhabitants (remembering my proposition of the city as the new American wilderness), we might conclude that, like Crockett, they have mastered its secrets, and in so doing, established themselves as attractive harbingers of a new religious age. Just as the career of Davy Crockett reveals him to be the archetypal Trickster, so also might the respective careers of many American Buddhist leaders be characterized. This is important, for "this trickery was salvific because it blended the ordering processes of culture with the disordering forces of chaos."[14] It is the degree to which Buddhism is successful in bringing order out of chaos that will determine its future development in America.

The second notable feature of charismatic leaders mentioned above concerns the methodology by which the American Buddhist leaders implement their "plan of action" on a personal level. In other words, the student-teacher relationship becomes of crucial importance. The chief problem for American Buddhists has not been the effectiveness of the teacher in bringing his students to a fuller realization of their various religious and individual ideals, but rather that, in their quest for numerical advances, the teachers have often assumed the role of religious advisor for more students than can be effectively handled in the intensely personal way required by Buddhist precedent. In so doing, the tradition as a whole suffers, and for the obvious reasons. I do not mean to say that American Buddhists must necessarily import more teachers, although this would be extremely helpful. Such a tactic is both unlikely and impractical. I do mean, however, that senior, mature students of the various teachers must be trained to fulfill this role in the future. Of course the stringent certification procedures mentioned above would have great application here. In

addition, by training American disciples to function in the role of
teacher, Buddhism in this country would take on a more distinctly
American flavor, aiding significantly in the acculturative process.
Some groups have already begun to do this, and while they need to
exercise much more care in quality control, they have taken the first
small steps in an important direction.

Supernormal Helpers

The second topic to be considered from Ellwood's typology concerns having "a band of supernormal helpers." Two aspects of the
Buddhist tradition are operative here. First, in the Mahāyāna and
Vajrayāna traditions, there is a full pantheon of celestial Buddhas
and Bodhisattvas, each of whom, through the notion of "transfer-
ence of merit," can provide aid to the Buddhist practitioner. Consequently, each American Buddhist in one of these traditions has an
array of supernormal beings to assist in his quest. Not only are these
celestial patrons significant through their offering of good merit to
the practitioner, but also because they engender, by their example, a
prototypic behavior that is founded on exemplary moral comport-
ment. Thus, American Buddhists are reminded to structure the ethical
dimension of their own lives around the cardinal practices of love,
compassion, sympathetic joy, and equanimity, therefore enhancing
their own progress on the Bodhisattva path. The transformative
function of these practices must not be underestimated, for they
yield a profoundly beneficial impact on society as well. In a culture
beset with so much moral uncertainty, these supernormal helpers
provide American Buddhists with an oasis amid despair and confusion. By inculcating the values they symbolize, the entire course of
American Buddhism is advanced.

In addition to the obvious supernormal helpers, Buddhism is
assisted by the tradition known as *lineage.* Each of the Buddhist
traditions maintains a rich literature regarding the various and famous recipients of the teaching. It matters little, from a pragmatic
viewpoint, whether the Dharma is transmitted from teacher to disciple
(as in the Zen tradition) or effected through an incarnation system
(as in Tibetan Buddhism). It could even be argued that edifying tales
concerning famous, accomplished theras and therīs in the Theravāda
tradition function in the same fashion as more proper lineages. In
any case, these bastions of the various Buddhist traditions establish,
through the lineage, not only a living reminder of the efficacy of the
respective teachings, but also a means by which it is possible, in each
successive generation, to maintain a link to Buddhist orthodoxy. In
this way, Buddhism is able to renew itself continually, while maintaining bonds with an increasingly authoritative historical tradition.
In studying and practicing with an American Buddhist teacher who
is in the Dharma line of a Dōgen or a Tsong-kha-pa, each disciple
shares in the religious power of that lineage, and draws on it freely
in pursuing his own experience of the Buddhist tradition. We have a

few cases of Dharma transmission to American Buddhists already, as noted elsewhere in this study, and it is not unreasonable to project, in the near future, an unbroken lineage of American Buddhist masters in the various traditions. I suspect that such an American lineage will have a profound effect on the assimilation of the Buddhist tradition in America.

A Desire to be Modern

The next point in the adopted typology concerns "a desire to be 'modern' and to use scientific language." It is here that Buddhism in America has faced serious difficulties. While it is generally true that Buddhism in this country is more modern than its Asian counterpart, this fact is more a product of American culture than Buddhist endeavor. The greatest advances have been made in the area of *human sciences,* particularly psychology. The reason is obvious: Buddhism has had throughout its history a deep concern for the mind and its function, as evidenced by the Abhidharma tradition and the meditative systems that grew out of it (some of which militated against it). It is commonplace for American Buddhist teachers to utilize more than a liberal sprinkling of psychological terminology and jargon in their public lectures and seminars, as well as in private instruction. Unfortunately, many of these teachers have little more than a layman's knowledge of formal psychology, doing it as much injustice as most Western psychologists do in treating Buddhist psychology. More complete knowledge of each of these traditions would certainly benefit the other, but this is not now (with few exceptions) being done. To be sure, the problem is quite as difficult in the other human sciences.

In the physical sciences, Buddhism has lagged severely. I suspect that this is less due to Buddhism's inability than it is to Buddhism's apologetic position. There is much in modern physics, for example, that has a deep resonance with Buddhist tenets. This has only been superficially explored. The same is true in such fields as chemistry and biology. Nevertheless, Buddhism attempts to *appear* scientific. American Buddhists tend to shy away from the tradition of reason and logic in Buddhist thought, although it represents the most significant stratum of Buddhist philosophy.

Perhaps the solution to the problem lies in a twofold approach. Needless to say, the first necessary step is the *decision to change.* The second step would enable Buddhism to exploit the simple fact that in this country its adherents are an extremely literate group, quite often including professionals from virtually all the scientific fields. The high level of educational training, as well as the professional positions of these American Buddhists, might be utilized to some degree in addressing problems common to Buddhism and science. As a corollary of this last issue, the question of Buddhism and vocation comes to the forefront. It appears that the time is ripe for American Buddhist teachers to more firmly emphasize education and career to their students and to encourage those with scientific background and leaning to pursue these studies further—but in a way consonant with American Buddhist needs and requirements. In so doing, Buddhism could forthrightly confront science and modernity in a more profound fashion than their predecessors. Technology, societal complexity, medicine, and the like will simply not wait for advancement until American Buddhists suddenly experience a collective "Eureka." And the longer Buddhists wait to pursue these avenues of research, the more difficult the problem becomes. The experiential lag that Buddhists are seeking to correct in their everyday lives through religious training rests on the verge of becoming a cultural lag that escalates the difficulty exponentially.

A Reaction against Orthodoxy

We turn now to Buddhism in America as "a reaction against orthodoxy." By orthodoxy, Ellwood means the established churches and, occasionally, the scientific orthodoxy. Of course it goes without saying that Buddhism currently lies outside the mainstream of modern American religion and represents, to some degree, an alternative to it. It has been argued (in Part I of this book) that throughout its history on the American scene, Buddhism was attractive to many Americans precisely because of its differentness, its rejection of the traditional modes of religious belief and practice. However, it was also argued that, from the standpoint of successful acculturation, it was not its unusual or exotic character that would lead to a continued or profound impact on America. Rather, I would maintain that Buddhism's sameness with American values, its affirmation of America's mission is the key that unlocks the door to Buddhism's future success in this country. By no means does this position condemn American Buddhism to a tacit acceptance of what has gone before. On the contrary, its distinctness in both ideological standpoint and methodological procedure must be promulgated in a context of mutual respect. That is to say, it must take its place on the religious marketplace with a hopefully better product—maybe even a revolutionary one—but without employing advertising that undermines the integrity of its competition. Americans tend to be inherently distrustful of a product that advertises itself by informing the public that its competitors will only lead one to headaches and heartaches, and in the secular, pluralistic world in which we live, we cannot ignore that religion too has become a commodity.

In order to emphasize its sameness with American religious ideals, Buddhism has had to violate yet another orthodoxy, namely, that of its own parent tradition in Asia. Although it has not broken with the Asian tradition of Buddhism altogether, American Buddhism has made many accommodations that certainly compromise traditional forms of practice, as well as the doctrinal bases of that practice. For many Buddhists in Asia and America, such alterations are considered outrageous, unthinkable, or at best, foolish. I would argue that such a reaction is both predictable and necessary, for it requires that American Buddhists face their identity crisis squarely. It is a crisis that Buddhism faced as it entered each new culture in Asia, and represents a healthy step toward developing a distinct national character in a new culture. As long as Americans pursuing Buddhism try to *be Japanese* or *be Tibetan* (or *be whatever*), there will never be anything resembling an American Buddhism, and this has been forcefully stressed by teachers like Chögyam Trungpa, who tell their students not to try to wear Tibetan Buddhism on their jeans like a patchwork of fine Tibetan brocade and American fabric. The way in which the tentative mixture of Buddhism and American culture finds its way into concrete religious and societal manifestations is highlighted in the next topic in our typology: "eclecticism and syncretism."

Eclecticism and Syncretism

The manner in which Buddhism in America reveals itself to be eclectic and syncretistic is most significantly demonstrated in its growing capacity for inclusiveness. Within the Buddhist tradition itself, many individual sects are now beginning to employ doctrines and practices that have formerly been considered in the domain of another sect. This tactic represents more than a merely tolerant attitude on the part of the various groups and appears to be political and pragmatic as well as religious. Perhaps the most striking example of this sort of strategy is that of the Sino-American Buddhist Association, which utilizes techniques from a wide variety of Buddhist traditions. It is now not unusual to find Zen meditation masters serving as invited instructors in Tibetan Buddhist centers, Tibetan Buddhist procedures cropping up in Zen centers, Theravādins teaching satipatthāna all over the Buddhist roadmap in America, and all the meditative strands of Buddhism teaching Pure Land adherents how to meditate. Contrary to what *might* be expected, the individual identity of the various Buddhist traditions and sects is not being compromised, but the seeds of mutual understanding and respect are being sown, fostering not only the previously suggested ecumenical attitude, but also a renewed commitment to the soteriological dimension that has always been a major component of Buddhist practice.

Buddhism, however, is also reaching outside of itself in its quest for integrity in an American setting. It is not being done, as Martin Marty suspects,[15] by ignoring the Asian Americans, but rather by implementing, as a unifying element, the (elusive) American character that provides the framework for all our endeavors, Buddhist and otherwise. By addressing rather than repressing the obvious tension between being Buddhist *and* American, the acculturative process is significantly advanced, first by awareness and then by positive and productive action. With regard to this latter issue, perhaps the chief item for consideration concerns the prior religious commitment and affiliation of persons now claiming to embrace Buddhism. As noted earlier in this study, clear guidelines pertaining to multilateral religious affiliation must be outlined in the near future, as well as a more explicit definition of what constitutes Buddhist membership and identity. Other areas of concern will be discussed below. Not all of Buddhism's attempts to expand its horizons in the search for meaningful acculturation can be applauded. To date, some of these attempts represent less than careful scrutiny of the cultural landscape. Agehananda Bharati is right when he says:

> The all-American mental retardation as I see it is pathological eclecticism
> —and I don't think the new anthropology can leave it at that with a shrug
> and a note—it has to be chastised. Aloha and amigo don't go together
> except in the realm of the phoney. Neither do yoga, Sikhism, kundalini,
> T'ai Chih', and macrobiotic diet.[16]

Thus it might be argued that American Buddhism would profit from a more discriminating attitude in absorbing various approaches, techniques, and practices into its fold. Without so doing, a new cultural-religious amalgam will most certainly develop, but it will have neither Buddhist nor American identity (nor a reasonable blend of the two), and it will be the salvation of nobody, despite what I am certain will be an enormous initial popularity.

By providing a true confrontation of Buddhist ideals and practice, and Buddhist culture, with American religious life and culture, it is possible to bring about the first American transformation of Buddhism. If the procedure is based on solid principles, nurtured for no short time duration, and carried out with utmost caution, it is likely that a real fusion can be effected, just as it has in the Buddhist cultures of Asia. In other words, *there is precedent.* It is the task of American Buddhists not to ignore the past examples of Buddhist acculturation, but to learn from it. Of course this will take much study and analysis, and it is my opinion that if the enterprise is too frivolously entertained, the Buddhist mission in America will advance only little beyond its current status.

A Monistic and Impersonal Ontology

The next item in our typology is "a monistic and impersonal ontology." Needless to say, Buddhism's position on the absolute is clear and explicit. Buddhism employs no god concept and must necessarily be regarded as nontheistic. Further, that which is ultimate, whether it be regarded as nirvāṇa (as in some traditions) or Buddhahood (in others), is nonpersonal or suprapersonal. To engage in a long and careful discussion of ultimacy in the Buddhist tradition would be outside the scope of this book (and tedious as well). Any number of reasonable books can be consulted for information: Rune Johansson's *The Psychology of Nirvana,* Nalinaksha Dutt's *Aspects of Mahāyāna*

Buddhism and Its Relation to Hīnayāna, and Guy Welbon's *The Buddhist Nirvāṇa and Its Western Interpreters*. Nevertheless, it is important to note here that Buddhism's ontological position does indeed put it in direct conflict with the mainstream of Judaeo-Christian theology—a situation that is not likely to be corrected, and represents some liability to the Buddhist movement in America. It is no accident that the Buddhist sect that comes closest to a "theological" position, Jōdo Shinshū, is the second largest Buddhist group in America. Of course the above in no way dismisses a following for Buddhism among those persons either accepting the death of God theology or expressly maintaining an atheistic stance, but these persons hardly can be categorized as anything but a minority in traditional American religion. Buddhism's lack of a theological position, so to speak, does not, however, eliminate the possibility of meaningful dialogue with other religious traditions. If Buddhists and adherents of traditional Western religions can understand that theology or its lack is a subservient issue to basic ontological questions, Buddhism's initially unacceptable appearance can be mitigated in the light of its abundant and profound literature on the latter.

Optimism, Success, and Evolution

We come now to "optimism, success orientation, and a tendency to evolutionary views." Quite often in the literature we find references to "Buddhist pessimism." The basic thrust of such an idea rests primarily on the emphatic statement of the First Noble Truth: all life is pain (or suffering, or dis-ease). It must be recognized, however, that by this statement, Buddhists do not mean to assert that the necessary condition of humanity *must* be so defined. Rather, Buddhists maintain that as long as there is craving for permanence in a rapidly changing world, as long as there is greed, hatred, and delusion, as long as people isolate themselves from the experience of the world "as it is" (yathābhūtam), such a condition will persist. Viewed from the opposite pole, from the standpoint that Buddha and countless other disciples through the ages actually attained the cessation of pain, the outlook is far brighter—perhaps even optimistic. In other words, if the outlook was as bleak as many critics claim, there would be absolutely no point in following the prescriptive path outlined by Buddhism. Balanced against this claim is the testimony of Buddhist literature (canonical, commentarial, and popular) that reveals the Buddhist path to have been truly liberating for those fearless and dedicated practitioners who were willing to brave its rigors.

That the positive fruits of the religious life may be voiced in negative terminology should surprise no students of the history of religions, for such is often the case in the world's great religious traditions. Nevertheless, it does call attention to the fact that while some Buddhist sects express the truth of the path positively, others simply employ the opposite approach, in Asia and America. If we

overgeneralize somewhat, it appears that the nonmeditative traditions within Buddhism tend to utilize optimistic language (and
success orientation), while the meditative groups stress the opposite.
In America, the nonmeditative groups include Nichiren Shoshu of
America and Buddhist Churches of America (Jōdo Shinshū). The
former group, it will be remembered, relies on the chanting of the
formula Nam Myoho Renge Kyo (homage to the Lotus Sūtra) to
effect religious goals, while the latter group exhorts the saving grace
of Amida Buddha through recitation of the nembutsu (Namu Amida
Butsu-Homage to Amida Buddha). To recall the basis for such
practice is, in this context, less important than noting that it is these
two groups, with their optimistic attitude and emphasis on success,
that represent the two largest Buddhist groups in America. We have
previously identified some of the ways in which these groups reso-
nate with patterns in mainstream American religion, and these will
not be reiterated here. Nevertheless, the two groups are highly consonant in their quest with the "American dream." They highlight the
benefits of the traditional work ethic in America, as well as the
fruits of a life of strong faith, calling to memory the myth of "rugged
individualism." In so doing, these two groups present a strong
potential for assimilation and acculturation in America, once their
internal struggles are resolved. The meditative groups (Zen, Tibetan
Buddhism, and Theravāda) present a different vision. More negative
in their rhetoric than Nichiren and Pure Land, they nevertheless
presume potential victory over the evils of unenlightened existence
by their emphasis on the possibility of religious realization, experienced after a long training period. I would argue that although the
descriptions vary from the former, nonmeditative groups, the intent
and expectation is the same: complete human wholeness in the
world. As in virtually all human experience, there is overwhelming
potential for self delusion, and it appears that the seeming pessimism
of the meditative groups in Buddhism is little more than a skillful
device to assist its adherents in avoiding this problem. Further, when
one considers the powerful transformation of consciousness that
hopefully results from meditative endeavor, such a device can be
witnessed to have strong purgative value. And it in no way contra-
dicts the strong tendencies for general suspicion that have come to
underlie the fiber of life in America. It is unfortunately the case that
the victor in many avenues of pursuit is not the participant who has
played the game fairly and properly, but the one who has played
more cleverly and thoroughly. The meditative traditions of Buddhism simply warn the practitioner not to be fooled—especially by
himself. In any case, the arduous path of meditation has much in
common with the classic American success story: a great victory
after a long and difficult period of preparation. Just as American
children have for generations been reminded that "anyone can become President," it follows that for American Buddhists, anyone can

become a Buddha. Neither claim may be realistic, but each is certainly optimistic. This optimism is a powerful ally of Buddhism's acculturation on the American scene.

Healing

The next item in our typology is the "emphasis on healing." Although the usual application of the word *healing* has little to do with traditional Buddhism, it does have some bearing on Buddhism in America. It must be stated at the outset that Buddhism in America hardly *emphasizes* healing. To some degree, Nichiren Shōshū of America did early on, but this is less commonplace now. Nevertheless, in both the physical and psychological domains, it does have a place. Buddhists have always recognized the clear relationship between physical and psychological health, resulting in the development of healing procedures that are holistic. Perhaps the highest expression of this sort of approach is Tibetan medicine. It is also possible to consider certain dietary regimens in Zen in this category as well. And of course such an emphasis has profound meaning in the nutritional wasteland in which many Americans live. As our culture becomes increasingly aware of the benefits of consuming genuinely natural products, it is beginning to understand what Buddhist cultures have known for years: there is a direct relationship between products consumed and physical health. The above is particularly relevant as more and more carcinogenic agents in our diet are being uncovered.

Holistic medicine, however, includes more than dietary matters. Two other features are significant as well. The first concerns the means by which we can improve bodily health through regulated exercise and activity. It is, for example, traditional in Zen monasteries that a day without work is a day without food. To be sure, the obvious basis of this practice is economic. However, it is also possible to view this approach from a medical standpoint, recognizing that sedentary existence (which could easily have become the monastic lifestyle) breeds physical disorder through lack of activity. In American culture, where so much leisure time activity is nonphysical (television, movies, bars, and the like), physical activity is a momentous therapeutic. And as American working life becomes more and more sedentary through the creation of technology's nightmarish production of gadgets, the need for physical maintenance becomes critical, lest we eventually mutate into a race of disembodied minds of the variety only previously witnessed on Star Trek. The Human Potential Movement has been quick to exploit this predicament, postulating such popular new phenomena as Inner Tennis. Dr. George Sheehan makes a similar argument in his book *Running and Being.* American Buddhists could well learn from these innovations and introduce a variety of activities that are not only physically beneficial, but also Buddhist-related. There is nothing mind-boggling about tennis, running, or gardening as a physical *and* meditative exercise.

The other feature to be noted under the category of healing is the emphasis on psychological healing in Buddhism. A few Buddhist groups have already embarked on healing-oriented projects (the Tibetan Nyingma Meditation Center's Human Development Training Program and Chögyam Trungpa's Maitri Project being but two examples). The rapidly growing world of biofeedback has great relevance to such projects. Enhanced by modern technological advances, psychologists can now assist in training people to develop mental patterns that are consistent with well-being. For the most part, Buddhists in America have ignored these technologically assisted breakthroughs. It might be suggested that as part of the greater scientific awareness suggested earlier, American Buddhists confront directly and utilize the fruits of these labors, not only in recognition of their (wanted or not) identity in twentieth-century America, but also in order to emphasize that the Buddhist quest is wholly consonant with Americans' search for physical and psychological completeness, as well as their unity.

Entry and Initiation

Following the emphasis on healing we have "a simple but definite process of entry and initiation." Among the Buddhist groups on the American scene there is an incredible variety of initiation procedures, ranging from utterly informal affairs to complex rituals. Underlying each of these avenues of entry to the Buddhist tradition, however, is the basic question of Buddhist identity. This question involves not only what constitutes a Buddhist, but also what constitutes a Buddhist *in America.* Concerning traditional Buddhism, the specifics of entry are clear cut if not actually practiced. As noted earlier, formal entry into the lay tradition of Buddhism rests on the twofold practice of taking refuge and accepting the five vows of the layman. It is not overstating the case to indicate that very few Buddhist groups in America employ both of these requirements. It is curious that while most meditative groups require the taking of refuge, it is only those groups that have an active monastic organization that require layman also to follow the layman's vows. Further, the "church" groups (Buddhist Churches of America and Nichiren Shōshū of America) tend not to require either practice. The above remarks tend to indicate that by traditional standards there are very few Buddhists in America, yet hundreds of thousands of Americans are currently professing Buddhism as their religious preference. Consequently, American Buddhists must directly confront the question: What (or who) is a Buddhist? My own suggestion for the remedy of this problem is an extension of a solution proposed by Agehananda Bharati for a similar situation regarding the definition of a mystic. Bharati says,

> . . . here is what I regard as a thoroughly operational definition of a mystic: *A mystic is a person who says "I am a mystic,"* or words to that

effect, *consistently*, when questioned about his most important pursuit. Further, his statement must be an *etic* statement—that is to say, it has to have a general widely applicable meaning, and must not be a term used only by a group of people in a manner peculiar to them, *emically*, that is.[17]

If we define a Buddhist as someone who says "I am a Buddhist" when questioned about "his most important pursuit," we not only abandon our attachment to a ritual formulary that is neither workable nor widely followed, but we also provide more than a modicum of freedom for the various American Buddhist groups—a freedom in which they can develop a procedure that is consistent with their own self-image and mission. In addition, we also circumvent the issue of determining Buddhist standing by such nonuniform methods as cash contributions, periodic meeting attendance, and the like. Bharati's is a simple standard, easy to enforce and tabulate, and lends itself to the widest possible flexibility. It also requires, however, that each Buddhist group establish criteria for maintaining membership "in good standing," lest the various groups become populated by those professing only minimal commitment. In other words, what appears initially as an outrageous definition of Buddhist affiliation serves the double purpose of providing a new standard and a simple method of professing Buddhist commitment while at the same time imposing a renewed sense of seriousness on all Buddhist groups.

Of course *any* working definition of "Buddhist" only confronts half of the problem facing Buddhists in America. The other half involves the manner in which Buddhist religious commitment functions in an American setting. I suggested earlier that for Buddhism to be successful in acculturating, multilateral affiliations must be conceded, or perhaps even affirmed. Here I simply reiterate that position with the added proviso that the entire process is undertaken in the context of the above discussion. I mean to imply that when individuals say they are Buddhists, they are referring to their "most important pursuit," and this should be understood to be a *religious pursuit.* On the other hand, when these individuals also state that they are Jews or Protestants (or Catholics or whatever), they are referring to their *cultural heritage,* to the complex of factors (ethnic and otherwise) that are primarily locational rather than religious. It is untenable to maintain, for example, Buddhist practice and Judaeo-Christian theology. It is mixing the proverbial apples and oranges. However, it is *not untenable* to assimilate Western cultural orientation into a Buddhist world view. Needless to say, such a venture must be performed carefully, remaining constantly aware of the traps and snares that may befall the careless entrant. Nevertheless, when the goal is human wholeness and completeness, we must realize that the pursuit is common to both East and West, and that the process outlined is precisely the same method that Buddhism has employed for over two thousand years in Asia as it moved from culture to culture.

Architecture of the Sacred Centers

For cultic groups Ellwood's typology postulates "in many cases the establishment of a sacred center." The issue of sacred center has been discussed in Part I above, where it was emphasized that Buddhism in America was sorely lacking in such an enterprise. Rather than simply repeat my argument for utilizing this means of developing religious identity and power, here I suggest that perhaps the highest expression of Buddhism's unwillingness to Americanize is manifest in its religious architecture. Of course in many cases American Buddhist groups have purchased already existing buildings and converted them according to need. Until quite recently this was even the norm. Consequently, it is not at all unusual to find old fraternity houses, public service buildings, and similar facilities flying Buddhist banners and other symbols of the religious tradition. As Buddhist groups become financially stable and geographically expansive, however, they are beginning to engage in the construction of *new* buildings, which affords them a greater sense of structural flexibility. Almost exclusively, the newly constructed Buddhist centers and buildings reflect the architectural style of the parent group in Asia. In fact, there is little attempt to harmonize Buddhist motifs with American stylistic expressions. On the one hand, such an enterprise is understandable, for the American Buddhist groups tend to want to preserve their Buddhist heritage. On the other hand, they fail to recognize that the vast majority of the Buddhists in America do not share that heritage; rather, they have emerged from the mainstream of Western culture. Needless to say, the solution is obvious. But however obvious the solution, its implementation is significantly more difficult to achieve, for it entails the creation of a new architectural form. And of course this new form must reflect the developing style of American Buddhism. Western expressions of Buddhist ideals, practices, ritual enactment, and the like must be sought out and fully manifested. In other words, Buddhists in this country must develop an American Weltanschaung and demonstrate it concretely in their architectural forms. In this manner, while the axis mundi remains in Asia, the sacred center in America is infused with the power inherent in its Buddhist *and* American delineation. In so doing, American Buddhists would begin to utilize and demonstrate a creativity that is uniquely theirs, and that has, up to the present, been latent rather than kinetic.

Whom Do the Groups Attract?

The next to last item in Ellwood's typology highlights the "tendency to attract isolated individuals rather than family groups." With the exception of Buddhist Churches of America and Nichiren Shōshū of America, this detail rather accurately describes the Buddhist movement in America. It also keynotes the problem of community life in Buddhism as well. Harvey Cox is quick to point out that "the movement from recovered interiority to renewed community is a perilous one."[18] Cox goes on to speak about the value of testimony in establishing a sense of community:

> Testimony, like everything else, is susceptible to debasement and trivialization. But in its essence testimony is the primal human act. It breaks the barrier we erect between the "inner" and the "outer" worlds. Telling my story is the way I dissolve this artificial distinction and create a lived and shared world. I do not abolish the chasm, either by surrendering my interiority to the outer or by keeping it entirely to myself. I break out by claiming the world as my own, weaving its stories into my story, and making it *our* world. My interiority, instead of being swallowed by the world or retreating to a well-guarded citadel, widens out to include the worlds of others in itself.[19]

To my knowledge, the only Buddhist group in America that actively incorporates testimony into its practices is Nichiren Shōshū of America. It is no accident, I think, that this group is the fastest growing of all Buddhist groups and the one possessing the most tightly knit and active community life. It has utilized testimony as a means of developing a meaningful community life and identity, from which it is possible to confront the world actively and with an intense sense of sharing.

It is in the above context that many Buddhists groups in America, including those emphasizing meditative practice, could employ the technique of testimony as a means of fostering community solidarity without compromising the major thrust of their religious endeavor. To be sure, great care would be required to prevent the notion of testimony from deteriorating into simple ego-tripping (promoting the very delusions which Buddhists are attempting to conquer). Nevertheless, it is a step worth taking, for it would enable American Buddhism to develop the firm community base from which to exercise its concern for social justice.

In noting the Eastern religions in America to be the descendants of the counterculture, a claim which is hardly accurate, Martin Marty states,

> Similarly, as we move toward the kin of these groups, Eastern religions, it must be recognized that much is private and invisible (except insofar as anything that an individual holds or does has some sort of bearing on the order around him or her).[20]

At least with regard to the Buddhist tradition in Asia *and* America, our esteemed commentator falls into the same trap that engulfs Winston King, namely, that the dynamic emphasis on social ethics by Buddhism is ignored. Of course it is convenient to ignore it, for such incognizance enables a wide variety of claims to be launched against the tradition. Nevertheless, these claims are grossly inaccurate, and it would serve the various Buddhist groups well to be a bit more vocal about their numerous activities and concerns in this domain.

In conclusion, the meditative groups in Buddhism must make serious effort to establish themselves as family traditions if they are to enjoy the communitarian success of the Buddhist church groups. Such practice would enable them to spread more dynamically in American culture than they have to date.

Emphasis on Participation

The final topic in our typology concerns "increasing emphasis on participation by all members in the ecstatic experience through group chanting, meditation, and so forth." Of course, religious experience is the summum bonum, the highest good, of the Buddhist tradition. It must be stated at the outset that virtually all Buddhist groups on the American scene engage their members in a religious practice that is designed to promote such experience, whether it be repetition of the nembutsu (in the Jōdo Shinshū tradition), the mantric chant paying homage to the Lotus Sūtra (in Nichiren Shōshū), or formal meditation. Despite the fact that one scholar posits that "most of the New Religions were obsessed with states of consciousness,"[21] the two largest Buddhist groups in America are nonmeditative. From my perspective, the problem with American Buddhist practice is not the practice per se, but rather the style and form in which it is undertaken.

Almost all Buddhist groups that require some form of chanting from its participants carry out this procedure in the native language of the tradition. Most of the participants, however, do not read or understand the native language. Consequently, the practice and its religious meaning remain largely a mystery. I would argue that American Buddhist chants and religious rituals, if they are to be more profoundly meaningful to an American clientele, ought to be translated into English. Such practice, in addition to "demystifying" the tradition and procedure, would reflect a cognizance of the necessity of developing an American character for Buddhist practice and would assist in the acculturation process. Going one step further, it might well serve Buddhist groups in America to develop profoundly *new* modes of Buddhist religious expression. Such activity might include developing an American Buddhist art: maṇḍalas utilizing American symbols and styles, for example. In other words, without compromising their proper emphasis on religious practice as the means by which religious experience and enlightenment are attained, American Buddhist groups must develop a Buddhist practice that is uniquely American and capable of being understood by persons other than those intensely interested in the Orient and its cultures. Until such strides are made, American Buddhism will likely remain an opaque, veiled mystery to the majority of Americans.

CONCLUSION

Throughout this study, I have made much of the fact that there is a singular relationship between Buddhism's degree of acculturation in its new American environment and its potential future role in American religious life. To my way of thinking, there is a clear yardstick by which acculturative growth may be measured, namely, the extent to which American Buddhist groups begin to identify with American civil religion. Conrad Cherry has pointed out that in American sacred ceremonies, "religious differences are transcended to the plane of a national faith made up of symbols and beliefs that Americans hold in common."[22] Just as ". . . the Memorial Day rite is a national service that unites Protestants, Catholics and Jews beyond their differences,"[23] Buddhists may too stand united under Peter Berger's "sacred canopy" in expressing the American character of their faith. Of course it might be argued that Buddhism must be excluded from these other groups because of its express denial of the God concept. Nevertheless, Robert Bellah notes:

> Some have raised the question of whether the Mahayana Buddhist concep-
> tion of sunyata, emptiness, might not be a more adequate symbol of the
> open transcendence legitimating a democratic political order than the
> biblical God.[24]

Further, Bellah goes on:

> The publicly institutionalized civil religion must remain as symbolically
> open or empty as possible, both for the reasons suggested by Richardson
> and in order not to exclude significant groups who could not share over-
> specific symbols.[25]

In fact, once we have dispensed with adherence to the God concept as a necessary requisite for civil religion, Buddhism's entry into this domain is much more readily seen. Martin Marty has revealed as much:

> It would also be a faith for "plural belongers," people who might be
> Presbyterian, Nazarene, Pentecostal, Zen Buddhist, a believer that "God is
> Red," and *still* within the circle of claims of Civil Religion."[26]

Needless to say, American Buddhist groups would be able to partic-
ipate fully in the American experience by emphasizing the unique qualities of freedom, equality, and justice held dear by so many Americans. It would also be beneficial for American Buddhist groups to manifest their American nature in their holiday observances, art, music, ritual life, and so forth. To date, this has remained an unfulfilled dream for Buddhists in this country. Yet the process is unques-

tionably the proverbial "two-way street," for as Harvey Cox has stated:

> Eventually the spiritual disciplines of the Orient will make a profound contribution to our consciousness and our way of life. Some day, somewhere, we will hear the message the East has for us. But we can only begin to know the real Orient when we are willing to let go of the mythical one.[27]

Notes

PART I INTRODUCTION

1. Bob Dylan, "Ballad of a Thin Man," Warner Brothers, Los Angeles.
2. Michael Novak, *The Experience of Nothingness* (New York: Harper & Row, 1971), p. 6.
3. Agehananda Bharati, *The Light at the Center* (Santa Barbara, Calif.: Ross-Erikson, 1976), p. 127.

CHAPTER 1

1. Martin Marty, *A Nation of Behavers* (Chicago: University of Chicago Press, 1976), p. 2.
2. Louise Hunter, *Buddhism in Hawaii* (Honolulu: University of Hawaii Press, 1971), p. 32.
3. Ibid., p. 33.
4. Shigetsu Sasaki Rōshi, "Excerpts From *Our Lineage*," Wind Bell 8, no. 1-2 (Fall 1969):8.
5. Louis Nordstrom, ed., *Namu Dai Bosa: A Transmission of Zen Buddhism to America* (New York: Theatre Arts Books, 1976), p. xix.
6. Ibid.
7. Ibid., pp. xix-xx.
8. Ibid., pp. 58-59.
9. Mary Farkas, "Footsteps in the Invisible World," Wind Bell no. 1-2 (Fall 1969):18.
10. Ibid., p. 17.
11. Elsie Mitchell, *Sun Buddhas Moon Buddhas* , author sketch, (New York: Weatherhill, 1973).

12. From an interview with Gary Snyder, published in *Wind Bell* 8, no. 1–2 (Fall 1969):29.

195
Notes

CHAPTER 2

1. Harvey Cox, *The Seduction of the Spirit* (New York: Simon and Schuster, 1973), p. 121.
2. Ruth Fuller Sasaki, quoted in Shigetsu Sasaki Rōshi, "Excerpts From *Our Lineage*," *Wind Bell* 8, no. 1–2 (Fall 1969):12.
3. Robert S. Michaelson, *The American Search for Soul* (Baton Rouge: Louisiana State University Press, 1975), p. 8. Also see Henri Bergson, *The Two Sources of Morality and Religion* (New York: Henry Holt and Company, 1935), p. 219.
4. Cox, *The Seduction of the Spirit*, p. 284.
5. Frederick Streng, *Understanding Religious Life*, 2nd ed., rev. (Encino, Calif.: Dickenson, 1976), p. 95.
6. Ibid., p. 102.
7. Joseph M. Kitagawa and Frank Reynolds, "Theravāda Buddhism in the Twentieth Century," in Heinrich Dumoulin, ed., and John Maraldo, assoc. ed., *Buddhism in the Modern World* (New York: Collier Macmillan, 1976), p. 55.
8. Ibid., p. 47.
9. Bruce Cook, *The Beat Generation* (New York: Charles Scribner's Sons, 1971), pp. 9–10.
10. Ibid., p. 152.
11. Theodore Roszak, *The Making of a Counter Culture* (Garden City, N.Y.: Anchor Books, 1969), p. 130.
12. Ibid., p. 134.
13. Gary Snyder (from a tape recording), "On Rinzai Masters and Western Students in Japan," *Wind Bell* 8, no. 1–2 (Fall 1969):23–24.
14. Kitagawa and Reynolds, "Theravāda Buddhism," p. 48.
15. Martin Marty, *A Nation of Behavers* (Chicago: University of Chicago Press, 1976), p. 142.

CHAPTER 3

1. Theodore Roszak, *Unfinished Animal: The Aquarian Frontier and the Evolution of Consciousness* (New York: Harper & Row, 1975), p. 15.
2. Theodore Roszak, *The Making of a Counter Culture* (Garden City, N.Y.: Anchor Books, 1969), p. 156.
3. Catherine L. Albanese, unpublished response to my paper "American Buddhism," presented to the faculty of the Department of Religious Studies, The Pennsylvania State University, University Park, February 17, 1977, p. 4.
4. Bruce Cook, *The Beat Generation* (New York: Charles Scribner's Sons, 1971), p. 89.
5. Ibid., p. 198.
6. Ibid., p. 196.
7. Charles Y. Glock, "Consciousness Among Contemporary Youth: An In-

terpretation," in Charles Y. Glock and Robert N. Bellah, eds., *The New Religious Consciousness* (Berkeley: University of California Press, 1976), p. 356.

8. Ibid., p. 358.

9. Robert N. Bellah, "The New Consciousness and the Crisis in Modernity," in Glock and Bellah, *The New Religious Consciousness,* p. 341.

10. Ibid., p. 339.

11. Peter L. Berger, *Sacred Canopy: Elements of a Sociological Theory of Religion* (Garden City, N.Y.: Doubleday, 1966), p. 134.

12. Ibid., p. 137.

13. Ibid., pp. 140–47.

14. Gregory Johnson, "The Hare Krishna in San Francisco," in Glock and Bellah, *The New Religious Consciousness,* p. 39.

15. Bellah, "The New Consciousness," p. 341.

16. Roszak, *The Making of a Counter Culture,* p. 163.

17. Ibid., p. 166.

18. Philip Slater, *The Pursuit of Loneliness* (Boston: Beacon Press, 1971), pp. 101–02.

19. Ibid.

20. Robert S. de Ropp, *The Master Game,* (New York: Delta Books, 1968), pp. 42–43.

21. Agehananda Bharati, *The Light at the Center* (Santa Barbara, Calif.: Ross-Erikson, 1976), p. 93.

22. Johnson, "The Hare Krishna in San Francisco," p. 36.

23. Donald Stone, "The Human Potential Movement," in Glock and Bellah, *The New Religious Consciousness,* p. 93.

24. Harvey Cox, *The Seduction of the Spirit* (New York: Simon and Schuster, 1973), p. 199.

25. Rosabeth M. Kanter, *Commitment and Community* (Cambridge, Mass.: Harvard University Press, 1972), p. 113.

26. Ibid., p. 121.

27. Mircea Eliade, *Cosmos and History* (New York: Harper Torchbooks, 1959), p. 28.

28. Ibid., p. 9. The images are Eliade's, the application mine.

29. Cox, *The Seduction of the Spirit,* p. 56.

30. Albanese, unpublished response to "American Buddhism," p. 5.

31. This phrase is Emma Layman's. See Emma McCloy Layman, *Buddhism in America* (Chicago: Nelson-Hall, 1976), p. 203.

32. Bellah, "The New Consciousness," p. 341.

CHAPTER 4

1. Paul Tillich, *Morality and Beyond* (New York: Harper Torchbooks, 1966), p. 55.

2. Harvey Cox, "The Meeting of East and West," lecture at Naropa Institute, Boulder, Colorado, July 30, 1975.

3. I have used the word *syncretistic* Zen for those groups that combine techniques from Rinzai and Sōtō Zen.

4. Martin Marty, *A Nation of Behavers* (Chicago: University of Chicago Press, 1976), p. 129.

5. Harvey Cox, *The Seduction of the Spirit* (New York: Simon and Schuster, 1973), p. 251.

6. Charles S. Prebish, *Buddhist Monastic Discipline: The Sanskrit Prātimokṣa Sūtras of the Mahāsāṃghikas and Mūlasarvāstivādins* (University Park: Pennsylvania State University Press, 1975), p. 42.

7. Harold K. Schilling, "In Celebration of Complexity," *Union Seminary Quarterly Review* 30, 2–4 (Winter–Summer 1975):85–93.

8. Emma McCloy Layman, *Buddhism in America* (Chicago: Nelson-Hall, 1976), p. 203.

9. Robert N. Bellah, "The New Consciousness and the Crisis in Modernity," in Charles Y. Glock and Robert N. Bellah, eds., *The New Religious Consciousness* (Berkeley: University of California Press, 1976), p. 347.

10. Layman, *Buddhism in America*, pp. 265–70.

11. Robert S. Michaelson, *The American Search for Soul* (Baton Rouge: Louisiana State University Press, 1975), pp. 27–28.

PART II INTRODUCTION

1. Robert Greenfield, *The Spiritual Supermarket* (New York: E.P. Dutton, 1975), p. 1.

2. Philip Slater, *The Pursuit of Loneliness* (Boston: Beacon Press, 1971), p. 109.

CHAPTER 5

1. *Buddhist Churches of America 75th Anniversary Commemoration Volume*, San Francisco, 1974, p. 19.

2. The Eastern Branch (Higashi Hongwanji) is represented in America by the Higashi Hongwanji Buddhist Church in Los Angeles.

3. The priests were Eryu Honda and Ejun Miyamoto. Cited in the *Congressional Record*, Washington, D.C., December 20, 1974, and referring to a speech made by Phillip Burton of California on the previous day.

4. Ibid.

5. Ibid.

6. Emma McCloy Layman, *Buddhism in America* (Chicago: Nelson-Hall, 1976), p. 41.

7. Ibid., pp. 41–42.

8. See the bulletin "The Institute of Buddhist Studies," 1973–74, prepared by Buddhist Churches of America, San Francisco, pp. 8–9.

9. Layman, *Buddhism in America*, p. 45.

10. Ibid., pp. 45–46.

11. Ibid., p. 47.

12. The "chairman" is the lay leader of the congregation.

13. This format for the service is quoted from Layman, *Buddhism in America*, p. 44.

14. Such a book is Tetsuden Kashima's *Buddhism in America: The Social Organization of an Ethnic Religious Institution* (Westport, Conn.: Greenwood

Press, 1977), but this includes much more than simply history. Kashima's book is not sponsored by the organization, but is an expansion of his doctoral thesis, "Buddhist Churches of America," University of California, San Diego.

CHAPTER 6

1. *NSA Quarterly* (Fall 1975):49.

2. Robert S. Ellwood, *The Eagle and the Rising Sun* (Philadelphia: The Westminister Press, 1974), p. 94. Ellwood is citing an NSA press release from November 1972. Kosen-rufu is the propagation of True Buddhism.

3. Ibid.

4. Emma McCloy Layman, *Buddhism in America* (Chicago: Nelson-Hall, 1976), p. 129.

5. Ibid., p. 130.

6. Ibid.

7. *NSA Seminar Report 1968–1971,"NSA Demographics"* (Santa Monica, Calif.: World Tribune Press, 1972), pp. 93–106, appendix 3. The figures presented are in-house extrapolations from a small sample. New figures are available.

8. Ellwood, *The Eagle and the Rising Sun*, p. 92.

9. Layman, *Buddhism in America*, pp. 132–33.

10. Ellwood, *The Eagle and the Rising Sun*, p. 105.

11. Ibid., p. 77.

12. Ibid., pp. 23–31.

13. Robert Thurman, questioned in "The Diamond Vehicle: 2 Conversations on Tibetan Buddhism and the West," *Parabola* 2, no. 1 (1977):105.

14. Ellwood, *The Eagle and the Rising Sun*, p. 25.

15. Ibid., p. 77.

16. Layman, *Buddhism in America*, p. 138. The quote is from the page cited, but also see pp. 135–39.

CHAPTER 7

1. "Zen in America," brochure on Zen Mountain Center prepared by San Francisco Zen Center.

2. Editor, in "City Practice," *Wind Bell* 9, no. 3–4 (1970–1971):23.

3. Much of this information was gathered by Peter Schneider when he was president of San Francisco Zen Center and *Wind Bell* editor, and presented in *Wind Bell* 11 (1972):7–10.

4. See Huston Smith's Preface in Shunryu Suzuki, *Zen Mind, Beginner's Mind*, 4th paperback ed., (New York: Weatherhill, 1973), p. 11.

5. Elsie Mitchell, *Sun Buddhas Moon Buddhas* (New York: Weatherhill, 1973), p. 189.

6. *Wind Bell* 11 (1972):10–14.

7. "Zen in America."

8. Claude Dalenberg, in "City Practice," *Wind Bell* 9, no. 3–4 (1970–1971): 15.

CHAPTER 8

1. Henepola Gunaratana, *Come and See*, vol. 1, *The Vihara Papers* (Washington, D.C.: Buddhist Vihara Society, n.d.), p. 6.

2. André Bareau, *Les sectes bouddhiques du petit véhicule* (Saigon: Ecole Francaise d'Extrême-Orient, 1955), pp. 30, 205–10.

3. See Janice J. Nattier and Charles S. Prebish, "Mahāsāṃghika Origins: The Beginnings of Buddhist Sectarianism," *History of Religions* 16, no. 3 (1977): 237–72.

CHAPTER 9

1. Hsüan Hua, "Great Uncle Know-It-All," *Vajra Bodhi Sea* 6, series 13, no. 66, p. 38; from a seminar delivered to college students at Redwood City, Calif., May 11, 1975.

2. I offer my deep gratitude to Upāsaka I Kuo-jung (R.B. Epstein) of the Sino-American Buddhist Association (San Francisco), who furnished much of the data presented in my account.

3. John Blofeld, "Smart Enough to Gnaw Their Way Straight Through," *Vajra Bodhi Sea* 6, series 13, no. 65, p. 21.

4. From the Translator's Introduction (by Bhikṣuṇī Heng Yin), *Records of the Life of the Venerable Master Hsüsan Hua*, vol. 1 (San Francisco: Sino-American Buddhist Association, 1973), p. xiii.

5. Upāsaka I Kuo-jung (R.B. Epstein), "A Short History of the Sino-American Buddhist Association," private document, pp. 4–5.

6. Emma McCloy Layman, *Buddhism in America* (Chicago: Nelson-Hall, 1976), p. 155.

7. I Kuo-jung, "A Short History," p. 30.

8. Heng Yin, *Records of the Life of the Venerable Master Hsüan Hua*, p. xiii.

9. Ibid.

10. I Kuo-jung, "A Short History."

11. See Holmes Welch, *The Practice of Chinese Buddhism, 1900–1950* (Cambridge, Mass.: Harvard University Press, 1967), p. 411.

CHAPTER 10

1. Alan Watts, "Progress Report on Odiyan."

2. Stephan Beyer, "Tibetan Buddhism," in Charles S. Prebish, ed., *Buddhism: A Modern Perspective* (University Park: Pennsylvania State University Press, 1975), p. 243.

3. Tilden Edwards, "The Human Development Training Program," *Gesar News* 1, no. 2 (Summer 1973):17.

4. Tarthang Tulku, *Gesture of Balance* (Emeryville, Calif.: Dharma Publishing, 1977), pp. 158–59.

5. See Emma McCloy Layman, *Buddhism in America* (Chicago: Nelson-Hall, 1976), pp. 106–07.

6. "The Structure," *Gesar News* 1, no. 1 (Spring 1973):17.

7. "The Sacred Thankas of Tibet," *Saturday Review of Education*, March 1973.

8. Layman, *Buddhism in America*, p. 106.

CHAPTER 11

1. Agehananda Bharati, "The Future (if any) of Tantrism," Rick Fields, ed., in *Loka: A Journal from Naropa Institute* (Garden City, N.Y.: Anchor Books, 1975), p. 129.

2. Robert Greenfield, *The Spiritual Supermarket* (New York: E.P. Dutton, 1975), p. 212.

3. Ibid., p. 220.

4. See, for example, Florentz Helitzer, "Bringing Meditation & Buddhism to U.S. Higher Education," *University: a Princeton Quarterly* 64 (Spring 1975): 14–18, or "Precious Master of the Mountains," *Time*, February 14, 1977, p. 86.

5. See my review in *Journal of the American Academy of Religion* 43, no. 2 supplement (June 1975):337–38.

6. Ibid., p. 337.

7. See my review in *Parabola* 2, no. 1 (Winter 1977):112–16.

8. Rick Fields, "How the Swans Came to the Lake. Chogyam Trungpa and His Holiness the Gyalwa Karmapa," *New Age*, March 1977, p. 52.

9. Chögyam Trungpa, *Cutting Through Spiritual Materialism* (Berkeley, Calif.: Shambhala Publications, 1973), p. 123.

10. Greenfield, *The Spiritual Supermarket*, p. 216.

CHAPTER 12

1. Louis Nordstrom, ed., *Namu Dai Bosa: A Transmission of Zen Buddhism to America* (New York: Theatre Arts Books, 1976), pp. xviii–xix.

2. I offer my thanks to Reverend Jitsudō Baran and Reverend Keiketsu Norton for supplying much of the data appearing in this chapter.

3. From Kōhō Zenji's Foreword to Jiyu Kennett, *Selling Water by the River* (New York: Vintage Books, 1972), p. vi. The revised edition is *Zen Is Eternal Life* (Emeryville, Calif.: Dharma Publishing, 1976).

4. See Jiyu Kennett Rōshi, Swami Radha, and Robert Frager, "How to be a Transpersonal Teacher Without Becoming a Guru," *Journal of Transpersonal Psychology* 7, no. 1 (1975):48–65.

5. "General Information," pamphlet published by Shasta Abbey, March 1975, p. 6.

6. Ibid., p. 3.

7. See Kennett, *Selling Water by the River*, p. 224. I have arranged the mantra linearly rather than as a verse, as the author does.

8. Jitsudō Baran and Isan Sacco, "Pitfalls in Meditation," *The Journal of Shasta Abbey*, special issue on Zen Meditation, 7, no. 9–10 (November–December 1976):56.

1. D.H. Lawrence, "New Heaven and Earth," in Gerald DeWitt Sanders, John Herbert Nelson, and M.L. Rosenthal, eds., *Chief Modern Poets of England and America*, 4th ed. (New York: Macmillan, 1962), vol. I, p. 221.

2. Philip Slater, *The Pursuit of Loneliness* (Boston: Beacon Press, 1971), p. 21.

3. Harvey Cox, "Why Young Americans are Buying Oriental Religions," *Psychology Today,* July 1977, p. 40 (adapted from *Turning East* [New York: Simon & Schuster, 1977]).

CHAPTER 13

1. Robert S. Michaelson, *The American Search for Soul* (Baton Rouge: Louisiana State University Press, 1975), p. 116.

2. Robert S. Ellwood, *Religious and Spiritual Groups in Modern America* (Englewood Cliffs, N.J.: Prentice-Hall, 1973), p. 2.

3. Ibid., pp. 2-3.

4. Barbara Hargrove, untitled paper presented to the Conference on New American Religious Movements held at Graduate Theological Union, Berkeley, Calif., June 16, 1977.

5. Harvey Cox, untitled paper presented to the Conference on New American Religious Movements held at Graduate Theological Union, Berkeley, Calif., June 15, 1977.

6. Harvey Cox, "Why Young Americans are Buying Oriental Religions," *Psychology Today,* July 1977, p. 39 (adapted from *Turning East* [New York: Simon & Schuster, 1977]).

7. Ibid., p. 40.

8. Ibid., p. 42.

9. Ellwood, *Religious and Spiritual Groups in Modern America*, p. 19.

10. Ibid., pp. 28-31.

11. Catherine L. Albanese, "Citizen Crockett: Myth, History, and Nature Religion," *Soundings* 6, no. 1 (Spring 1978):87-104.

12. Ibid., p. 100.

13. Ibid., p. 93. Here she quotes Joseph Arpad, "David Crockett, an Original Legendary Eccentricity and Early American Character," Ph.D. dissertation, Duke University, Durham, N.C., 1968), p. 193.

14. Ibid., p. 100.

15. Martin Marty, *A Nation of Behavers* (Chicago: University of Chicago Press, 1976), p. 144.

16. Agehananda Bharati, *The Light at the Center* (Santa Barbara, Calif.: Ross-Erikson, 1976), p. 11.

17. Ibid., p. 25.

18. Harvey Cox, *The Seduction of the Spirit* (New York: Simon and Schuster, 1973), p. 95.

19. Ibid.

20. Marty, *A Nation of Behavers,* pp. 139-40.

21. Ibid., p. 131.

22. Conrad Cherry, "Two American Sacred Ceremonies: Their Implications

for the Study of Religion in America," *American Quarterly* 21 (Winter 1969): 751.

23. Ibid., p. 741.

24. Robert N. Bellah, "American Civil Religion in the 1970s," in Donald G. Jones and Russell E. Richey, *American Civil Religion* (New York: Harper & Row, 1974), p. 258.

25. Ibid.

26. Marty, *A Nation of Behavers,* p. 181.

27. Cox, "Why Young Americans are Buying Oriental Religions," p. 42.

Bibliography

BOOKS

Ames, Van Meter. *Zen and American Thought*. Honolulu: University of Hawaii Press, 1962.

Bareau, André. *Les sectes bouddhiques du petit véhicule*. Saigon: Ecole Française d'Extrême-Orient, 1955.

Bellah, Robert N. *Beyond Belief: Essays on Religion in a Post-Traditional World*. New York: Harper & Row, 1970.

———. *The Broken Covenant: American Civil Religion in a Time of Trial*. New York: Seabury Press, 1975.

Berger, Peter L. *Sacred Canopy: Elements of a Sociological Theory of Religion*. Garden City, N.Y.: Doubleday, 1966.

Bergson, Henri. *The Two Sources of Morality and Religion*. New York: Henry Holt and Company, 1935.

Bharati, Agehananda. *The Light at the Center*. Santa Barbara, Calif.: Ross-Erikson, 1976.

Bradbury, Ray. *Zen and the Art of Writing*. Santa Barbara, Calif.: Capra Press, 1973.

Bridges, Hal. *American Mysticism from William James to Zen*. New York: Harper & Row, 1970.

Cherry, C. Conrad. *God's New Israel; Religious Interpretations of American Destiny*. Englewood Cliffs, N.J.: Prentice-Hall, 1971.

Cook, Bruce. *The Beat Generation*. New York: Charles Scribner's Sons, 1971.

Cox, Harvey. *The Feast of Fools*. Cambridge, Mass.: Harvard University Press, 1969.

———. *The Secular City*. New York: Macmillan, 1966.

———. *The Seduction of the Spirit*. New York: Simon and Schuster, 1973.

de Ropp, Robert S. *Drugs and the Mind*. New York: St. Martin's Press, 1951.

———. *The Master Game*. New York: Delta Books, 1968.

Dhiravamsa. *A New Approach to Buddhism.* Lower Lake, Calif.: Dawn Horse Press, 1974.

Dumoulin, Heinrich, ed., and Maraldo, John, assoc. ed. *Buddhism in the Modern World.* New York: Collier Macmillan, 1976.

Eliade, Mircea. *Cosmos and History.* New York: Harper Torchbooks, 1959.

Ellwood, Robert S. *Religious and Spiritual Groups in Modern America.* Englewood Cliffs, N.J.: Prentice-Hall, 1973.

——. *The Eagle and the Rising Sun.* Philadelphia: The Westminster Press, 1974.

Fields, Rick, ed. *Loka: A Journal from Naropa Institute.* Garden City, N.Y.: Anchor Books, 1975.

——. *Loka Two: A Journal from Naropa Institute.* Garden City, N.Y.: Anchor Books, 1976.

Fromm, Erich, Suzuki, D.T., and DeMartino, Richard. *Zen Buddhism and Psychoanalysis.* New York: Harper & Row, 1960.

Fung, Paul F., and Fung, George D., trans. *The Sutra of the Sixth Patriarch on the Pristine Orthodox Dharma.* San Francisco: Buddha's Universal Church, 1964.

Ginsberg, Allen. *The Fall of America: Poems of These States, 1965–1971.* San Francisco: City Lights Books, 1972.

——. *The Gates of Wrath: Rhymed Poems, 1948–1952.* Bolinas, Calif.: Grey Fox Press, 1972.

——. *Howl, and Other Poems.* San Francisco: City Lights Books, 1959.

——. *Kaddish, and Other Poems.* San Francisco: City Lights Books, 1961.

——. *Open Head.* Melbourne: Sun Books, 1972.

——. *Planet News, 1961–1967.* San Francisco: City Lights Books, 1968.

——. *Reality Sandwiches, 1953–1960.* San Francisco: City Lights Books, 1967.

——. *Wichita Vortex Sutra.* London: Housmans, 1966.

Glock, Charles Y., and Bellah, Robert N., eds. *The New Religious Consciousness.* Berkeley: University of California Press, 1976.

Graham, Dom Aelred. *Conversations: Christian and Buddhist.* New York: Harcourt Brace Jovanovich, 1968.

——. *Zen Catholicism: A Suggestion.* New York: Harcourt Brace Jovanovich, 1963.

Greenfield, Robert. *The Spiritual Supermarket.* New York: E.P. Dutton, 1975.

Gunaratana, Henepola. *Come and See,* vol. 1. *The Vihara Papers.* Washington, D.C.: Buddhist Vihara Society, n.d.

Hanh, Thich Nhat. *Vietnam, Lotus in a Sea of Fire: The Buddhist Story.* New York: Hill and Wang, 1967.

Heng Ch'ien, Bhikṣu, trans. *The Essentials of the Dharma Blossom Sūtra,* vol. 1. With commentary by Ven. Hsüan Hua. San Francisco: Sino-American Buddhist Association, 1974.

Heng Ch'ih, Bhikṣuṇī, trans. *A General Explanation of the Vajra Prajñā Pāramitā Sūtra.* With commentary by Ven. Hsüan Hua. San Francisco: Sino-American Buddhist Association, 1974.

Heng Yin, Bhikṣuṇī, trans. *Records of the Life of the Venerable Master Hsüan Hua,* vol. 1. San Francisco: Sino-American Buddhist Association, 1973.

——. trans. *The Sixth Patriarch's Dharma Jewel Platform Sūtra and Commentary.* With commentary by Ven. Hsüan Hua. San Francisco: Sino-American Buddhist Association, 1971.

——, and Kuo Chen, Upāsaka, trans. *A General Explanation of the Essentials of the Śrāmaṇera Vinaya and Rules of Deportment.* With commentary by Ven. Hsüan Hua. San Francisco: Sino-American Buddhist Association, 1975.

Hua, Hsüan. *Pure Land and Ch'an Dharma Talks.* Trans. by Bhikṣuṇīs Heng Yin and Heng Ch'ih. San Francisco: Sino-American Buddhist Association, 1974.

——. *The Ten Dharmarealms Are Not Beyond a Single Thought.* Trans. by Bhikṣuṇī Heng Ch'ih. San Francisco: Sino-American Buddhist Association, 1973.

Humphreys, Christmas. *Sixty Years of Buddhism in England (1907–1967).* London: The Buddhist Society, 1968.

——. *Zen Comes West; the Present and Future of Zen Buddhism in Britain.* London: George Allen & Unwin, 1960.

Hunter, Louise. *Buddhism in Hawaii.* Honolulu: University of Hawaii Press, 1971.

Huxley, Aldous. *The Doors of Perception, and Heaven and Hell.* New York: Harper & Row, 1956.

I Kuo-jung, Upāsaka, and Heng Yin, Bhikṣuṇī, trans. *A General Explanation of the Buddha Speaks of the Amitābha Sūtra.* With commentary by Ven. Hsüan Hua. San Francisco: Sino-American Buddhist Association, 1974.

Ikeda, Daisaku. *The Complete Works of Daisaku Ikeda,* vols. 1–4. Tokyo: The Seikyo Press, 1967–71.

James, William. *The Varieties of Religious Experience.* New York: Modern Library, 1929.

Johnston, William. *The Still Point.* New York: Fordham University Press, 1970.

Jones, Donald G., and Richey, Russell E. *American Civil Religion.* New York: Harper & Row, 1974.

Kanter, Rosabeth M. *Commitment and Community.* Cambridge, Mass.: Harvard University Press, 1972.

Kaplcau, Philip. *The Three Pillars of Zen.* New York: Weatherhill, 1965.

——. *The Wheel of Death.* New York: Harper & Row, 1971.

Kashima, Tetsuden. *Buddhism in America: The Social Organization of an Ethnic Religious Organization.* Westport, Conn.: Greenwood Press, 1977.

Kennett, Jiyu. *Zen Is Eternal Life.* Emeryville, Calif.: Dharma Publishing, 1976. Revised edition of *Selling Water by the River.* New York: Vintage Books, 1972.

Kerouac, Jack. *Big Sur.* New York: Farrar, Straus, and Cudahy, 1962.

——. *Desolation Angels, a Novel.* New York: Coward-McCann, 1965.

——. *The Dharma Bums.* New York: Viking Press, 1971.

——. *Maggie Cassidy.* New York: Avon Book Division, Hearst Corp., 1959.

——. *Mexico City Blues.* New York: Grove Press, 1959.

——. *On the Road.* New York: Viking Press, 1959.

——. *Scattered Poems [by] Jack Kerouac.* San Francisco: City Lights Books, 1971.

——. *The Scripture of the Golden Eternity/Jack Kerouac,* 2nd ed. New York: Corinth Books, 1970.

——. *The Subterraneans.* New York: Ballantine Books, 1958.

——. *Visions of Cody.* New York: McGraw Hill, 1972.

Kornfield, Jack. *Living Buddhist Masters.* San Francisco: Unity Press, 1976.

Layman, Emma McCloy. *Buddhism in America.* Chicago: Nelson-Hall, 1976.

Leary, Timothy. *The Psychedelic Experience: A Manual Based on the Tibetan Book of the Dead.* Seacaucus, N.J.: Citadel Press, 1976.

Lilly, John. *The Center of the Cyclone.* New York: Bantam Books, 1973.

Luckmann, Thomas. *The Invisible Religion.* New York: Macmillan, 1974.

Maezumi, Hukuju Taizan, and Glassman, Bernard Tetsugen. *On Zen Practice,* vols. I and II. Los Angeles: Zen Center of Los Angeles, 1976, 1977.

Mahasi Sayadaw. *Practical Insight Meditation.* San Francisco: Unity Press, 1972.

Marty, Martin, *A Nation of Behavers.* Chicago: University of Chicago Press, 1976.

McFarland, H. Neill. *Rush Hour of the Gods.* New York: Macmillan, 1967.

Merton, Thomas. *The Asian Journals of Thomas Merton.* New York: New Directions, 1973.

——. *Mystics and Zen Masters.* New York: Farrar, Straus & Giroux, 1967.

——. *Zen and the Birds of Appetite.* Philadelphia: New Directions, 1968.

Michaelson, Robert S. *The American Search for Soul.* Baton Rouge: Louisiana State University Press, 1975.

Mitchell, Elsie. *Sun Buddhas Moon Buddhas.* New York: Weatherhill, 1973.

Naranjo, Claudio. *The Healing Journey.* New York: Ballantine Books, 1975.

——, and Ornstein, Robert. *On the Psychology of Meditation.* New York: Viking Press, 1971.

Needleman, Jacob. *The New Religions.* Garden City, N.Y.: Doubleday, 1970.

Nordstrom, Louis, ed. *Namu Dai Bosa: A Transmission of Zen Buddhism to America.* New York: Theatre Arts Books, 1976.

Novak, Michael. *The Experience of Nothingness.* New York: Harper & Row, 1971.

Ornstein, Robert E. *The Psychology of Consciousness.* New York: Viking Press, 1972.

Pirsig, Robert. *Zen and the Art of Motorcycle Maintenance.* New York: Bantam Books, 1975.

Powell, Robert. *Zen and Reality.* New York: Viking Press, 1975.

Prebish, Charles S. *Buddhist Monastic Discipline: The Sanskrit Prātimoksa Sūtras of the Mahāsāṃghikas and Mūlasarvāstivādins.* University Park: Pennsylvania State University Press, 1975.

——, ed. *Buddhism: A Modern Perspective.* University Park: Pennsylvania State University Press, 1975.

Reich, Charles. *The Greening of America.* New York: Bantam Books, 1971.

Robinson, Richard H., and Johnson, Willard. *The Buddhist Religion,* 2nd ed., rev. Encino, Calif.: Dickenson, 1977.

Roszak, Theodore. *The Making of a Counter Culture.* Garden City, N.Y.: Anchor Books, 1969.

——. *Unfinished Animal: the Aquarian Frontier and the Evolution of Consciousness.* New York: Harper & Row, 1975.

——. *Where the Wasteland Ends.* Garden City, N.Y.: Anchor Books, 1973.

Rowly, Peter. *New Gods in America.* New York: David McKay Co., 1971.

Sanders, Gerald DeWitt, Nelson, John Herbert, and Rosenthal, M.L., eds. *Chief Modern Poets of England and America,* 4th ed. New York: Macmillan, 1962.

Shaku, Soyen. *Zen for Americans.* Trans. by D.T. Suzuki. LaSalle, Ill.: Open Court, 1974. Originally published as *Sermons of a Zen Abbot.*

Slater, Philip. *Earthwalk.* Garden City, N.Y.: Anchor Books, 1974.

——. *The Pursuit of Loneliness.* Boston: Beacon Press, 1971.

Snyder, Gary. *The Back Country.* London: Fulcrum Press, 1967.

——. *Myths and Texts.* New York: Totem Press, 1960.

——. *Regarding Wave.* New York: New Directions, 1970.

——. *Six Sections from Mountains and Rivers Without End.* San Francisco: Four Seasons Foundation, 1965.

——. *Turtle Island.* New York: New Directions, 1974.

Streng, Frederick. *Understanding Religious Life,* 2nd ed., rev. Encino, Calif.: Dickenson, 1976.

Suzuki, D.T. *Essays in Zen Buddhism,* 1st series. New York: Grove Press, 1961.

——. *Essays in Zen Buddhism,* 2nd series. London: Rider, 1958.

——. *Essays in Zen Buddhism,* 3rd series, 3rd ed. London: Rider, 1958.

——. *Manual of Zen Buddhism.* New York: Grove Press, 1960.

——. *Mysticism, Christian and Buddhist.* New York: Harper & Row, 1957.

——. *Shin Buddhism.* New York: Harper & Row, 1970.

——. *The Training of the Zen Buddhist Monk.* New York: University Books, 1965.

Suzuki, Shunryu. *Zen Mind, Beginner's Mind,* 4th paperback ed. New York: Weatherhill, 1973.

Swearer, Donald. *Buddhism in Transition.* Philadelphia: The Westminster Press, 1970.

Tart, Charles T., ed. *Altered States of Consciousness.* New York: John Wiley and Sons, 1969.

Tarthang, Tulku. *Gesture of Balance.* Emeryville, Calif.: Dharma Publishing, 1977.

Tillich, Paul. *Morality and Beyond.* New York: Harper Torchbooks, 1966.

Trungpa, Chögyam. *Born in Tibet.* Baltimore: Penguin Books, 1971. Originally published in London by Allen & Unwin, 1966.

——. *Cutting Through Spiritual Materialism.* Berkeley, Calif.: Shambhala Publications, 1973.

——. *Meditation in Action.* Berkeley, Calif.: Shambhala Publications, 1969.

——. *Mudra.* Berkeley, Calif.: Shambhala Publications, 1972.

——. *The Myth of Freedom.* Berkeley, Calif.: Shambhala Publications, 1976.

——, and Fremantle, Francesca, trans. *The Tibetan Book of the Dead.* Berkeley, Calif.: Shambhala Publications, 1975.

——, and Guenther, Herbert. *The Dawn of Tantra.* Berkeley, Calif.: Shambhala Publications, 1975.

Watts, Alan. *The Book; On the Taboo Against Knowing Who You Are.* New York: Collier Books, 1967.

——. *Cloud-Hidden, Whereabouts Unknown: A Mountain Journal.* New York: Pantheon Books, 1973.

——. *Does It Matter?* New York: Pantheon Books, 1970.

——. *In My Own Way: An Autobiography.* New York: Pantheon Books, 1972.

——. *The Joyous Cosmology: Adventures in the Chemistry of Consciousness.* New York: Pantheon Books, 1962.

——. *Psychotherapy East and West.* New York: Random House, 1961.

——. *The Spirit of Zen.* New York: Grove Press, 1960.

——. *This Is It, and Other Essays on Zen and Spiritual Experience.* New York: Pantheon Books, 1960.

——. *The Two Hands of God: the Myth of Polarity.* New York: George Braziller, 1963.

——. *The Way of Liberation in Zen Buddhism.* San Francisco: American Academy of Asian Studies, 1955.

——. *The Wisdom of Insecurity.* New York: Vintage Books, 1951.

Welch, Holmes. *The Practice of Chinese Buddhism, 1900–1950.* Cambridge, Mass.: Harvard University Press, 1967.

Wolfe, Tom. *The Electric Kool-Aid Acid Test.* New York: Farrar, Straus & Giroux, 1968.

Zaehner, R.C. *Mysticism, Sacred and Profane.* Oxford: Clarendon Press, 1957.

——. *Zen, Drugs, and Mysticism.* New York: Pantheon Books, 1972.

Zaretsky, Irving, and Leone, Mark, eds. *Religious Movements in Contemporary America.* Princeton, N.J.: Princeton University Press, 1974.

JOURNALS OF THE GROUPS STUDIED IN THIS VOLUME

Buddhist Churches of America, San Francisco, *Wheel of Dharma.*

Nichiren Shōshū of America, Santa Monica, Calif., *NSA Quarterly* and *World Tribune.*

San Francisco Zen Center, *Wind Bell.*

Buddhist Vihara Society, Washington, D.C., *Washington Buddhist.*

Sino-American Buddhist Association, San Francisco, *Vajra Bodhi Sea.*

Tibetan Nyingma Meditation Center, Berkeley, Calif., *Annals of the Nyingma Lineage in America, Crystal Mirror,* and *Gesar News.*

Vajradhatu and Nalanda Foundation, Boulder, Colo., *Garuda, Loka,* and *Sangha Newsletter.*

Shasta Abbey, Mount Shasta, Calif., *The Journal of Shasta Abbey.*

Index